BETWEEN CRAFT AND CLASS

BETWEEN CRAFT AND CLASS

Skilled Workers and Factory Politics in the United States and Britain, 1890–1922

JEFFREY HAYDU

UNIVERSITY OF CALIFORNIA PRESS
BERKELEY   LOS ANGELES   LONDON

University of California Press
Berkeley and Los Angeles, California

University of California Press, Ltd.
London, England

© 1988 by
The Regents of the University of California

Library of Congress Cataloging-in-Publication Data
Haydu, Jeffrey.
    Between craft and class: skilled workers and factory politics in
the United States and Britain, 1890–1922 / Jeffrey Haydu.
        p.   cm.
    Bibliography: p.
    Includes index.
    ISBN 0–520–06060–1 (alk. paper)
        1. Labor and laboring classes—United States—Political activity—
History. 2. Labor and laboring classes—Great Britain—Political
activity—History. 3. Artisans—United States—History.
4. Artisans—Great Britain—History. 5. Social classes—United
States—History. 6. Social classes—Great Britain—History.
I. Title.
HD8076.H39 1988
322'.2'0941—dc19   87–22169
                                                                         CIP

Printed in the United States of America
1   2   3   4   5   6   7   8   9

To Colin

Contents

Acknowledgments

In writing this book I have learned a great deal about two kinds of craftsmanship: that of the skilled worker and that of the scholar. My guides to the former are amply footnoted. For the latter I am most grateful to Michael Burawoy, Thomas Laqueur, and William Kornhauser. Michael Burawoy championed the role of theory in organizing historical interpretation when I began to revel in the details; Thomas Laqueur defended the integrity of historical actors against my sociological perspective; and William Kornhauser upheld the need for analytical rigor when I got sloppy. I like to think that no one book could ever meet each of these men's standards. If mine will fully satisfy none of them, it has still benefited from their distinct perspectives. None, moreover, requires public absolution for persisting deficiencies. The book's shortcomings are actually to these scholars' credit: each pressed his points but supported my efforts to find my own way.

Along that way, Craig Heron's thorough reading and constructive criticisms of one draft provided encouragement and direction for subsequent revisions. Victoria Bonnell, Harold Wilensky, and Neil Smelser offered useful advice on individual sections of the manuscript. Among Kathy Mooney's many contributions to the book, I will single out only one: her editorial counsel made the manuscript more literate and its author appreciate yet another craft, that of writing. Thanks are also owed to my new colleagues in the Department of Sociology at Syracuse University. I joined them too recently for this book to reflect their influence, but their warm welcome and encouragement helped me complete final manuscript preparations in good time and in good spirits.

Those who offered access to and help with archives include Richard Storey of the Modern Records Centre, University of Warwick; the Coventry Engineering Employers' Association's A. P. Berry and Francis Moe; R. Lissaman and the staff at the Amalgamated Union of Engineering Workers' Coventry offices; W. E. Kinchin of the Engineering Employers' Federation; David Palmquist in the Bridgeport Public Library; and Robert Rodden of the International Association of Machinists. The University of California, Berkeley, and a Charlotte W. Newcombe Dissertation Fellowship provided money for research travel and writing; the hospitality of conveniently located family and friends helped make that money last. My thanks to them all.

Chapter One

Factory Politics and
Selective Mobilization

For most of the nineteenth century, manufacturing practices in the machine trades relied, as in other industries, on the skills and judgment of craftsmen. Craftsmen commanded indispensable knowledge of production techniques, gained through long apprenticeships. Their skills supported a privileged economic position and a wide range of controls over workshop affairs. By the late nineteenth century these privileges and controls had come under attack from employers eager to cut costs, increase output, and secure a more compliant work force. Employers pursued these goals by installing new machinery, subdividing work tasks, introducing novel wage payment methods, tightening supervision, and placing unapprenticed men and women on jobs previously performed only by craftsmen.

This book examines the development of craftsmen's goals and struggles at work—what will be called "factory politics"—as skilled workers confronted industrial change. During the early years of this century, the agenda for industrial conflict was unsettled. Craftsmen could pursue varied policies in response to management offensives; indeed, changes at work forced skilled workers to reappraise the traditional goals and strategies of craft unionism and to confront alternatives. They could, for example, defend their customary privileges and powers at work, trade traditional job controls for larger economic rewards, or demand a greater voice in the introduction of new technology and the conduct of shop-floor management. In their battles with employers, craftsmen could stand alone, or they could ally with employees of different trades and skill levels to oppose management. One goal of this book is to explain why, at different times and places, craft protest turned in one or another of these directions.

In retrospect, the transition from craft manufacture to mass production is typically associated with a straightforward shift in factory politics. After rearguard action to protect exclusive craft controls failed to halt industrial progress, succeeding generations of workers accepted basic management prerogatives and concerned themselves with expanding economic benefits and defending narrow occupational interests.[1] But this trend was actively contested and perhaps not inevitable. Different factions within the labor movement put forward rival programs for the proper aims and organization of workers, and it was by no means clear which would win the support of rank-and-file workers. Traditions of craft control sustained the popular appeal of more democratic workshop life, moral standards made skilled men unwilling to exchange customary workplace responsibilities for consumer satisfactions, and labor aristocrats at times proved willing to ally with less privileged industrial workers. The trend in the machine trades between 1890 and about 1917 was actually toward broader solidarity in support of innovative demands for workplace control—not toward the more familiar accommodation between capital's right to manage and labor's right to job security and higher living standards.

Eventually, this crisis of transition was resolved in favor of management control and economistic, defensive, and sectional factory politics. What accounts for this outcome? The answer is developed by first examining the development of radical factory politics: broadly based alliances of workers (rather than sectional movements) supporting ambitious programs for workers' control (as against either economistic goals or the defense of the craft status quo). Analyzing the conditions that made movements for workers' control possible sets the stage for the second major task: to explain how radical factory politics were contained, and economistic and sectional alternatives consolidated.

The focus is on American machinists and their British counterparts, the engineers, between 1890 and the 1920s. These workers were the most important machine trades craftsmen, in their num-

bers, their organization, and their relationship to changing manufacturing practices. A more detailed study of two World War I
munitions centers—Coventry, England, and Bridgeport, Connecticut—shows how movements for workers' control failed, and
more familiar patterns of industrial contention triumphed. Comparative analysis—between the two cases, between time periods
in each country, and between sectors within each national industry—highlights the contributions of the labor process,[2] the unions,
industrial relations, and the state to the rise and fall of radical factory politics among engineers and machinists.

This book belongs to a growing literature on craft radicalism.
Scholars examining the history of working-class politics have shown
that the most privileged sectors of the labor force were not always
the most conservative. Artisans were at the forefront of socialist
movements and revolutionary politics in Western Europe, Russia,
and North America. Challenges to their status at work—as well as
distinctive corporate traditions and changing economic fortunes—
are often cited as predisposing craftsmen to political radicalism.[3]
There is also ample historical evidence of skilled workers' involvement in industrial militancy. Pre–World War I craftsmen often
formed the vanguard in mass strikes and in syndicalist and industrial unionist tendencies within the labor movement. Here, too,
craft radicalism developed as the traditional workplace powers and
privileges of skilled men came under attack.[4]

Skilled metalworkers of the late nineteenth and early twentieth
centuries were leading examples of this larger category of craft radicals. This book concentrates on a still narrower occupational
group: craftsmen who made machinery.[5] Such selectivity helps
make research manageable. In addition, historical sources on engineers and machinists are relatively rich. These workers are the
target of investigation not because they are representative, but because they are significant. Unionized machinists and engineers
played leading roles in their national labor movements by virtue of
their exceptional strength and militancy. The struggles of these
craftsmen thus had an importance extending beyond the borders
of the trade. Innovations in technology and management practice
affected the work lives of large numbers of skilled workers in this
occupational group (as compared to other metalworkers, such as
boilermakers and patternmakers) and incited lively debate over ap-

propriate responses. It was among engineers and machinists, too, that movements for workers' control enjoyed the greatest support, providing a clear if not typical case for examining conditions that favored and undermined radical factory politics. Finally, it was during World War I that movements for workers' control both reached their greatest strength and were defeated—a defeat that came in part from unprecedented government intervention in labor relations. The story of wartime worker militancy and government control of industrial relations is above all the story of engineers and machinists.

Radical Factory Politics in Historical Perspective

Like craftsmen of other trades, engineers and machinists turned to militant industrial action as changes at work devalued their skills and diminished their status. This interpretation is consistent with a growing body of historical scholarship. This book, however, is not primarily concerned with craft militancy in general; instead, it emphasizes and explains the different organizational and ideological forms that craft militancy took. Explanations tend to be multicausal and specific to time and place. For any given case particular constellations of historical conditions—arrangements at work, industrial relations practices, union and government policies—are seen to channel craft protest in certain directions.

Beneath the empirical complexities and detail lies a straightforward argument. Radical factory politics has been described provisionally in terms of class solidarities (in contrast to sectional identities) and an orientation to workers' control (rather than defensive efforts to preserve craft restrictions or the pursuit of economic rewards). But in day-to-day shop life grievances concerning control of production were more often divisive than unifying. Most important, the interests of different occupational groups were sharply opposed on certain questions of control. While deskilling and piecework threatened the position of craftsmen, for example, these same innovations promised less skilled workers opportunities for upward mobility. Control issues were also divisive because of their idiosyncrasy. Workers of a given craft employed in different departments or factories did not usually face the same grievance at the same time, nor did skilled members of different trades. Engineers or machinists at one plant might be ordered to accept piecework while those elsewhere—or molders and patternmakers in the same plant—continued to enjoy standard hourly pay. Obnoxious discipline could be a problem in one shop, while in others easygoing supervision prevailed.

Features of the labor process thus might inhibit concerted action on control issues even among engineers and machinists. More important, the pursuit of such interests could alienate workers of other trades and grades. Economic grievances, by contrast, might be widely shared and demands for higher wages more likely to mobilize solidary action.

Craft unionism tended to reinforce the influence of working conditions. For historical, organizational, and practical reasons (elaborated in Chapter Three), the unions of the day were committed to monopolizing occupational jurisdictions and privileges at the expense of other craftsmen and less skilled workers.[6] Union structures, policies, and leaders favored working-class solidarity no more than did the labor process. Union executives were also more likely to support local action in pursuit of economic interests than demands for control.[7] This pattern reflects in part an accommodation to employer policies. Employers typically declared themselves willing to negotiate wages and hours, but reserved basic issues of workshop control for unilateral management prerogative. Such preferences were in some cases enshrined in formal agreements with trade unions. Union policies and industrial relations agreements, in turn, could strongly influence rank-and-file action. Workers often relied on their executive officers for benefits, protection, and assistance and benefited from formal grievance procedures. To the extent that they did so, they had clear incentives to follow official priorities and industrial relations rules in their demands and disputes.

Characteristics of the labor process, unions, and industrial relations shaped the kinds of demands and alliances engineers and machinists made. All else being equal, struggles over shop control would likely be fought on a sectional basis and for exclusive ends; industrial action uniting workers of different crafts and grades would be favored only where economistic interests were at stake.[8] Solidary movements for workers' control, by contrast, faced considerable obstacles. These obstacles were not immutable, however, and all else was not equal.

From 1890 through World War I, engineers and machinists, acting in a changing environment, developed new forms of organization to advance their interests. Industrial relations and state intervention, as well as features of the labor process and trade unionism, gave rise to new local agencies for rank-and-file protest. These altered the organizational terrain on which industrial conflict was mobilized. A variety of shop and citywide committees brought together workers of different crafts and skills, helping bridge divisions created at work and by trade union structures. These institutions became increasingly independent of sectional union authority, evading the constraints imposed on factory politics by executive policies. Although such "unofficial" joint organization did not necessarily *originate* with popular commitments to solidarity or rebellion, it did enhance the *possibilities* that engineers and machinists could develop policies in common with other metalworkers and act on them, if necessary, in defiance of national union officials and industrial relations agreements. These possibilities were in fact realized, in part because new forms of local organization also gave radicalized craftsmen greater opportunities for influence. Organizational innovations not only facilitated alliances among workers of different trades and skills; they also made possible alliances between progressive leaders and rank-and-file engineers and machinists of quite varied political inclinations.[9]

New styles of rank-and-file organization overcame major obstacles to radical factory politics laid down by the labor process, craft unionism, and industrial relations. As independent, joint organization gained strength, the prospects increased for mobilizing solidary (rather than sectional) action in pursuit of control (rather than economistic) demands. The following account of the rise and fall of radical factory politics, accordingly, concentrates on the development and ultimate demise of autonomous, solidary rank-and-file organization.

In these developments ideology as well as organization shaped the terrain of conflict. A secondary goal of this book is to show how the changing prominence of different issues affected prospects for worker solidarity over control issues. Metalworkers had varied grievances and interests, some of which divided employees along the lines of trade and skill. But others—such as resentments against the arbitrary and unilateral exercise of management authority—were more widely shared.

Events or demands that highlighted common rather than sectional concerns would naturally enhance the prospects for united action.[10] In particular, certain claims for workers' control favored alliances even between self-interested craftsmen and less skilled workers. The demand that employers recognize innovative shop committee schemes, for example, recalls more traditional devices for defending craft rules, yet moves beyond sectional interests to a broader concern with workers' rights to a voice in shop management. The demand could thus mobilize an alliance between craftsmen, many of them guided by traditional preoccupations, and less skilled workers, who shared with engineers and machinists a desire for more equitable and rule-bound supervision. Similarly, the call that employers assure minimum wage rates and negotiate job classifications could move craftsmen beyond opposition to dilution to a demand for joint control over employment policies. And this created common ground with less skilled workers, equally concerned to check arbitrary hiring, job assignment, and firing.[11] Besieged craftsmen, in short, embraced radical factory politics under specific organizational and ideological conditions—conditions examined in some detail in subsequent chapters.

The terms "radical factory politics" and "movements for workers' control" summarize a type of industrial conflict different from either traditional craft union policies or more recent patterns of collective bargaining. The major distinction of radical factory politics is to involve workers of varied trades and skills in common struggles for control over production practices. It is the *combination* of control demands and solidarity that is decisive. Craft unions were always preoccupied with control issues, but their regulation of shop affairs aimed to safeguard exclusive privileges—privileges maintained at the expense of other work groups. Joint action with members of rival trades or workers of lesser skill signified a break with craft consciousness. On the other side, contemporary collective bargaining gives highest priority to economic interests, and concerns for job control again reflect exclusive occupational interests.[12]

The combination of control demands and solidarity represents an exceptional challenge to management as well as to prevailing union policies. In the face of such movements, employers could introduce new techniques or win concessions on work practices neither by offering economic payoffs nor by playing one occupational group off against another. Here a progressive potential in the craft tradition is clear: while craft standards survived, the exercise of autonomy, judgment, and skill at work—control—remained a high priority, not to be bargained away for higher wages.

The actual goals pursued in movements for workers' control also differ from those dominating either craft policies or contemporary industrial relations. Demands and work rules advanced by craft unions were typically defensive or, in Carter Goodrich's terminology, "negative."[13] They aimed to block employer encroachments on customary privileges and shop practices. Current collective bargaining attends to similar priorities, albeit with greater formality. Detailed rules and precedents dictate what managers may *not* do.[14] Initiative usually lies with employers today: management acts, and unions grieve. Movements for workers' control, by contrast, were far more aggressive (or "positive"), demanding new powers for employees rather than protecting old ones. They did not merely limit the rights of management but also called for new arenas of control for workers.

Workers' control demands, finally, sought to democratize shop life and collective bargaining. Among the new rights claimed for labor were those of participation in workplace decisions, not simply by union representatives, but by rank-and-file workers themselves. The call for expanded shop-floor democracy is related to broadened solidarities. Craftsmen, by virtue of their indispensable skills, had long enjoyed a voice in organizing production. The radical alternative aimed to involve a wider range of employees in "management" decisions. But the call for industrial democracy signifies another break from traditional policies. Rather than defending customary work rules (if possible, by unilateral regulation), skilled men accepted technical innovation but demanded a role in guiding change.

The emphasis on shop-floor participation stands opposed to contemporary practices in two respects. First, the rank and file rejected bureaucratic collective bargaining as the appropriate agency for labor's involvement in regulating working conditions. Workers' control should instead originate in the shops. Second, industrial democracy would not be limited to legalistic restrictions on employers' freedom of action. It would instead extend worker participation in the actual management of production. Here too craft traditions could play a progressive role. Skilled men were accustomed to making a wide range of decisions in the course of their work and relied more on work group cohesion than on outside union representatives to uphold the standards of the trade. This double autonomy—from management and from union officialdom—would contribute to the ideal of shop-floor democracy.

None of these ideal-typical distinctions alone proves unambiguous in sorting out the real world of factory politics, but, taken together, they suggest a distinctly different agenda for industrial conflict. Although few disputes met all the criteria for "radical" factory politics, the demands advanced in many were "radical" when even limited workplace rights were still in question and when even moderate demands for control were often pursued with remarkable militancy and under socialist or syndicalist banners. Both the realities and the limitations of radical factory politics will become clearer in subsequent discussions of specific conflicts and programs.

Theoretical Approaches to Factory Politics

The question of factory politics during the transition from craft production to modern manufacture has been presented in historical terms. But explaining factory politics involves theoretical problems, and the historical arguments made in this book are guided by a more abstract analytical scheme. Stated in general terms, the theoretical problem is that protest is highly selective. Among those in a common social setting, grievances and interests may vary, both for each individual and from one individual or group to another. Given this variety, there are diverse goals around which alternative coalitions may rally. Why, at any one moment, are certain of these interests, goals, and alliances—and not others—mobilized in collective action? Returning to the example of craft protest may clarify this theoretical problem.

Management attacks on craft control had many components and

generated varied grievances among skilled workers.[15] Craftsmen faced deskilling (or "dilution") as employers subdivided work tasks and introduced more automatic machinery. Employers also sought to assume control over production at the expense of the workers' customary autonomy, and payment by results challenged traditional notions of a fair day's work for a fair day's wage. Dilution and piecework undermined basic mechanisms by which craft unions defended their members' working conditions and standard of living. More rigorous and intrusive supervision violated craftsmen's standards of "manliness," independence, and integrity.

The grievances these changes produced were not of a piece. Dilution and piecework, for example, tended to reduce earnings; but they also threatened skills and craftsmanship of which skilled workers were intensely proud. Closer supervision undermined the autonomy and judgment traditionally exercised and highly valued by skilled men; yet it also violated commitments to liberal rights and freedoms that had little to do with occupational or class identities. Nor were grievances equally distributed. Because establishments would rarely modernize all at once, some trades would suffer while others remained, for the time being, secure. And innovations such as dilution undermined the position of craftsmen while offering less skilled workers opportunities for upward mobility.

Engineers and machinists could pursue a number of goals and alliances in response to these diverse grievances. They might concentrate on issues of shop control, attempting either to preserve customary standards or to create a new role for workers in managing industrial change. Alternatively, craftsmen might agree to trade traditional shop rights and privileges for economic rewards—permitting the introduction of new machines and the displacement of some skilled men, for example, in exchange for higher wages for those still employed. As for alliances, workers of one craft might fight their battles alone, apart from other tradesmen and aloof from the workplace rabble. Or they might join with workers of different trades, or even less skilled employees, to oppose management.

Historically, these alternatives combined in three ideal-typical patterns of factory politics.[16] First, engineers and machinists might seek to preserve their craft prerogatives at the expense of both management control and the interests of workers of other trades and skills. Regulations restricting machine operation to duly apprenticed men, for example, would both limit employers' discretion in job assignment and block the advancement of laborers. Demarcation rules, similarly, at once denied employers the right to assign workers to machines as they pleased and curtailed job opportunities for members of rival unions. Whatever the specific strategies, these tactics represent a policy of craft sectionalism.

A second possibility was for skilled men to trade in their job control and restrictive work practices for economic concessions—what would now be called "productivity bargaining." They might do so in cooperation with workers of other crafts and grades, acting together to secure higher wages. They might not. In either case this is a policy of economism (or instrumentalism).

A third possibility involved solidarity with employees of other trades and skill levels, but not at the expense of control over production practices. This has been termed a movement for "workers' control," dedicated to some principles of joint authority over workplace techniques, employment policies, and discipline and involving the participation and interests of a wide range of employees.

Each of these alternatives had its proponents among labor leaders and its partisans among the rank and file. Given the multiple grievances machine trades workers suffered, the theoretical problem is not to explain the occurrence of collective action.[17] The problem is rather to explain why specific grievances, goals, and alliances were favored—and others inhibited—in the mobilization of protest. How, in different times and places, were craft interests selectively mobilized? The combination of selected goals and alliances yielded particular patterns of factory politics. More concretely, processes of selective mobilization influenced the popular support enjoyed by competing leaders representing rival agendas for industrial conflict.

This conceptualization of the issues points to a basic analytical strategy. The focus should not be on workers' ideas and interests so much as on how these are translated into collective action. It is clearly necessary to show that certain grievances and proposed solutions were in fact available for mobilization. But having done this, explanatory arguments shift to considerations of selective mobilization. In brief, what are the chances that a given issue (e.g., dilution) or program (e.g., workers' control in one guise or another) can become the basis for collective action? Specifically, what groups within the labor force are likely to experience such an issue as a grievance? What are the chances that other groups in other departments, plants, or cities will share this grievance? What opportunities exist for aggrieved workers to communicate their dissatisfactions and their demands for redress? How do various conditions affect their ability to act in unison on this issue?

Because these influences will differ from one issue and demand to another, it is possible to gauge the prospects that some issues rather than others will form the basis for collective demands and to identify the origins and breadth of support for those demands. This approach offers a way of understanding the selective mobilization of goals and alliances in factory politics. The procedure will, to begin with, yield credible arguments only for why factory politics *should*, under specific conditions, assume a particular form. The analysis will gain added plausibility in two ways. First, the estimates for the relative prospects of certain kinds of factory politics may be confirmed from strikes, because strikes reveal goals and alliances in action. Second, it may be shown through comparisons—over time, between countries, and among sectors within a country—how the character of industrial conflict varies with contrasting conditions for mobilizing different issues and coalitions and does so in the expected ways.

The conditions affecting selective mobilization emphasized in this book are the labor process, union structures and policies, industrial relations, and state intervention. These may be conceptualized as conditions favoring or inhibiting mobilization on behalf of certain issues by specific work groups. The clearest contribution of the labor process to selective mobilization lies in the distribution of grievances and strategic power among the work force. Grievances concerning control of production often divided workers. Depending on the plant or department in which they worked, skilled men confronted different problems at any one time. Managers might hire rate fixers to study jobs in one shop while craftsmen elsewhere retained their customary freedom from close supervision. Changes in production techniques often blurred traditional distinctions between trades and incited demarcation disputes. And whereas deskilling undermined craft monopolies, it promised less skilled workers better pay and status. For such reasons the labor process favored sectional action on control issues. Economic grievances and demands had broader appeal and offered a more plausible basis for concerted action across skill and trade lines.

Just as the grievances experienced at work varied from one employee group to another, so too did the ability of different groups to act on their grievances. Skilled workers typically enjoyed greater influence with employers by virtue of their central role in production and the greater difficulty in replacing them. Being fewer in number and enjoying greater freedom to move about the shop, they faced fewer problems than less skilled workers in discussing grievances, formulating demands, and coordinating action. Craftsmen, accordingly, were often in a good position to act alone, without compromising their sectional interests. For these reasons, too, the labor process favored exclusive interests and conflicts in matters of control.

These influences varied from one country, industrial sector, and time to another. Some control issues were less divisive than others. Although skilled workers and machine tenders were at odds on the merits of deskilling, both resented arbitrary or "bullying" supervision. When the latter emerged as an important issue, alliances regarding aspects of shop control were possible. Changes in production techniques could lower the barriers separating employees of different skills and reduce the independent power of craftsmen.[18] But the creation of a more homogeneous, semiskilled work force would also erode the social base for control struggles—craftsmen and their traditions of autonomy at work. And other changes (e.g., the development of payment by results or job ladders) might introduce new obstacles to labor solidarity.[19] Such variations influence mobilization patterns.

The role of unions in shaping industrial conflict may be viewed in similar terms. Workers contemplating action on a given issue usually must evaluate the prospects that their union will support them with strike pay, negotiating skills, and boycotts. If they consider going out with other tradesmen, they may ask if other unions will offer similar support to their allies and thus preserve a united front. Similarly, local officials will need to weigh the chances for executive sanction and the costs of disobedience—in strike bene fits for which the local is not reimbursed and, at the extreme, in fines, suspensions, or expulsion.

It will be argued that national union leaders typically favored

sectional action and economic demands. They did so in part because they undertook the same kind of analysis advocated in this
book: calculating chances for mobilizing effective strike action, and
thus the likely return on a given investment of union funds. What
are the chances that this particular strike can be won? How firm is
our members' support? How strongly will management resist this
demand? Can we count on sympathetic support from other trades?
What are the possible rewards of success (and costs of failure) in
terms of membership, organization, and the basic standards of
working conditions for our constituents?

The answers to these questions generally favor economistic policies. It is usually easier to mobilize broad support for wage demands than for idiosyncratic disputes over workplace control.
Employers are more disposed to concede pay increases than to
compromise their "managerial rights." And by securing real im-
provements for their members, union leaders improve their own
positions. Finally, executive officials are wary of involving their organizations in strikes by workers of different skills and union affiliations (though naturally they welcome the support of others in
their own disputes). Such strikes involve an unpredictable and po-
tentially large drain on the treasury, have less certain prospects,
and, even if successful, may bring disproportionately small rewards in terms of increased membership and improved organization.[20]

Union policies, then, channel rank-and-file unrest toward sectional action and economistic goals, at least to the extent that workers depend on their executives for support and respond to union
sanctions against unofficial action. These constraints may be more
or less forceful from case to case. During economic booms, when
profits are high and labor scarce, workers can expect that strikes
will be short and (if strikers are fired) new jobs easily found. They
are thus in a better position to forgo union support. In some instances negotiations with employers (or employer associations) and
control over union benefits are highly centralized; in others local
lodges (or even shop committees) retain greater autonomy in their
conduct of trade policy.[21] Factory politics would be less constrained
by national perspectives and priorities in the latter case. It may
happen, too, that uncongenial national policies and union bureaucracy heighten the appeal of local autonomy, thus creating ideological conditions favorable to radical factory politics.

A third determinant of factory politics is industrial relations—the rules and conventions governing relations between labor and employers. Of special interest here are procedures and policies for resolving disputes. Employers often claim that certain control issues (e.g., selecting foremen, assigning workers to machines, or discharging undesirable employees) are nonnegotiable, falling within the realm of unquestionable management rights. Wages, by contrast, are declared a legitimate subject for consultation. Employers may also agree to meet with employee representatives and discuss grievances, but only if the employees remain at work while conferences proceed. Union officials often accept these rules of the game as the safest and fastest route to union recognition and organization.

If workers take advantage of conciliation procedures, they have to accept definitions of "legitimate" grievances laid down by management and endorsed by their unions. They also have to cede responsibility for negotiation to union representatives and thus in practice follow the agenda for factory politics sanctioned by officials.[22] To a lesser degree the same restrictions apply even where (as in the United States prior to the 1930s) open shops prevail. Given employers' resolute opposition to any encroachments on their right to manage, but their professed willingness to discuss wage matters (albeit only with their own employees), union leaders and members alike would tend to follow the path of least resistance, which favors action on behalf of economic rather than control interests. In either instance these constraints on factory politics will be more or less binding from case to case. Favorable economic conditions, tight labor markets, and strong local organization, for example, give rank-and-file workers the capacity to act effectively without regard for industrial relations sanctions. Here, too, excessive restrictions on workers' freedom of action may contribute to radical factory politics by widening the appeal of "direct action" and shop-floor control.

Thus, the impact of the labor process, unions, and industrial relations on factory politics is not uniform. A crucial source of variation is government intervention.[23] Between 1890 and 1920, the British and American governments actively involved themselves in day-to-day work relations only during World War I. The effects of this involvement can be traced through determinants of factory politics already discussed and treated in similar terms. Government-sponsored changes in production techniques both intensified the grievances and enhanced skilled workers' bargaining power. Both governments gave legal support to union policies that discouraged control struggles and independent rank-and-file action; yet they also inadvertently impaired unions' capacity to enforce these policies on their members. Both governments sought to centralize industrial relations procedures, ban strikes, and restrict disputes to economistic issues. Here, too, however, war mobilization made defiance of these restrictions less costly to workers and forced government officials to settle disputes in war industries even over employers' objections. Government action could also alter the ideological terrain for factory politics. At some times state policies highlighted issues (e.g., dilution or military exemptions) that divided the interests of craftsmen and less skilled workers; at other times wartime policies accentuated common grievances (e.g., over workplace authority).

Finally, government intervention encouraged the development of unofficial rank-and-file organization, which put metalworkers in a position to mobilize around control issues despite the impediments of the labor process, unions, and the government itself. Ultimately, however, the state—even more than scheming capitalists or reactionary trade union leaders—spurred the union and industrial relations reforms that undermined workers' control movements. The economistic and sectional priorities so familiar in contemporary factory politics reflect in part the success of government intervention in a crucial period of industrial change.

Workshop organization—how workers more or less formally cooperate at work to advance their interests—is a critical factor mediating the effects of the labor process, unions, industrial relations, and state intervention. These four elements affected rank-and-file organization within the shops—its strength, independence, and sectional or solidary character. They did so directly, influencing the opportunities for and constitution of workshop organization, and indirectly, as workers developed their own agencies for collective action in response to shop conditions and their institutional environment. Yet the effects of the labor process, unions, and industrial relations may be offset—or reinforced—by rank-and-file organization. Features of the labor process tend to divide workers, especially on questions of control. But insofar as employees discuss grievances in shop meetings, hammer out joint demands, and select common representatives to deal with management, these divisions may be overcome. Unions may favor exclusive action and defensive goals, while industrial relations arrangements limit the aims and scope of worker militancy. Yet workshop organization can provide an agency through which employees can conduct bargaining and handle disputes in defiance of union officials and industrial relations rules. Such arrangements create a favorable organizational terrain for mobilizing control demands and solidary action. It is equally possible, of course, that workshop organization along sectional lines, under union control, and incorporated into industrial relations procedures may more strongly inhibit united action for workers' control.

These theoretical propositions complement the earlier historical argument. Both suggest the peculiar importance of workshop organization in explaining movements for workers' control. The historical discussion identified certain obstacles to radical factory politics and raised the possibility that these might be overcome by independent, solidary organization. Conceptualizing the labor process, unions, and industrial relations as conditions favoring or impeding mobilization on behalf of certain issues leads to similar conclusions. Each factor typically favored sectional action and an economistic agenda. But in each case this influence varied, and rank-and-file organization is a crucial source of that variation.

This approach to factory politics thus adapts general principles for analyzing goals and alliances in collective action to the study of a particular historical problem: the rise and fall of workers' control struggles. It is a method of connecting certain social conditions not directly to ideology but to ideological practices, not to the ideas of workers but to the principles they pursue in action.

Recasting the question of factory politics as a problem of selective mobilization suggests guidelines for historical explanation. The more formal propositions concerning selective mobilization in craft protest also facilitate comparisons among distinctive individual cases. Analytically separating the contributions of unions, industrial relations, workshop organization, and the labor process to selective mobilization does some injustice to historical realities. "Unions," "industrial relations," and "workshop organization" are not sharply demarcated in practice. Nor are they fully *independent* variables: for example, the labor process strongly influences union strength and industrial relations practices.

Despite their empirical fuzziness, these distinctions are useful. They highlight variations in the relations among causal factors that prove important for the development of factory politics. The term "industrial relations," for example, normally includes unions, but the influence of formal contracts or informal labor-management understandings is partly independent of union policies. Although two unions may take an equally dim view of unofficial strikes, only one may agree with employers to ban such strikes in exchange for regular grievance procedures. Similarly, rank-and-file leaders (such as shop stewards and committees) may be official union representatives with a recognized role in collective bargaining. The chapters that follow, however, emphasize variations in the connections between workshop organization and unions or industrial relations procedures—formal or informal, cooperative or antagonistic, dependent or independent. These variations can then be used in comparative analysis to identify more clearly the role of specific factors in selective mobilization.

This method of analyzing factory politics has other justifications. One is historiographical. Documentation of the ideas and shop culture of metalworkers is meager, and what exists is not necessarily representative. The approach advocated here sidesteps this problem of evidence by emphasizing action rather than motives and by examining how types of action are selected from a range of possibilities. For the study of factory politics, whether or not employees have personal commitments to workers' control is irrelevant if they do not act accordingly, and quite varied interests might contribute to alliances in pursuit of workers' control.

There are virtues in this historically dictated shift in focus. Above all, principles of selective mobilization establish more compelling links between the organization of work and factory politics than students of the labor process generally offer. A common approach in this literature is to attribute the weakness of rank-and-file radicalism to employers' divide-and-conquer strategies. Thus some see job ladders or spurious occupational distinctions as operating to block worker solidarity.[24] But pointing to divisive arrangements only begins the analysis of factory politics. Although labor's internal divisions are important, it is also necessary to consider the opposite side of "divide and conquer": alliances and resistance. Workers do, after all, act together—along some lines—and do oppose management—on some issues. A more complete account must show how specific divisions and weaknesses among workers impede some alliances but not others and inhibit battles on certain but not all issues. *Normally,* workers of different skills have conflicting interests with regard to issues of workshop control, and employer policies may encourage these conflicts. But these same workers may share other concerns (e.g., the length of the work day). Thus employees may be divided and conquered on one front but ally and fight back on another. These considerations are obviously important in analyzing factory politics.

A second strategy for connecting work relations to labor politics, evident especially in Michael Burawoy's work, narrows the gap left by divide-and-conquer theories. He views workplace arrangements as generating particular interests and orientations among workers and as shaping their capacity to act on those interests. In Burawoy's comparative study of factory regimes and working-class politics,[25] workers' *goals* are traced to interests and ideologies produced within the factory gates. Thus factory regimes that institutionalized patriarchy at work favored industrial and political action by male cotton spinners to defend their economic privileges against encroachments by women and children. By a similar logic, internal labor markets encouraged individualistic attitudes and production politics among machinists in the United States, and the absence of such devices led to more equalitarian orientations on the part of British engineers.

Different *capacities,* in turn, account for different *levels* of conflict. Paternalistic factory regimes, Burawoy argues, denied workers an independent base for protest. This explains the relative absence of industrial protest in Lancashire during the third quarter of the nineteenth century. Differences in workers' control over production processes and in the stability of labor forces between Moscow cotton factories and St. Petersburg metalworks, similarly, led to greater levels of conflict in the latter.

Ronald Aminzade's study of artisans in mid-nineteenth-century Toulouse is narrower in empirical focus and owes more to resource mobilization theory than to structuralist Marxism.[26] The links he makes between the workplace and worker politics, however, are similar to Burawoy's. Changes in the organization of production and consequent threats to artisans' status generated key grievances over wages and control of production; these grievances, in turn, shaped artisans' political goals. The same changes at work (together with broader cultural and political developments) also fostered working-class associations that gave artisans the capacity to act on their grievances. For example, factory production undercut traditional trade controls over wages and working conditions. The resultant development of more encompassing class organizations enhanced workers' ability to defend their interests.

A different method for connecting work and factory politics is adopted in this book. Although it is necessary to uncover the grievances and interests generated at work, such orientations cannot explain the goals of industrial protest. Workers had a variety of interests and possible courses of action. Explaining factory politics requires understanding the processes by which some of these interests and alternatives are selected for mobilization. And if interests alone do not sufficiently account for collective goals, workers' "capacities" are relevant to much more than levels of protest. The logic of resource mobilization adopted by Aminzade[27] and (less explicitly) by Burawoy tends to invoke interests and capacities to explain different sorts of outcomes—the goals and the extent of collective action.

An alternative approach highlights how interests shape capacities and capacities shape interests. On one side, the kinds of capacities workers enjoy—such as the bargaining power of specific work groups or the alliances formed among them—are crucial for determining which interests will be mobilized and which goals pursued. On the other side, the salience of specific grievances and goals in different contexts influences the formation of alliances by workers and between work groups; such alliances, in turn, affect workers' capacities for concerted action.

As many recent studies emphasize,[28] the interests and capacities that guide working-class protest are not generated solely on the job. Community concerns (over food prices, rents, and local politics) and institutions (pubs, dance halls, ethnic associations, political clubs) interact with experiences and resources at work to influence patterns of protest. Chapter Eight suggests how analysis sensitive to selective mobilization and to the interplay of interests and capacities may be usefully applied to studies of community life and broader working-class political behavior. The focus in this book is confined strictly to factory politics, in which the key determinants of selective mobilization, and especially of the *differences* in factory politics between cases, are to be found in the organization and institutional setting of work.

To emphasize the selective mobilization of goals and alliances rather than the beliefs of flesh-and-blood individuals may appear contemptuous of real people. It is not. The goal is to steer a middle course between two competing scholarly agendas—one preoccupied with structural determinants of social action, the other with the subjective experiences and creative action of real men and women. In the practical business of explaining social phenomena, one must adopt explanatory principles from each camp. This book does attend less to people making their own history than to the conditions, not of their own choosing, under which they do so. But it also acknowledges how conditions shaping factory politics themselves become objects of contention among the rank and file, union leaders, employers, and government officials. The outcomes of these contentions are new conditions. More important, these conditions are interpreted in terms of the dilemmas and opportunities faced by workers and their leaders. For example, by emphasizing how the labor process or industrial relations systematically favors some alternatives for action over others, an element of human choice is at least preserved conceptually within largely structural explanations. And to some degree this analytical strategy mirrors the deliberations of workers and union officials in choosing among different courses of action.

Preview

The existence of competing agendas for factory politics has been traced to a period of transition from craft control to modern production and management techniques. This book begins, accordingly, with a survey of craft control in the late nineteenth century, how it came under attack by employers, and the varied grievances that followed among skilled workers (Chapter Two). Much of this discussion is broadly applicable to the entire period 1890–1922. The mobilization of protest against management initiatives, how-

ever, was shaped by characteristics of unions and industrial relations in the 1890s. These influences are evaluated in Chapter
Three, along with the development of factory politics—developments that culminated, in both countries, in industrywide disputes
and attempts to solve "the labor problem" in the metal trades on a
national scale.

The outcomes of these disputes were new and divergent environments for factory politics. British employers relied on trade
agreements and union discipline, American employers on open
shops and union busting. Chapter Four reviews this altered context for protest and analyzes its consequences for factory politics—
the emergence of new forms of rank-and-file organization and how
these organizational changes, in combination with union policies
and industrial relations conditions, facilitated alliances behind new
goals and leaders. Chapter Four concludes by evaluating persisting
obstacles and limitations to radical factory politics.

A final group of chapters focuses on World War I and its aftermath. Chapter Five describes the war's impact on the labor process, unions, and industrial relations and the role of government
intervention in these areas. The culmination and containment of
movements for workers' control are analyzed in separate studies of
Coventry (Chapter Six) and Bridgeport (Chapter Seven). The impact of the war in these cities—introducing new workshop practices, increased rank-and-file bargaining power, union restraint
in the national interest, major departures from prewar industrial
relations procedures, and unprecedented government intervention—is typical of munitions centers throughout Britain and the
United States.

In one important respect Coventry is not representative of national conditions. As the home of Britain's most progressive engineering sectors (automobiles and motorcycles), the city experienced wartime changes in production techniques and organization
that were less abrupt than elsewhere. The radical potential of craft
traditions was thus less fully expressed in Coventry. The relative
degree of wartime militancy (within or between countries) is not of
primary concern, however. Rather, these chapters emphasize the
contrasting structural bases of that militancy and the corresponding differences in the containment of radical factory politics. For
these purposes struggles over the status and organization of shop

committees in Coventry and Bridgeport are unusually clear examples of conflicts occurring throughout the two countries. The resolution of these struggles also helped set the pattern for each nation's industry as a whole. The settlement of Coventry's 1917 shop stewards strike was national in scope and subsequently incorporated into the 1919 and 1922 industrywide agreements. Similarly, the system of works committees the National War Labor Board established for Bridgeport in 1918 reflected general government policies and paved the way for company unionism in the metal trades during the postwar period. Chapter Nine evaluates contrasting patterns of radicalization and containment in comparative perspective and clarifies the analytical lessons for selective mobilization.

The arrangement of chapters reflects an effort to divide historical developments into periods. The first period extends up to the national disputes and their resolutions (1898 in Britain, 1901 in the United States), the second to 1914 (with the American metal trades involved in the war long before the U.S. government entered), and the third through the war and immediate postwar years. This periodization is designed in part to help organize comparative analysis.

Comparison is the principal method used to identify and sort out the complex connections between the labor process, unions, industrial relations, and state intervention on one side and factory politics on the other. The major comparative focus is on the two national (or city) cases. Engineers and machinists shared certain grievances at work but acted under different industrial relations and union environments before World War I and different government policies during the war. Contrasting patterns of factory politics in the two cases help clarify the effects of trade unionism, industrial relations, and state intervention on the mobilization of protest.

Further comparisons *within* each country, focusing on varied combinations of the key explanatory factors, allow refinements in the causal argument while providing rough controls on national differences. One such comparison is between time periods. Industrial relations in British engineering, for example, changed with the settlement of the 1897–1898 lockout. Juxtaposing factory politics before and after the lockout suggests the influence of the national trade agreement imposed in 1898. Similar use may be made of contrasts between workshop organization during World War I and conditions, in either country, before or after the war. A second type of internal comparison is between different sectors within each national industry. American railroad repair shops display relatively traditional manufacturing practices, strong unions, and recognized collective bargaining procedures. Because these were unusual traits for the United States, differences between factory politics here and in more typical metal trades sectors are especially instructive. So too are contrasts between Coventry—with its relatively modern auto plants and, before World War I, weak craft societies—and more traditional engineering centers of Britain.

These comparisons do not offer rigorous scientific tests. The determinants of factory politics are too numerous and their interactions too complex to systematically isolate the precise role of each independent variable. Comparison is used instead in a Weberian spirit, as a method for refining concepts and checking the application of broad theories to particular cases. The transition from craft control to modern production and management opened up alternative lines of development for factory politics. Certain sociological concepts are advanced as analytical tools to account for the selection of some alternatives rather than others. These concepts may be useful in other empirical settings, but they are not general laws, to be tested and confirmed or rejected by comparative study. Rather, the principle of selective mobilization offers basic guidelines for research. The results of comparative analysis will be a better understanding of how common dilemmas were resolved, or how a similar range of possibilities was narrowed, in specific ways and in historically distinct settings.

The primary evidence on factory politics is drawn from strikes. Sometimes particularly important or large-scale disputes are examined in detail; occasionally aggregate strike data are invoked to verify an argument or suggest a trend; and at many points the facts of a dispute are used in more anecdotal fashion.

Strikes merit close attention because they speak to most of the key issues in this book.[29] They are a gauge of solidarities and alliances—who came out? They indicate the goals of collective action—what did the strikers demand? They offer signs of the relations between the rank-and-file workers and their union and the influence of different factions and organizations within the labor movement—who called the strike? Was it sanctioned by union executives? Which leaders or committees conducted negotiations, made key decisions, and arranged a return to work? Finally, strikes suggest the role of industrial relations rules in shaping conflict. Were grievances processed through established channels and according to formal procedures? Did union officials hold members in check until constitutional remedies had been exhausted? Were some demands abandoned in the course of negotiations?

Strikes thus provide useful information, which comes in a form especially suitable for analyzing selective mobilization. On the one hand, strikes complement a largely structural interpretation of factory politics by exposing the commitments and ideals of ordinary workers. Indeed, strike participation is a more rigorous indicator of individual values than a vote on a union resolution or an answer to a survey question, for here one sees people sacrificing income, perhaps putting their jobs at risk, and, during World War I, incurring public censure and even government reprisals in support of some goal. The goal may not have been a noble one, but evidently it was highly valued. On the other hand, even if one could systematically uncover individual worker attitudes, the information would not be adequate for explaining factory politics. Where grievances are many and interests varied and possibly conflicting, strikes show which issues ultimately became the basis for collective demands. And when the historical record is sufficiently rich, it is possible to see this process of selective mobilization in action.

Chapter Two

The Employers' Challenge
to Craft Standards

Engineers and machinists of the 1880s exercised a wide range of controls over workshop life. Trade customs and the craftsman's own judgment sharply circumscribed employers' roles in training apprentices, assigning workers to machines, choosing manufacturing techniques, setting the work pace, and supervising workers. Within a single generation craftsmen would see many of these powers won by management and used to enforce employers' standards and interests. By reorganizing and retooling production, managers reduced their dependence on skilled workers. Through new wage payment methods, employers gained greater control over the pace and details of manufacturing operations. By more closely directing and supervising work tasks, managers secured for themselves a large measure of the control over shop life that craftsmen had formerly enjoyed.

Deskilling, payment by results, and new authority relations developed in response to the pressures and opportunities of changing markets, technological innovation, and workplace conflict. The same basic trajectory and causes of change are found in both Britain and the United States from the late nineteenth century into the 1920s. Yet the development of the labor process was uneven. In each country dilution, wage incentive schemes, and novel modes of supervision were more advanced in newer industrial sectors with large, standardized product markets—cycles, autos, electrical goods—than in traditional centers of the trade. Change generally came earlier in American than in British shops, occurred more rapidly, and assumed more systematic forms (including that of "scientific management"). The position of skilled workers and their unions varied accordingly within and between the two countries. As subsequent chapters show, these variations had important consequences for factory politics. It is best to begin, however, by emphasizing the challenges and discontents that engineers and machinists shared. Contrasting patterns of industrial protest developed from a similar stock of perceived injustices. Juxtaposing craftsmen's common tribulations with their divergent responses demonstrates the limited explanatory power of popular grievances alone.

The diversity of skilled workers' grievances is what makes the development of factory politics problematic. Craft control rewarded engineers and machinists with economic privileges and professional pride. Management strategies threatened both the financial well-being and the collective moral standards of craftsmen. This double challenge to skilled workers helps explain the intensity, if not the specific character, of conflict over industrial change. Craft ethics also prevented employers from resolving these conflicts by sharing the fruits of increased productivity. Economic enticements alone would not lead machinists and engineers to abandon their customary powers and standards at work. And under favorable conditions this moral code would lead craftsmen from a defense of the status quo to demands for workers' control.

Craft Control

Late-nineteenth-century craftsmen in the metalworking trade, as in other industries,[1] discharged most of what later would be called "management" functions. These included the recruitment and training of skilled workers. Employers chose apprentices, but customs and union rules limited the number they could take on, usually one for every four or five journeymen. Over the apprentice's four-year term he received meager wages from his employer and most of his education from journeymen. At its start this training was not technical—the apprentice might spend the first six months sweeping up—but social, an initiation into the "traditions, customs, and usages" of the workshop and the trade. Loyalty to one's craft and mates, a manly pride in one's work, a skeptical attitude toward the technical competence of employers, and an outright contempt for unapprenticed "monkey wrenches and Ho Bo machinists" were part of the apprentice's early education.[2] Under the tutelage of journeymen, apprentices eventually worked their way through the different machine shop tools and techniques. Although young journeymen would probably develop some specialized competence—fitting or turning in Britain, using some class of machine tool in the United States—by the end of their terms they could turn their hands at most machine shop operations. Versatility was the hallmark of the fully qualified craftsman.[3]

Apprenticeship helped engineers and machinists control the labor market. Its aim was to produce broadly trained workers in sufficiently small numbers to avoid flooding the trade. Particularly for smaller firms doing a variety of work, the system also had advantages for employers. It did produce well-trained, all-around workers, and for the last year or two of an apprenticeship, the employer got the services of such workers for very low wages. In 1896, the *American Machinist* found active apprenticeship programs in more than 70 percent of firms surveyed, and Charles More finds the system surviving in British shops well into the 1910s.[4] Journeymen's control over recruitment and training was supplemented in some cases by their powers to hire, fire, and pay their own helpers.[5]

The extent of craft control was most clearly shown in the skilled metalworker's responsibility for getting the work out. When an order came in, the craftsman might act as his own draftsman and, at the very least, would interpret designs and drawings and determine the appropriate sequence of operations for producing the required pieces. He would plan out each individual operation, setting up the machine, finding and grinding his own tools, and doing the work. Because few shops could afford to provide for every contingency, engineers and machinists often improvised with materials and tools (with union and trade journals proudly reporting the inventive makeshifts of "practical men"). The assembly of individual parts required a fine eye and considerable dexterity with the file to achieve a good fit. With his command of skill came the craftsman's independence. "The machinist was allowed to operate on the particular piece of work given him according to his own ideas of what was fit and proper, having tools dressed and ground as he wished and choosing his own speeds and feeds."[6] Similarly, engineers and machinists were often free to move about the shop, from one machine to another, to the grindstone and tool room, and to work at their own pace, according to their own notions of "a job well done."[7] Employers often objected to their craftsmen's discretion and work pace, but, given the indispensability of skilled workers and the absence of any alternative means for getting the work done, there was little they could do about it.

Craft control of production was formalized in the rule that only craftsmen were eligible to run machines and handle tools. In U.S. shops of the 1860s, "there were but few 'handy men,' so-called— none at all who ever touched a machine tool to operate it, or otherwise than as a laborer to help shift jobs. This would have been resented promptly by the workmen, and though not given to striking they would have left the shop in a body if laborers had been allowed to handle tools."[8] Such regulations were embodied in the branch constitutions of the International Union of Machinists and Blacksmiths of the United States of America in the 1860s and in the rules of the International Association of Machinists (IAM) and the Amalgamated Society of Engineers (ASE). Local practice varied. Where possible, "skilled" work was restricted to apprenticed craftsmen or union members; elsewhere union branches insisted that employers pay the craft rate for skilled work. In neither case could employers assign operators to machines as they saw fit, and machine shop work was generally split between relatively high-wage craftsmen, responsible for most production tasks, and unskilled laborers and helpers, who fetched materials, helped lift heavy pieces, and cleaned up. By ensuring that journeymen were recruited only through apprenticeships, unions reinforced this division over time.[9]

A final aspect of craft control involved engineers' and machinists' considerable freedom from direct supervision. Their principal overseer was likely to be the foreman, who could be hard on subordinates. But the supervisor's authority had clear limits. By virtue of their skill, craftsmen would not be told how to do their work or (within reason) how long it should take. Bullying foremen would lose their best workers (and see their reputations suffer as a result), for engineers and machinists strongly resented any challenge to their "manhood" and autonomy.[10] The foremen, who usually came up from the ranks and often retained their union membership, had some sympathy for craft customs and some tolerance for the idiosyncrasies of skilled men. There were rarely formal rules or explicit instructions from above to direct them otherwise.[11] The craftsmen's responsibility for training new workers, their management of production, and their freedom from close supervision meant that employers exercised but slight, informal, and indirect control of their own shops.[12]

Challenges to Craft Control

Engineers or machinists completing their apprenticeships around 1890 would live to see profound changes in their trade. Over the next thirty years craft control would be undermined and management prerogatives emphatically asserted and exercised in new ways. This transformation did not occur all at once, but in fits and starts, varying in character and extent from one shop or sector to another. The trend was clear, however. Indeed, because changes at work were the subjects of wide debate and contention, the trend was perhaps as clear to managers and workers at the time as it is to the historian today. Its principal features were deskilling, the spread of piecework, and more exacting and detailed management supervision of workers. From the craftsmen's point of view, manual skills were parceled out to specialists and transferred to new machines, and knowledge and control of production were centralized in management hands and embodied in specific instructions and finely calculated piece rates.

The most far-reaching challenge to craftsmen's position was deskilling (or "dilution"), three aspects of which are particularly important: the transfer of knowledge and control to management, the transfer of skills to machines, and the fragmentation of craft work into specialized tasks.

Management, not craftsmen, gradually took charge of production. Instead of handing skilled workers rough drawings and leaving the rest to them, management planned out the job before it ever reached the shop floor. The order in which work should proceed, the routing of materials and parts from one machine or department to the next, and even how each individual operation should be done (which machine to use, the requisite speeds, feeds, and cutting angles) were increasingly determined in the office by management rather than on the floor by craftsmen and foremen. In the well-managed shop of the 1910s and 1920s, materials, tools, and instructions would be provided to machinists or engineers as required; they could then devote their full attention to productive work.[13]

Skill was transferred to machines as well. Even before the 1890s, specialized machine tools joined other, more versatile machines as part of the standard machine shop equipment. Accomplishing varied tasks on a general-purpose lathe demanded highly skilled workers. Many of the new tools, designed for specific operations (e.g., drilling machines and screw or gear cutters), did not. Others, such as millers, slotters, or grinding machines, performed operations previously done by hand. With single-purpose machines came specialists, operators skilled in a narrow line of work. In their own line they turned out work equal in quality to that of all-around craftsmen, and did so for lower wages.[14]

Newer machine tools in the 1890s and after took this process further. Where large quantities of a standard piece could be sold, employers increasingly adopted automatic machinery. Once set up, turret or capstan lathes, screw machines, and some milling or grinding machines could conduct a series of operations without human intervention. Operatives, who only had to place the piece in the machine, start it up, and remove the finished product, needed little manual skill or technical knowledge. Moreover, with machine tools able to turn out standard pieces to close tolerances, skilled fitting of parts gave way to less skilled assembly. Eventually, this trend led to assembly lines. And with both specialized manual machines and automatic ones, management claimed the right to assign operators as it saw fit, regardless of union rules or customs.[15]

New technology combined with reorganization to change the functions and reduce the numbers of fully skilled workers. If employers were to pay for craftsmen, they sought to get their money's worth. A variety of tasks customarily performed by skilled men (e.g., getting and grinding their own tools, fixing belts, and chasing after work materials) required neither their skills nor their time. Some of these tasks management assigned to specialists in tool grinding or belt repair. Others were facilitated by installing cranes and trolleys and by making more rigorous provision for delivering the appropriate materials and tools to workers at their machines. Skilled men thus found themselves gradually confined to their posts, working with little interruption for the full day and often at a single machine—or even several machines of the same type.

The goal of many managers was to shift craftsmen out of production altogether. Production departments would be staffed by less skilled specialists and operatives, turning out large quantities of standardized parts. Skilled workers would be responsible for setting up machines, for repairs, and especially for the varied tasks and limited output involved in making tools, jigs, fixtures, and gauges.[16] Their numbers declined accordingly. In 1910, "nearly three-fourths of all jobs in the auto shops were classified as skilled work. By 1924, skilled workers were estimated as five to ten percent of the work force of the auto shops."[17] An extreme case—the Ford Motor Company—shows the proportion of skilled mechanics falling from 28 percent in 1910 to 2.4 percent in 1917.[18] Among firms belonging to the British Engineering Employers' Federation, 60 percent of workers were classified as skilled in 1914, 34 percent in 1928.[19]

While the numbers of fully skilled workers diminished, the numbers of specialists and semiskilled machine tenders increased. In British engineering firms the proportion of the work force classified as semiskilled stood at 20 percent in 1914 and 53 percent in 1928.[20] At Ford 26 percent of employees were specialists in 1910, 55.3 percent in 1917.[21] Between 1910 and 1920, the number of journeymen and apprentice machinists in the United States grew 82.8 percent and then declined by 22 percent over the next decade. By contrast, machine operatives in auto and farm equipment increased 473.1 percent during the years 1910–1920, and their numbers continued to expand at a slower pace over the following ten years.[22] Semiskilled workers formed a new stratum in the workshops, blurring the traditional distinction between skilled men who operated machines and laborers who fetched and carried. The latter also declined in numbers as management improved work flow coordination and installed mechanical conveyances (e.g., cranes, trolleys, and moving belts) to help move materials.[23]

One corollary of dilution was the decline of union apprenticeship regulations. The value of apprenticeship for employers diminished as the proportion of semiskilled workers increased. Managers who planned manufacturing tasks, divided jobs, and adopted specialized machinery had less need for broadly trained workers. The ASE and the IAM sought to preserve a system under which a limited number of youths acquired all-around skills and to place only workers thus trained on the machines. With increasing success, employers instead hired apprentices and learners in excessive numbers, kept them in one line of work indefinitely, and assigned them to machines claimed by craftsmen.[24] In the United States apprenticeship declined to a point where employers complained that they could not find the few all-around machinists still required. By 1910, efforts were under way to increase the supply of skilled labor through company training programs and technical education. Unfettered by union regulations, these schemes promised employers as many workers as needed, with training tailored to the demands of modern manufacture. If, through government-supported technical schools, this cost employers little and removed boys "during the formative period, from the union atmosphere," so much the better.[25]

Dilution circumscribed the tasks skilled workers performed. Yet it also transferred from craftsmen to management control over assignments to machines and methods for doing the work. On the surface, payment by results seemed merely to base earnings on output rather than on time worked. Here, too, however, a great deal more was involved. Through payment by results employers sought to wrest from skilled workers and foremen their customary control over the pace, character, and costs of machine shop production.

In 1886, 5 percent of men and youths in British engineering and boilermaking were paid by the piece; by 1906, 27.5 percent of them were paid in this fashion; and in 1927, the figure had grown to 49.5 percent. Among specialists, women, and workers in industries characterized by repetitive production, piecework was even more popular with employers. In 1906, 47 percent of "machine men" (specialists), 52 percent of women workers, 52.8 percent of cycle makers, and 67.6 percent of railway carriage and wagon builders were paid by results.[26] Comparable figures do not exist for the United States; but reviewing the period from July 1, 1907, to June 30, 1909, IAM President O'Connell estimated that more than

50 percent of the strikes involving union members resulted from attempts to introduce piecework and that the IAM had been largely unable to prevent the spread of the system. Certainly, piecework would have been even more prevalent in nonunion shops, and contemporary observers found a greater resort to payment by results in the United States than in Britain.[27] By 1922, of twenty-eight metal trades plants studied by the Federated American Engineering Societies, sixteen had well-developed wage incentive plans, and only three had no such plan.[28]

The earliest, simplest, and most widely used system of payment by results was straight piecework. Instead of being paid so much per hour, workers received a certain sum for each piece produced. Particularly after 1900, more exotic systems gained attention and popularity. These differed in operation and name but shared a basic principle. A certain time would be set to complete a job or produce a certain number of pieces. The time saved or the amount by which the quota was exceeded formed the basis for calculating a bonus. Exactly how that bonus was figured varied and could be quite mystifying. In perhaps the most straightforward system (the "Halsey" plan), a job time might be set at ten hours. Workers who completed the job in eight hours earned their hourly time rate for those eight hours plus a bonus of 50 percent of the time saved— that is, they received nine hours' pay for eight hours' work. Other schemes were considerably more complicated.[29]

Whatever the system, the tendency was to relieve foremen of responsibility for fixing rates, this duty falling instead to specialized personnel ("rate fixers" and, eventually, time and motion experts). If the work resembled that done in the past, rates might be fixed from the office on the basis of records of previous times and estimates of how long a machine "should" take to complete the job, given the relevant variables (the materials being used; the amount of metal being removed; the appropriate speeds, feeds, and cutting angles; and the desired finish). Particularly with new work, the tools of scientific management—the stopwatch and the motion study—were deployed to determine how quickly a job could be done. Depending especially on the strength of union organization in the shop, rates might be subject to negotiation or imposed unilaterally.

Payment by results presupposed a degree of standardization

and repetition in machine shop operations. Where output consisted of only a few pieces of a kind, as in much tool room and
repair work, it did not pay to invest the time and money required
to estimate rates and calculate bonuses. Elsewhere, however, incentive schemes had considerable advantages for employers. Pay
ment by results helped centralize control over incentives and work
pace. Craftsmen would no longer be allowed to define "a job well
done" or "a fair day's work."[30] Increased control over effort levels,
in turn, allowed management to lower the costs of supervision and
to estimate more accurately costs and delivery dates for prospective customers.[31]

A final component of the employers' challenge involved efforts
to substitute tighter management control over workshop tasks for
the discretion and autonomy enjoyed by skilled workers. Instead
of relying on their workers' seasoned judgment, managers increasingly issued detailed instructions to their hands, specifying how
machine tools were to be set up, the speeds and feeds at which
each job should be run, and the specific dimensions of the finished
piece. Such orders were necessary above all for less skilled employees, for whom clear directions substituted for personal knowledge. Cheap workers required costly supervision; deskilling thus
forced managers to assume new responsibilities. But the detailed
direction of tasks applied to skilled men as well. Increasingly, work
was given out with job cards attached, indicating precisely how the
job should be done and the piece rates or bonus times allowed.[32]
Management sought to dispense with craftsmen's judgment in favor of central planning and direction of work performance.

Once instructions were issued, of course, they had to be enforced. Employees of all skill grades faced closer supervision and
scrutiny to ensure obedience to rules, adherence to instructions,
and constant application to their work. Time discipline became
more relentless and exacting as the Bundy time recorder gained
favor, and metalworkers faced the prospect of losing from fifteen
minutes' to a half day's pay if they arrived moments past starting
time. Once at work they might have to clock in and out of each job
to ensure compliance with production standards, provide employers with accurate information on times and costs, and prevent
worker "fiddling" with premium bonus times. Later, even this
check proved too rough and ready, and time discipline narrowed

its focus to individual motions, measured in hundredths of a second.[33] All increased supervision was not so impersonal, however. Particularly as firms grew in size and management assumed new responsibilities, engineers and machinists found themselves "watched and dogged by a whole army of non-producers."[34] At Ford in 1914, one foreman supervised an average of fifty-three workers; in 1917, there was a foreman for every fifteen.[35] An array of new supervisory personnel—rate fixers, speed and feed men, progress chasers, inspectors—confronted workers at every turn, leaving few aspects of machine shop life to the discretion of employees.

At first new supervisory tasks, together with responsibilities for recruitment, job assignment, and piece rates, were added to foremen's duties. Such power could corrupt, and foremen were often found tyrannical and abusive by their subordinates and unreliable by their employers. Gradually, the foreman's functions were parceled out to specialists and centralized in planning and personnel departments.[36] The foreman's responsibility slowly narrowed to ensuring that standards set elsewhere were met by those under him. In this way skilled workers, who might have compensated for their loss of autonomy by informal influence with foremen, found even this form of control circumscribed.

Dilution, incentive pay, and tighter authority were familiar to engineers and machinists employed in large or progressive plants and were widely advocated in trade journals by the mid-1890s. The movement for "scientific management," which developed after 1900, was not in practice the revolutionary innovation heralded by its promoters. Scientific management extended trends already under way: deskilling, payment by results, and more exacting methods of supervising work and workers.[37] The new management systems that gained favor in the United States and to a lesser degree in Britain may be distinguished from earlier developments in three respects.

First, these changes were achieved less through mechanical innovations than through administrative reform. Scientific management did not aim for technical change; it sought instead more efficient means of organizing and disciplining the work force. This reflected a common managerial sentiment of the period: "The greatest problem before us today is not so much the further improvement of machinery, but the development of an increased efficiency in men."[38] Thus under scientific management employers pursued deskilling through organizational and supervisory techniques that transferred skill in the planning and execution of work from operatives to new staff experts. Two such techniques occupied a prominent place in scientific management. One was job analysis, sometimes involving time and motion study and sometimes not. Through a careful scrutiny of machine shop operations, management identified less skilled tasks that could be split off and assigned to less skilled workers. Scientific management also demanded systematic attention to the routing of work, the sequence of operations, and the provision of all equipment necessary for each task. Rather than relying on the operative to determine what tools and equipment were needed and to secure and modify those materials as required by the job at hand, employers would undertake those responsibilities. Once such provisions had been made, the narrowed task of running each machine operation could be left to less skilled men or women.[39]

Second, changes after 1900 represented a more self-conscious and systematic approach to shop management and were more likely to be introduced by self-proclaimed "experts" brought in for the purpose of improving efficiency throughout the firm. Despite their wary reception of Taylorism, employers increasingly accepted the view that organizational changes could not be made on a piecemeal basis. Unlike earlier workshop innovations, scientific management entailed a more thoroughgoing, interconnecting reorganization of accounting procedures, layout, work flow, and planning, production, and supervisory tasks.[40] Scientific managers' approach to incentive pay, for example, involved more centralized and systematic setting of production standards and premiums. Establishing output quotas and corresponding incentives, in turn, would increase production only if steps were taken to eliminate delays in the movement of materials. And all these tasks required experts.[41]

Third, and most important, scientific management was intended to be a coherent system of employer control to *replace* the controls exercised by craftsmen.[42] Managers sought to decrease their reliance on the manual and mental skills of machinists and to develop reliable mechanisms through which they, rather than their employees, could control the workplace. The first goal necessitated the second. As employers replaced fully qualified machinists with less experienced and less versatile workers, they had to assume responsibility for planning and organizing production—often in considerable detail. Scientific management was designed to handle these tasks,[43] and here more exacting methods of supervision played a major role. Closer monitoring of work enabled management to discover the less skilled components of tasks. Combined with more extensive use of time clocks and stopwatches, job study permitted employers to fix production norms on which premium bonus systems then would be based. By issuing detailed instruction cards, tightly supervising workers, and providing systematically for the proper equipment at work stations and the flow of materials, managers hoped to ensure that quotas would be met and tasks performed adequately by relatively inexperienced operatives. Such new functions brought new personnel—rate fixers, progress chasers, speed and feed men, inspectors, tool room clerks, production planners—organized along bureaucratic lines into specialized departments and offices.[44] Scientific management developed for employers a set of standards and mechanisms of control to replace those of craftsmen.

In the United States, fully developed scientific management systems existed more in theory than in practice. Employers typically picked from among its techniques those that suited their business and seemed relatively easy and inexpensive to install. Scientific management also represented novel approaches to traditional goals—dilution, incentive pay, and closer supervision and control. With these same provisos scientific management appeared in British engineering well before World War I.[45] Particularly in new sectors of the industry, employers devoted greater attention to organizing and administering work and hired new personnel to devise and implement more systematic production planning. As in the United States, the goal was to preempt craft control in the shops. But in Britain changes in management practices were less systematic and less successful in imposing alternatives to craft control.

With or without the trappings of scientific management, dilution reduced craftsmen's control of production tasks and diminished their hold on the supply and training of skilled labor, piecework eroded their control over work pace, and these together with new authority relations diminished skilled workers' discretion and autonomy. Responsibility for shop practices increasingly lay in the hands of managers. What accounts for this transformation at work?

Sources and Contrasting
Patterns of Change

Above all, changing market conditions shaped the adoption of new production and managerial techniques, although other factors played a role. Technological innovation offered employers cost-cutting, labor-saving equipment, the fractiousness or unreliability of craftsmen and foremen encouraged managers to replace skilled workers and centralize control, and the professional activities of industrial engineers provided manufacturers with convenient models of managerial expertise. Yet market conditions determined whether or not technical and administrative alternatives to craft control were profitable.

The most important market development in both countries involved the emergence of new product lines that generated extensive consumer demand.[46] Bicycles, sewing machines, typewriters, small arms, certain electrical products, and automobiles included standardized components that could be manufactured on a repetitive basis. Where markets permitted large batch production, heavy initial investments in specialized equipment and elaborate reorganization of shop tasks and administrative duties were amply repaid. This type of manufacture did not require the all-around skills of craftsmen on routine production work, and repetitive tasks favored piecework. New methods pioneered in these sectors gradually spread through the industry.[47]

U.S. firms created similar opportunities in another way. Machine builders increasingly specialized in some narrow line rather than offering a wide range of products or taking orders for special designs. At the extreme, one American machine tool firm sold only turret lathes, and only in a single size.[48] Where but few firms shared the market for a given machine, each could plan and equip for standardized parts and manufacture in large quantities. As repetition production in cycles and automobiles stimulated the development of single-purpose, automatic machine tools, so specialization in machinery construction contributed to new manufacturing practices elsewhere in the trade: large-scale production made new machine tools cheaper.[49]

Labor as well as product markets influenced workshop practices. In the United States skilled labor, whether organized or not, was expensive. American managers had incentives to use craftsmen efficiently and sparingly, particularly when competing with foreign firms employing cheaper workers. Where possible, employers replaced skilled men with automatic machinery tended by poorly paid immigrants and women. Machinists remained necessary for some machines and tasks, but employers could at least use the craftsmen economically—assigning them to operate several machines simultaneously and arranging work and piece rates to ensure that machinists applied themselves diligently to the tasks at hand.[50] British employers, of course, paid similar premiums for skilled labor relative to their own European competitors and from the late 1890s became increasingly concerned with their deteriorating position in the international economy. Managers, trade journals, and government commissions agreed that heightened foreign competition demanded a more economical use of craftsmen—along with greater control over costing, scheduling, and job times to fill orders punctually and profitably.[51]

A quickened pace in the development and adoption of new metalworking technologies also contributed to changes on the shop floor. Trends in machine tool design were toward single-purpose machines and automatic operation. Only where markets existed to justify long runs were many of these machines worthwhile investments. Still, even traditional sectors and smaller firms allowed room for innovation. Standard machines could be outfitted with "foolproof" jigs and fixtures. The construction of jigs and fixtures and the proper setup of machines required skilled workers, but production runs did not. New cutting tools, economical even for small batch production, accelerated the work pace and (according to production engineers) demanded scientific expertise in machine setup rather than the rule-of-thumb knowledge of practical machinists. Attention to tolerances and interchangeability rather than a handcrafted fit further replaced the craftsman's judgment and fine eye. Working with "go–no go" gauges, semiskilled workers could produce parts requiring little subsequent fitting and could do so cheaply enough to discard aberrant pieces.[52]

The implications of new technology went further than deskilling. Expensive equipment increased the importance of accurate costing and encouraged employers to get the most out of their investments through piecework, tighter discipline, closer instruction, and extensive overtime. Costly machine tools increased the importance of eliminating the human bottlenecks—the restrictions on machine assignment and output characteristic of craft control. Technical innovation did not in itself cause all of these changes in metal trades manufacture, but new technologies were available when managers, responding to market pressures, sought alternatives to traditional production practices. Once adopted, new production methods combined with economic incentives developed a logic and momentum of their own.

Fast production with high-speed steel on a turret lathe was of no value unless plans had been made to utilise the time saved. Up-to-date milling and drilling machines were liabilities unless the cutters, jigs and gauges had been planned and made before the job went into production and steps taken to ensure the continuity of production and elimination of hold-ups. New methods would end in confusion unless all parts of the factory worked at a smooth tempo with a steady cooperative discipline. This type of planning called for new men in the workshops, or for old men with new titles and functions. In the offices, works engineers, planners, rate fixers and progress men began to appear. . . . The office staff had no longer merely to design a detail as in the past but "also to determine exactly how the machining should be carried out," the numbers required, the type of jigs and the estimated time to be taken. . . . In the workshops these new methods meant job-cards, drawings in place of sketches, gauges, "work hustlers," "speed-and-feedmen," and increased supervision. . . . Increased inter-dependence of one process on another and higher overheads made time-keeping an economic problem for the employer. . . . While the craftsman was far from disappearing . . . an industry in which the technicians and craftsmen assisted and led a number of less skilled workers, who themselves were developing special skills, was the next stage in the evolution of the industry.[53]

Less impersonal forces operating within the employer's own plant also contributed to new workshop practices. Centralized control, dilution, piecework, and tighter discipline were prerequisites for meeting competition and exploiting new machines, but they also might eliminate problems posed by skilled workers and unreliable foremen.

Engineers and machinists presented a number of liabilities to employers, particularly when unionized, as perhaps half of engineers and 11 percent of machinists were in the decade before the war.[54] They commanded higher wages than less skilled workers—some two-thirds higher in prewar Britain and slightly more still in the United States.[55] They also insisted on shorter working hours and on enhanced rates (from time and a quarter to double time) for overtime work. But the penalty for relying on skilled labor was not merely financial; machinists and engineers endorsed customary methods and craft restrictions that ran counter to an increasingly strident assertion of employers' unfettered right to manage their own shops. Craftsmen also tended to strike on what seemed slight provocation and without much warning.

Under these conditions, the eagerness with which some employers seized opportunities to substitute new machines and green hands for craftsmen reflected more than a desire to cut labor costs. To be sure, less skilled workers cost less—an important consideration where wages represented about a third of employers' total costs.[56] But they were also less likely to be organized, less given to striking, and often more amenable to shop discipline. During World War I employers praised women workers for their willingness to do as they were told. "Once a woman employee is taught how to use a gage or learns what constitutes satisfactory work, the good work produced in the afternoon will be exactly the same as that produced in the morning. The judgment which is frequently so disastrous on the part of our men employees will not enter into the work of the woman operative. She will follow instructions absolutely."[57]

Similarly, the ideal of replacing recalcitrant men with machines exercised some hold on the entrepreneurial imagination. James Nasmyth, an important mid-century British machine tool inventor and manufacturer, argued that skilled engineering workers gave "an increased stimulus to the demand for self-acting machine tools, by which the untrustworthy efforts of hand labour might be avoided. The machines never got drunk; their hands never shook from excess; they were never absent from work; they did not strike for wages."[58] Employers never reached this promised land. Reducing the functions, powers, and independence of skilled men, however, brought management not just profits but a more manageable work force—and perhaps the satisfaction of putting the aristocrats of labor in their places.[59]

Managers had another headache within their shops and another incentive to centralize control: their foremen. Foremen were seen to err in one of two directions. They were either too hard on the workers or too easy. The "bulldozing" foreman created resentment, caused the best employees to quit, and could spark strikes. At the other extreme, the easygoing foreman too often placed the interests and goodwill of his workers ahead of loyalty to management. Such foremen condoned a comfortable work pace, winked at output restriction, and failed to insist on the observance of directions from above.[60] Worse still, where foremen belonged to trade unions, they helped enforce union work rules, favored unionists in hiring, and facilitated a thorough unionization of the shop. In their efforts to employ less skilled men and nonunionists during the 1897–1898 lockout, the Engineering Employers' Federation (EEF) noted "how prejudicially in many cases the members' interests are affected where their trusted agents belong to a union."[61] After a strike in Chicago in 1904, the National Metal Trades Association (NMTA) complained that "one of the greatest difficulties encountered by the manufacturers in their attempts to reorganize the shops with non-union men, was the widespread disloyalty . . . of the foremen," foremen who would harass nonunionists and "act as employment agents for union men out of work."[62] Such "disloyalty" was a serious risk, given the typical foreman's responsibility for hiring and firing, fixing piece rates, and much production planning, as well as discipline. By taking these functions out of the foreman's hands, managers could better protect their own interests. Moreover, not even the most loyal foreman could be expected to retain personal control over shop operations as the scale and complexity of production grew.[63]

Employers aiming to assume control over functions once exercised by skilled workers and foremen could scarcely take personal responsibility for recruitment, training, job assignment, rate fixing, production planning, and discipline. Such tasks fell to middle-level managers with appropriate qualifications, and they had an agenda of their own. Most important, this agenda included a strong belief that management tasks demanded experts. Scientific managers such as Frederick Taylor not only denied the competence of workers or foremen to determine the "one best way" to do a job, but they also claimed that employers, too, lacked the necessary scientific training and specialized skills. A second tenet followed: expertise should be recognized by employers and rewarded accordingly in terms of positions, salaries, status, and authority. One scholar finds in scientific management a "strategy of creating and monopolizing bodies of knowledge as a means of perpetuating and expanding professional job opportunities."[64] Personnel managers, similarly, argued that "hiring men and discharging men are serious affairs. Only big men can handle matters like these."[65] Third, many industrial engineers and personnel managers advocated opening these positions only to those with formal qualifications and, increasingly, educational credentials. Those engaged in employment management "must prepare, and in time will be bound to prepare, as for a profession."[66] In fact, a technical education was becoming a prerequisite for the practice of engineering by the early 1900s.[67] Finally, in such bodies as the American Society of Mechanical Engineers and the local and national Employment Managers' Associations, aspiring experts had professional societies to lobby for their interests and to instill a corporate identity.

These goals imply a strategy of monopolization, an effort to establish a profession with a lucrative and protected niche in industry.[68] The niches were administrative positions in which responsibilities formerly undertaken by craftsmen and foremen came into the hands of professional managers. In this way professional strategies reinforced employer incentives to remove control from the shop floor. Through the meetings of professional societies and the countless articles and debates in professional journals, American engineers elaborated alternatives to craft control at a time when employers needed them. However suspicious managers might have been of theoretical "systems," if dissatisfied with hourly wages and a fair day's work, they had well-publicized incentive schemes from which to choose. If they faced bottlenecks in the progress and coordination of work, there existed a wide array of plans for keeping track of jobs, minimizing handling time and costs, and integrating work flow. In addition, men and women knowledgeable in such fields were always available for hire, as consultants or permanent staff. This body of knowledge developed not just to meet the practical needs of capital, but also to justify and advance the status of a new group of aspiring professionals.

Contrasts in the Development of the Labor Process

Two ideal types have been drawn. One depicts workshops in which skilled engineers and machinists exercise considerable control over the recruitment and training of workers, the production process, and the pace of work; and they do so with a high degree of discretion and autonomy. The second pictures factory production by less skilled workers, with craftsmen, in relatively smaller numbers, confined to auxiliary functions. Here management takes responsibility for training, plans out the details of manufacture, seeks to control effort levels through incentive payment, and closely supervises the work force. This transformation reflects the impact of market forces, technological change, problems within the shops, and the influence of professional engineers and management theory. These factors made it profitable for employers to invest in the mechanical and administrative equipment needed to replace craft control.

Although these ideal types indicate the general trend in both countries during the period, two sets of contrasts in the development of the labor process do stand out: differences between the "average" British and American shop and between advanced and traditional sectors within each national industry. The erosion of craft control began earlier and went further in the United States than in Britain. This was true in most details of manufacturing practice: use of specialized and automatic machine tools and of less skilled employees to run them; assignment of one worker to two or more machines; reliance on jigs, fixtures, and gauges, enabling less skilled operatives to turn out interchangeable parts; centralized direction of work tasks; and payment by results. American firms were also more likely to organize these innovations into coherent policies of "scientific management."[69]

The more extensive development of the labor process in the United States is clear from a comparison of productivity in both individual sectors and the industries as a whole. The ratio of net value of output per employed person in the United States (1907) and Britain (1909) was 2.17 for engineering and shipbuilding.[70] In Britain net output per wage earner in the cycle and motor trades stood at 124 pounds in 1909. Two years earlier the figure for the U.S. bicycle and motorcycle industry (including parts) was 261 pounds, and for automobiles and auto parts, 320 pounds.[71] Between 1903 and 1904—well before the company's key breakthrough to mass production—Ford employed three hundred workers to make seventeen hundred cars. Before 1914, no British firm exceeded one car per worker per year.[72]

The reasons for these differences are not hard to find. Virtually all the factors leading to changes at work operated with greater force in the United States. Product markets were larger and more standardized,[73] individual firms were bigger and more specialized,[74] and labor was scarcer and more expensive.[75] To the extent that American shops needed skilled machinists, the unions' relative weakness left employers freer to use them as they saw fit.[76] Professional engineers were both more numerous and more widely accepted in America.[77] The U.S. metalworking industry also enjoyed the flexibility of youth. British firms had considerable capital tied up in older equipment and tended to rely on this equipment to turn out new products. By contrast, sewing machine, cycle, or small arms manufacturers, starting from scratch, could utilize specialized and automatic machine tools. A large demand for such tools, in turn, lowered their cost and made it cheaper for firms in other sectors to adopt them.[78]

The result was not only that comparable sectors of the industry were more advanced in the United States than in Britain, but also that the most progressive sectors in both countries (sewing machines, electrical products, cycles, typewriters, automobiles) developed earlier and employed a larger proportion of metalworkers in the United States than in Britain.[79] In 1907, less than 4 percent of Britain's engineering operatives worked in the cycle and motor trades; more than 16 percent were employed in shipbuilding and marine engineering. Two years later shipbuilding occupied less than 4 percent of American metal trades employees, as against 6.2 percent in the automobile and cycle sector.[80] As late as 1907, Britain still had twice as many engineers in shipbuilding as in the electrical, auto, cycle, and aircraft trades combined; and in output, two traditional sectors—textile machinery and railway locomotives— far outstripped all others.[81] The relative progress of new industrial sectors again reflects America's larger domestic markets. To domestic markets were added foreign ones as more economical production enabled U.S. firms to sell their wares more cheaply than their British competitors—including, in some cases, in Britain itself. From 1897 to 1901, for example, the value of U.S. exports of cycles and cycle parts was nearly three times greater than that of British exports.[82]

Similar contrasts in the development of the labor process appear within each country's metal trades. Newer British industries manufacturing for relatively large, standardized product markets were more progressive in shop organization and methods than traditional sectors such as shipbuilding and heavy machinery. Thus firms in Coventry—a center for the cycle trade in the 1890s and automobiles thereafter—featured unusually advanced production techniques with a high proportion of semiskilled workers, widespread use of incentive pay, and more methodical management practices.[83] Being located in a city with little history as an engineering center, Coventry employers, like many American ones, enjoyed greater flexibility in deploying labor and installing up-to-date equipment. In the United States large numbers of machinists found employment in railroad shops, where market conditions did not allow the manufacture of standardized parts in large batches. Such shops engaged primarily in repair work, which could not be consolidated in a single location to permit larger volume production; repair shops had to be widely distributed along the lines. For such bespoke manufacture skilled labor was essential, piecework less widely used, and detailed production planning inappropriate.[84]

These differences in the development of the labor process had clear consequences for the status of skilled workers. Traditional production methods relied on craftsmen. Less extensive and rapid changes at work preserved the jobs and strength of skilled men. British engineers, accordingly, typically enjoyed greater security and bargaining power than American machinists, as did railroad shop craftsmen compared to those elsewhere in the United States.

The position of skilled workers reflected more than the state of the labor process; it also reflected the relative *timing* of workplace change and craft organization. Engineers and machinists alike were under siege. When British employers mounted their offensive against craft control in the 1890s, however, they confronted well-entrenched craft unions. The ASE, for example, was forty years old, enrolled a large proportion of engineers, and had secured through local agreements and customs a substantial measure of control over shop practices. In the United States, by contrast, workshop innovations were well under way before the IAM (founded in 1889) was on its feet, particularly in the technically most progressive industrial centers of the Northeast. Unlike the ASE, the IAM was playing catch-up ball. For machinists, customary practices had neither the support of a strong union nor the sanction of work rules and agreements. Progressive management and a weaker union, moreover, reinforced each other. With the IAM a relative newcomer and its members in a less entrenched position in the shops, U.S. employers had a freer hand both in reorganizing production and in keeping unions out.[85]

Both the extent and the timing of workplace change enabled engineers to meet challenges at work from a position of strength. Ultimately, the relative development of production techniques is less significant than engineers' greater ability to protect their interests in the face of change. Dilution, for example, was certainly more advanced in the United States than in Britain. U.S. metalworking shops employed a higher proportion of specialists and women, relied less on traditional apprenticeship, and divided more sharply skilled tool room work from semiskilled production.[86] More important, *despite* new machinery and an increasing division of labor, engineers more than machinists managed to maintain rights to jobs or machines that once had required skilled hands, even if they no longer did, and more successfully monopolized the financial rewards, if not the substance, of craft work.[87]

Similarly, incentive pay, and especially the bonus systems associated with scientific management, were more widely used in the United States. But when more than half of engineers in certain sectors and centers experienced piecework, and nearly one in ten ASE members worked under premium bonus systems, quantitative contrasts with the United States had little subjective significance. Engineers, however, managed (through formal agreements, strong workshop organization, and informal pressures) to preserve collective bargaining over piece rates and bonus times, enforce union wage scales, and prevent a fragmentation of individual earnings.[88] Machinists, for the most part, did not.

Finally, it appears that U.S. employers relied more heavily on centralized planning, experts, and close direction of work tasks.[89] These developments were by no means absent in Britain, but engineers were more successful in influencing (or if necessary sabotaging) management initiatives and personnel. Through their unions and shop organization, engineers retained greater control over how work was done, at what pace and price, and by which workers.

The same contrasts appear within each country. Innovative managers faced stiffer opposition from railroad shop craftsmen, and were more often forced to compromise with unions, than employers in most other sectors of the American metal trades. During the early development of the cycle and auto industries, Coventry manufacturers enjoyed a freedom from effective craft opposition to new production methods that was unusual by British standards. This internal contrast is less sharp than that between the two countries, however, for Coventry engineers soon had the backing of a strong national union. Railroad machinists did not.

Dilution, piecework, and centralized control made greater headway in the United States than in Britain and at greater cost to American craftsmen. Yet it would be a mistake to conclude that machinists thereby felt more threatened. Engineers evaluated working conditions not with reference to America but in comparison to their own past; and for engineers, too, departures from the workshop status quo seemed radical and abrupt.

The Craftsmen's Grievances and the Craft Ethic

Two themes dominated skilled workers' resentment of managerial initiatives: economic insecurity and moral outrage. Engineers' and machinists' economic concerns were fairly straightforward, for changes at work directly threatened their earnings and jobs. Their sense of injustice is more elusive, partly because of its roots in a craft ethic rare today. It is important, however, to show how in both countries noninstrumental aspects of the craft tradition[90] formed a vital component of skilled men's grievances. Without a clear sense of this craft ethos, it is difficult to understand not only the intensity of conflict between skilled workers and their bosses but also the unwillingness of engineers and machinists to exchange craft customs for economic concessions and their receptiveness to proposals for workers' control.

Dilution put the economic position of craftsmen at risk. The use of unapprenticed men ("handymen"), women, or youths on tasks hitherto defined as "skilled" undermined the system of apprenticeship and job rights by which engineers and machinists monopolized privileges and kept wages up. Excessive numbers of apprentices and handymen threatened to flood the trade. Indirectly, so did the practice of one employee running more than one machine, for in the workers' view this meant that one man took the jobs of two. The result in either case would be a surplus of labor, falling wages, and unemployment. Naturally, it was the most highly skilled worker, who had invested time and money in an apprenticeship and commanded the best wages, who stood to lose the most from the influx of cheap labor. More broadly, the result would be to undercut craftsmen's privileged status relative to mere laborers. A New York brassmaker noted in 1885 that "a mechanic was considered somebody, and he felt he was somebody; he was a skilled mechanic, and he was considered above the poor laborer on the street." With the decline in skill and, accordingly, wages in the trade, brass workers were increasingly forced to live among "the cheapest class."[91]

Opposition to dilution involved more than concern over wages and jobs, important as these were. At stake too were craft control and the standards of "the trade." Dilution attacked skilled men's customary rights to decide how work should be done and by whom. It devalued the all-around skills of apprenticed craftsmen— skills from which they derived not only income but also tremendous self-esteem. "As a rule, [machinists] took pride in their tasks, and considered a bad job a serious reproach upon their ability and worried on it as if it were a personal matter."[92] A common complaint by the turn of the century was that "the trade has been subdivided and those subdivisions have been again subdivided, so that a man never learns the machinists' trade now."[93] Specialization denied craftsmen an opportunity to develop or deploy their full capabilities and could threaten their independence by confining them to the one shop in which their specific skills had been learned.[94] Technical changes inflicted further indignities. "The engineer," lamented a union journal, "Is being largely evolved into a mere attendant or looker-on, tending or watching the machine which now—as if possessed with intelligence—automatically takes the place of skill."[95]

In articulating their grievances against dilution, a code word for engineers and machinists was "the trade." Dilution meant "the ruination of the trade"; the successful defense of craft standards was essential to "the salvation of the trade." Saving the trade, again, meant more than protecting economic positions. "The trade" referred to a set of skills that were acquired with great difficulty over a long period and were the source of great pride. It also referred to a community of craftsmen bound together by common training, shared skills, and collective dignity (along with a good deal of tramping about in search of work). Union charges that handymen spoiled work or turned out shoddy goods had, of course, some public relations value. But these allegations also reflected a commitment to craftsmanship—with a job well done affirming both self-esteem and corporate standards—along with a corresponding arrogance and contempt for those outside the brotherhood. When manufacturers spoke of "the trade," they spoke of aggregate employment, invested capital, output, and sales. "The trade" in the language of craftsmen defined the industry, and the good of the industry, in terms of the moral standards and workmanship of producers. The trade was the *craft* of metalworking.

The economic and ethical dimensions of craft grievances came together in the antagonism to handymen, green hands, and women in the trade. These workers were threats to the craftsman's standard of living because they brought down wages and reduced employment for skilled men. But they also undermined the standards of the craft. The indignation directed toward handymen who presumed to do skilled work owes a good deal to the fact that they were not brought up to the trade; they had not made the craft their calling. "The handy man spreads himself over everything, and one never knows what he may handle next. He can groom a horse, and drive a tractor engine, and mend watches, and sole boots, and cut the children's hair, and wash a baby, and peel potatoes and do the Saturday's marketing. He can build anything—from a rabbit hutch to a gasometer, and he fills his spare time making steam engines— and things."[96] The reference to "women's work" performed by handymen also points to suspicions that they lacked "manhood"— the sturdy independence of craftsmen in standing up for craft rights and union rates and refusing to take work and bread from other men by operating two machines. A fear that skilled workers would be reduced to the same "effeminate" condition comes out most clearly when the dilutees were female. "Employers are plac- ing women on every job that they possibly can, where heretofore men have been employed. . . . If this keeps up at the rate it is being done, the men can attend the matinees and pink teas and the women can support the families."[97]

Similar preoccupations run through responses to the introduc- tion of piecework. Craftsmen viewed incentive schemes as a threat to their livelihood: directly, as rates were cut if workmen earned too much; indirectly, as jobs were divided up or done by new ma- chines at lower wages and as a quicker work pace lowered overall employment. Even if earnings remained the same, they came only at the price of greater effort.[98] Machinists at the Springfield Ar- mory charged that "the piece-work man had things down so fine that in order to make a decent week's pay they refused to respond to the call of nature during working hours."[99] Particular grievances display a similar concern for earnings. Engineers and machinists complained that under payment by results insufficient allowances were made for poor materials, unavoidable delays, or proper facil- ities for doing the job; that excessive penalties were levied for spoiled work; that overtime work was not adequately compensated; and that "debts" on one job (where piecework earnings fell below a guaranteed day rate) were carried over to others.[100]

Yet skilled men's concerns extended well beyond the contents of their pay envelopes. They felt that piecework, by forcing them to rush their work and think only of their earnings, undercut a crafts- manly pride in their work, favoring shoddy products and concealed defects. A machinist at the Watertown Arsenal testified that "on day work I endeavor to do that work to the best of my ability; now, if I am given a bonus or a premium to get out more work it is only natural to suppose that I would slight my work every bit I can, just to get it by the inspection, in order to make more money. . . . It would hurt my reputation severely."[101] The judgment and discretion engineers and machinists customarily exercised were often jeopardized under premium bonus systems, because with each job came cards specifying how to do each operation and how quickly. Payment by results also contributed to the erosion of craft standards as journeymen worked two machines or specialized in some narrow line of work in order to increase their earnings.[102]

Economic concerns and commitment to craft standards merged in the common charge that piecework undermined collective bargaining and, particularly in the United States, even the union minimum rate. Instead, workers were given a price, take it or leave it, or at best negotiated individually with foreman or rate fixer. Sometimes, too, prices were set according to the fastest man's pace, leaving average operators to struggle for decent pay.[103] The effect was both to reduce wages and to undermine craft solidarity and shop-floor camaraderie. Men would compete for good jobs, curry favor with foremen, work two machines to run up earnings, and conceal defects and abuse tools to the detriment of those on the next operation or shift. Engineers and machinists feared that piecework would ultimately undercut unionism as well. Piecework "brings out all that is selfish in men. . . . Under its blighting influence, shop-mates and brothers become Ishmaelites toward each other, one man's hand raised against the other in the fierce competitive struggle. . . . It encourages greed, is immoral in its tendencies, and does more to create discord and make a perfect hell of a harmonious shop or factory of our craft, than all the evils that escaped from Pandora's box."[104]

Both themes run through a final charge leveled against incentive pay schemes. The administration of payment by results, engineers and machinists noted bitterly, required a horde of officials—rate fixers, speed and feed men, efficiency engineers—whose salaries came out of the workers' wages. Such parasites were not only an economic burden, however; they were also viewed as nonproducers, "inexperienced clerks" presuming to set time limits from "theoretic charts." For these reasons their power to fix rates without consultation, drive the workers, and tell them how to do their jobs seemed especially outrageous. "The employee is not taken into consideration in setting prices; they are arbitrarily set by the efficiency engineers, who arrogate to themselves the terms upon which the employee shall work. We believe it is an effort to standardize men and conditions . . . to subordinate the mechanical initiative to others. . . . The workman is simply an automaton, and loses his mechanical identity."[105]

Grievances regarding new authority relations had little to do with wages and most clearly demonstrate the moral ethos of craftsmen. The exercise of management control threatened skilled workers' customary autonomy in doing their jobs, their sense of manhood, and their notions of fairness and "the square deal." Engineers and machinists were a prickly lot who valued their independence at work. They resented supervisors who watched them too closely, who attempted to speed them up, and who told them how to do their work. "Nothing irritates a man who really knows his business so much as for a manager or foreman to come constantly to him in a patronizing way, and, with considerable assumption of superior knowledge, 'show him how to do it.'"[106] Orrin Cheney, a machinist at the U.S. government's Watertown Arsenal, protested the imposition of orders from an efficiency expert and told the lieutenant in charge, "I could not follow this man's instructions out and do my work and do it properly. I told him that I never had a man tell me what speed and feed I should run my machine on. My work was always given to me." The commanding officer was not sympathetic: "Shut right up; you will carry out these instructions to a letter."[107]

Such treatment was more than an insult to the craftsman's skill; it was also emasculating. Endowed with a strong sense of "manly dignity" and insistent that they should be treated with respect and tact, engineers and machinists felt outraged by "bullying" or "tyrannical" supervision. "There will be no diminution of workshop discontent . . . no softening of the exasperation the worker feels, while he is treated as a social inferior, watched like a convict, and punished like a naughty school-boy."[108] Instruction cards, driving supervision, or the stopwatch deprived the craftsman of his manhood and dignified competence. The "objection of the average man . . . to what is generally termed here the stop watch . . . and to methods that are described in the various efficiency or scientific systems, lies very much in the fact that the man who feels within himself the power to successfully perform the duties of the trade to which he belongs . . . objects to being made an automaton and a cog in a wheel."[109]

Discontent grew also out of a commitment to equity and justice in workshop life. New authority relations were not necessarily tainted with favoritism or caprice. But tightened supervision and the transfer of control from workers to management created ample opportunities for abuse, particularly in the transitional period when new powers rested with foremen. Engineers and machinists complained, for example, that supervisors rewarded their "pets" with the best jobs, the easiest piece rates, secure employment, and promotion, without regard to skill or seniority. "Is a self-respecting workingman going to get down on his knees to youngsters who are the pets of or relatives of the men who own the plants . . . ? There is more politics played in some of the factories of Bridgeport than anywhere else in the city. And this is very demoralizing."[110] Coventry engineers frequently complained that foremen were not impartial in giving out work or in enforcing rules and, like engineers and machinists elsewhere, often struck for the removal of "arbitrary" and "obnoxious" foremen, rate fixers, or speed and feed men.[111] A similar commitment to fairness informed the workers' protest that foremen exceeded their jurisdiction or that penalties were out of proportion to the offense (e.g., unjustifiably large docking of pay for being late or fines for spoiled work or tools).

Some spokesmen for business and labor believed that once managers offered their employees a "square deal"—reasonable rules, impartially and tactfully applied—harmony would reign in the shops. If management would treat the workers fairly, discuss grievances with them or their representatives, and clearly set forth lines of authority and the duties and responsibilities of all, the labor problem would vanish.[112] The IAM sometimes argued that railroads and other corporations could obtain efficient and loyal service "by holding its officials to a strict accountability for any tyrannical or arbitrary exercise of power and by making the lowest servant feel that he will be protected against injustice at the hands of the highest official superior."[113] In this area, at least, some accommodation of craftsmen's grievances and some reconciliation between the craft ethic and management control seemed possible: a reconciliation based on the rule of law and at the expense of the foreman's powers and prerogatives.

Machinists attacked the system of scientific management in much the same terms as they did its constituent parts—dilution, incentive pay, and tightened supervision.[114] It is not surprising that, of all the features of scientific management, time and motion study was so often the focus of machinists' hostility. Time and motion study was a condensed symbol of the evils of scientific management. It was a new device for securing the old management goal of deskilling and a key tool for setting new standards of effort and implementing premium bonus systems. It was used to prepare detailed instruction cards and was conducted by new personnel, outsiders often lacking practical experience and insulated from shop-floor pressures. Add to these considerations the new assault on machinists' dignity and integrity in having such incompetents standing over a craftsman, stopwatch in hand, and it is easy to understand the outrage generated by time and motion study.

Such new approaches to older employer goals thus appeared to represent a concerted effort to replace craft autonomy with a *system* administered by new, distant personnel and outside experts. Under scientific management, machinists charged, "it was not necessary for a mechanic to possess any extraordinary amount of brain or ability; he was merely expected to become a part of the machine and [the] system would do the rest."[115] "Under no conditions will [machinists] aid and abet in the introducing of any system that would reduce them to mere souless machinery, mechanical in action, denuded in thought and which would rob them of their manhood."[116] Machinists opposed the system also because it undermined their *collective* control over workshop affairs, recognizing only individual employees and personal merit rather than craft standards and union rates. Even given the incomplete installation of scientific management in most shops, the very codification of these changes into a coherent management "science" and the widespread debate over its merits served to clarify and publicize antagonisms over workplace control.[117]

Running through grievances against dilution, piecework, and new authority relations, then, was a craft ethic and a corresponding language of injustice. This ethic was dominated by craftsmen's pride in their knowledge and skill—a pride sometimes expressed in arrogant contempt for laborers and handymen. It involved as well a testy sense of manhood, dignity, and sturdy independence in standing up for one's rights—an attitude as easily turned against more menial male and female workers as against overbearing supervisors. Neither pride nor manliness, however, should be seen as the products of belligerent individualism. Skill and knowledge belonged to a trade with which engineers and machinists identified. A manly and dignified bearing was a virtue befitting, and demanded of, a member of the craft. In standing up for one's rights against dilution, piecework, or tyrannical supervision, one made a stand for the integrity of the trade and the prerogatives of craftsmen. At the extreme, a brother was expected to give up or refuse a job rather than betray the standards of the craft. Obviously, this occupational solidarity had economic benefits; among the standards of the craft was the union rate of wages. And many engineers and machinists were quite willing to sell their trade rights for a mess of pottage. The tenacious resistance to management offensives, however, can be understood only against the background of a widespread moral commitment to the trade and to a community of craftsmen.

Engineers and machinists did not always express their resentments in the same idiom. American metalworkers' rhetoric of injustice is peppered with the ideals of political freedom, individual rights, and American citizenship. Abuses at work are often viewed not as examples of the hardships of wage labor, but as of a piece with the despotism suffered by American colonists, southern blacks, or Russian serfs. What appears here is not capitalist oppression but political authoritarianism, wrongs perpetrated not by property owners but by tyrants no different from George III, the slave owner, or the tsar.

When craftsmen denounce such autocracy, the standards of the trade shade into the rights and freedoms of American citizens, and the manly bearing of mechanics becomes the independence of every man in the land of the free, the home of the brave. "In the centuries of the past, surfism [*sic*] and slavery and vassalage [were] probably the proper thing, but not so now. The mechanics of the Denison shops had rights as sacred as the President of the United States, and in violating them Master Mechanic McIlvary has shown himself to be the tyrant that he is."[118] A committee of molders at the Watertown Arsenal, denouncing the introduction of scientific management, told government investigators, "We object to the stop watch on the ground that such a method applied to the finer sensibilities of the American workingman acts the same as a slave driver's whip on the negro."[119] Adapting wartime patriotism to his own purposes, an IAM business agent in Newark reports that, while wage earners are fighting in Europe, "we who comprise Uncle Sam's industrial army can not stand idly by and see the 'Kaisers' of American industry continue their un-American practices in the workshop."[120]

This rhetoric reflects a populist rather than a class perspective. Machinists' commitment to American freedoms and individual rights could mask class antagonisms and block class solidarities. This indeed was and continues to be a common stereotype of the American worker—ambitious, self-reliant, impatient with communal restraints, applying at work the individualism and liberty acquired in the exercise of political rights.[121] Yet populist traditions (particularly strong in the IAM, with its roots in southern and western railway shops) were rallied to the defense of craft standards. Craft ethics and populist language run together, for example, in testimony against scientific management. On one side, machinists complained that scientific management robbed them of their skill and dignity. "That system lessens a man's knowledge. . . . Too much direction is not a good thing . . . because the mechanic is supposed to know his business."[122] "I do object to their standing over me with a stop watch as if I was a race horse or an automobile. . . . A workman has just as much honor, manhood, and self respect as a business man or a manufacturer; and more so, I believe, than these scientific shop-management experts."[123]

The other side of machinists' protest, however, drew on populist sentiments. Scientific management, they charged, was un-American. It was all very well for efficiency experts to claim that "we all believe in liberty, but we recognize, or are capable of being shown, that true liberty is liberty under law."[124] For machinists the laws of scientific management were autocratic and demeaning, and the use of a stopwatch was an insult to the free-born American.[125] Allied with craft traditions, moreover, populism could lay the groundwork for democratic assertions of workers' control. "The men . . . should and ought to have a chance to work together voluntarily. [Scientific management] is despotic management, rather than voluntary cooperation. . . . That is, the men are forced to do as they are told. Orders come down absolutely from above. We believe that the men should have definite rights, and that they should be allowed to express their rights through their committees and through their organization."[126]

In both countries, then, craftsmen subscribed to a clear moral code—an implicit social contract, in Barrington Moore's terms—by which they evaluated new conditions at work and found them wanting. At the core of this code was a craft ethic, a shared commitment to the standards and dignity of the trade. Among machinists this ethic is overlaid with more populist rhetoric, in which the values of political liberty, equality, and participation are directed against the confinements, subordination, and despotism of the factory. This commitment to the rights of the individual and the citizen in a free society did not offer a promising foundation for class solidarity and for challenges to capitalist (as against autocratic) control of production.[127] But it could be a powerful source of antagonism to management policies, and one that resonated with craftsmen and less skilled workers alike.

The broader importance of the craft ethic for the development of factory politics is twofold. While this ethic survived, engineers and machinists were unwilling to trade craft control and craft standards for economic compensation. And traditions of craft control and autonomy lay behind engineers' and machinists' assertions of their right to a voice in workshop management. These ensured that workplace conflicts would be contentious and politically charged. At the same time, however, when this ethic was directed from managers to other workers, its characteristic expression was exclusive and arrogant. While craft traditions survived, engineers and machinists remained reluctant to ally with less skilled workers. The remainder of this book examines how these potentials and ambiguities in the craft tradition were mobilized in concrete strategies, organizations, and goals.

Chapter Three

In Defense of the Trade:
From Local Struggles to
National Settlements,
1890–1901

Skilled workers' responses to industrial change during the 1890s were largely defensive and sectional. Engineers and machinists sought to protect their exclusive privileges by blocking dilution and banning piecework, and they relied on their craft power and sectional strategies to enforce work rules.

Features of the labor process favored the mobilization of protest along defensive and exclusive lines. Skilled men still occupied an important place in manufacturing processes. Their position at work permitted effective action on an independent basis, with no need to compromise sectional interests. The organizational vehicles for protest reinforced this outcome. Rank-and-file protest in both Britain and the United States developed in a context of unsupportive national unions and localistic and informal industrial relations. Machinists and engineers, accordingly, relied on district and shop-floor organization to pursue their interests. Before 1900, these local bodies were constituted along narrow craft lines, and this too favored the mobilization of exclusive goals and disputes.

Local autonomy in defending craft privileges created problems for union leaders and employers. The problems for union executives included internal discipline and obstacles to the organization's recognition as a responsible bargaining partner. For employers, locally based craft protest meant opposition to managerial innovation, the inconveniences of sporadic strikes, and competitive inequalities in labor conditions from one shop or city to another. These irritations led in both countries to national confrontations—the 1897–1898 engineering lockout and the 1900 and 1901 machinists' strikes. The initial outcome in each case was a national trade agreement designed to resolve the dilemmas of employers and union leaders alike. In neither industry did these agreements meet employers' ambitions. Yet Britain's Terms of Agreement endured, whereas American metal trades employers turned instead to the open shop after 1901. This divergence would provide the basis for subsequent contrasts in the development of factory politics, creating a new framework for the selective mobilization of craft grievances.

Local organization played a crucial role in the factory politics of the 1890s. District and shop committees, organized on a sectional basis, channeled protest along exclusive lines. They also resisted the authority of both employers and union officials, resistance that contributed to national disputes. The character and importance of local organization, in turn, may be traced to the union and industrial relations conditions under which craftsmen pursued their interests.

The Context of Protest in the 1890s

Unions

In their efforts to defend traditional rights and practices at work, engineers and machinists of the 1890s found their own union executives at times unhelpful and at times actively hostile. Neither the International Association of Machinists (IAM) nor the Amalgamated Society of Engineers (ASE) had firm, coherent, national policies to meet management offensives against craft control. The IAM constitution prohibited members from working two machines or accepting piecework. But the union executives did not specify whether new machines were to be run exclusively by unionists, by apprenticed men, by "skilled" operators (e.g., those who had worked four years in the trade, whether apprenticed or not), or by those in receipt of the standard craft rate (which varied from one locality to another). Nor did ASE leaders provide such guidelines. The IAM had no rules regulating the operation of payment by results when such systems were in force; and after 1892, the ASE explicitly left control of piecework issues to district committees. In these matters, and even more so with regard to contentions over workshop discipline, the unions involved themselves in shop-floor struggles only after local negotiations broke down or strikes occurred.[1]

Even at such times, however, union executives often proved reluctant to sanction strikes or back local struggles over control issues. For two years after the IAM's founding in 1889, its constitution formally eschewed strikes, advising members "to act in a manner becoming men of our calling, and treat with our employers as gentlemen in making known our wants, and we are satisfied we will receive the proper consideration."[2] Even after constitutional changes permitted strikes, union officials remained cautious. IAM leaders, like their ASE counterparts, feared not only for the union treasury: excessive resort to strikes, in their view, could also endanger the union's respectability and its prospects for recognition and collective bargaining rights. These considerations appeared particularly pressing when periods of high unemployment strained union budgets and diminished the chances for victory.[3] Even if strike calls eventually won approval, union rules required that local and then national officials (who might have little familiarity with conditions in individual shops) review grievances and attempt negotiations. By the time constitutional procedures for declaring a strike were complete, the grievance may have smoldered for some weeks.[4]

But union leaders were not indiscriminately cautious. It was precisely over grievances concerning control issues that they exercised the greatest restraint. They had good reasons to do so. Compared to demands for shorter hours or higher wages, struggles against dilution or piecework represented a risky investment of strike benefits. A local demand for a wage increase would benefit all members; as a result, their loyalty during a strike was likely. Union representatives could more easily justify the demand in public on the grounds of an improved standard of living and more easily argue the case in negotiations on the grounds of equity with employees elsewhere and the employer's ability to pay. On the employer's side, wage demands did not threaten sacred management rights and could be offset with changes in work practices. At the least, compromise was always possible. The combination of broad member support and employers' willingness to compromise gave strikes for wages or hours a practical appeal to union leaders. By contrast, control issues tended to be sectional in appeal, illegitimate in employers' eyes, and harder to negotiate. When employers introduced piecework in one department, for example, some members welcomed the opportunity to increase their earnings. Members in other departments and plants, for the moment secure, might be reluctant to strike in sympathy. A ban on piecework challenged employers' freedom to manage their own business and pay their workers according to individual merit. They could generally count on favorable press coverage and public sympathy in their resistance to such trade union tyranny. On the question of whether or not to introduce piecework, finally, workers and managers could scarcely split the difference.[5]

Union leaders did not make these calculations in a vacuum. They found them amply confirmed by the strike statistics of their own organizations. At the 1897 IAM convention, President O'Connell reviewed the most important strikes over the two previous years. Four strikes had concerned wages, and all had resulted in compromise. Four others had involved control issues—one for the closed shop, and one each against dilution, piecework, and an obnoxious superintendent. Of these four, three had been lost.[6] The policy implications seemed clear to O'Connell. During the convention and throughout the late 1890s, he argued that the spread of piecework could not be halted; members should instead make concessions regarding piecework in exchange for the nine-hour day.[7] ASE leaders reached similar conclusions respecting dilution, urging attention to the earnings rather than the specific qualifications of machine operatives.[8]

Industrial Relations

In their defense of craft control, engineers and machinists received from national leaders only loose guidance and support that often was too little and too late. These weaknesses in union policy contributed to and reinforced a system of industrial relations characterized by localism and informality. Even in well-organized American cities negotiations between machinists and employers took place on a firm-by-firm basis and concerned issues peculiar to the individual shop. By the 1890s, districtwide agreements on wages and hours were common in Britain, but questions of control remained subject to plant-level bargaining.[9] Such bargaining was in both countries relatively informal. Custom rather than contracts ratified craft control. Employers who infringed on these standards would be visited not by a union official but by ad hoc deputations of their own employees.[10] Failing an amicable settlement of the dispute, the workers might turn to guerrilla tactics (restriction of output, refusal to instruct dilutees, or simply quitting) to press their claims.[11] Union officials, particularly national ones, entered the fray only as a last resort. And settlements, if any, usually took the form of verbal understandings or, especially in the United States, the posting of new work rules without explicit reference to any agreement between management and the men or their unions.[12] The industrial relations of the 1890s, like union policies, thus made the battle against employer policies a responsibility of union locals and, above all, the workers in the shops.

Britain

Factory Politics up to the 1897–1898 Lockout

How did engineers respond to employer attacks on their customary prerogatives and standards? In terms of goals, most engineers directed their energies to defending the craft status quo. In terms of tactics, they relied on sectional action and local organization. Conservative goals and sectional action reflect the continued importance of skill in production. Craftsmen acting alone still had great bargaining power and, having little need for allies, they faced no pressure to compromise their exclusive interests. District and shop-floor organization filled gaps left by union policies and conformed to the local and informal nature of industrial relations. By reproducing the exclusiveness of trade unions at the shop level and enhancing the strength of skilled employees at work, rank-and-file organization also channeled protest toward defensive goals and sectional action.

Engineers countered management encroachments on craft standards with work rules specifying conditions under which unionists would accept employment. These rules varied from one district to another. In well-organized centers ASE district committees ruled that only apprenticed engineers could do work undertaken in the past by engineers. The rule banned not only unapprenticed workers but also members of other crafts from the performance of certain tasks (e.g., fitting) and operation of certain machines (e.g., lathes): disputes over demarcation were almost as common as those over "illegal men."[13] Elsewhere district committees insisted that "skilled" work be done by men in receipt of the local craft rate rather than by those who had served their time; or they simply demanded that certain wage rates be attached to given classes of machines, regardless of who worked them.[14] Although this strategy opened the door to unapprenticed workers, it still aimed to protect craft standards of pay against dilution. Other rules combating dilution included an outright ban on one worker running more than one machine and on instructing handymen or setting up jobs for less skilled operatives.[15] If new semiautomatic machines did work formerly done by skilled men, engineers claimed those tools as their exclusive preserve, to be operated at the standard craft rates.[16]

Strongly organized districts also refused to allow the introduction of payment by results. In weaker areas or in shops where piecework had existed for some time, rules stipulated the conditions under which unionists would accept the system. For example, rates had to be mutually agreed between foremen and workers and extra pay offered for overtime. Both to discourage the system and to prevent such abuses as rate cutting, some districts also limited members' earnings (e.g., to time and a third). Such restrictions were undoubtedly still more prevalent on an informal basis.[17]

Engineers did not at first negotiate these defensive rules with employers. Although work rules often reflected traditional practices long accepted by management, they were unilateral in character, laying down the conditions under which ASE members would work. Bargaining and compromise played little role. An engineer asked to run two lathes was obligated to refuse, under penalty of fines or expulsion from the union. This was the first line of defense against new shop practices. Many employers abandoned innovations rather than lose their skilled workers. Unrepentant employers faced strikes, picketing, and the blacking (boycott) of their work or products at other firms. By selecting one shop at a time for attack, district committees both conserved strike funds and discouraged the spread of objectionable practices to other companies.[18]

These were exclusive policies aimed at defending engineers' status and jobs against all comers, including members of other trades and less skilled workers. Engineers opposed piecework for themselves, but rarely engaged in sympathetic action to aid other workers faced with the same evil. The tactics with which these goals were pursued were no less sectional. Engineers' refusal to accept or retain employment in offensive shops relied on the indispensability of skilled workers—a strategy not available to less skilled workers. When engineers resorted to strikes, they received union benefits, and the ASE often did its best to support skilled nonmembers who otherwise might have acted as blacklegs (scabs). In most cases no such support was extended to the laborers inevitably thrown out of work during strikes; because laborers could rarely replace craft workers, unions could safely ignore them.

Engineers relied on local and workshop organization to defend craft privileges, and it is here that the influence of unions and industrial relations is clearest. The basic cell of the ASE was the union branch, composed of members residing within a certain area. The key agency of local policy, however, was the district committee. In each industrial center a district committee, elected by local members, took responsibility for regulating the trade. Because the ASE Executive failed to initiate trade policy, district committees formulated work rules and disciplined members who ignored them. Because employers were organized at most on a local basis, and industrial conditions varied, work rules differed from one district to another. District committees laid down the work rules, but organization within the shops carried them out. Well before the 1890s, active unionists on the shop floor assumed the tasks of enrolling new hands, reporting on working conditions to their branches, and presenting shared grievances to management. Gradually, these functions were formalized in the shop stewards' duties. Workers would select (informally or by vote) one person in a department to represent them in dealings with management. District committees, for their part, recognized shop stewards as union representatives in the works charged with recruiting new members, making sure old members were paid up, and reporting any encroachments on local work rules—by employers or by other unions. The 1896 ASE convention formally conferred on district committees the power to appoint shop stewards.[19]

Shop steward organization helped local engineers overcome some liabilities of trade union structure and policy. Residentially based branches were ill equipped to deal with grievances shared by workers in the same shop who belonged to separate union branches. In any case the workers were often unwilling to wait for the weekly meeting to air their concerns and decide on appropriate action. They could press their demands more promptly and present a united front to employers through shop meetings and workplace organization. The shop steward system was also adapted to industrial relations in which conditions varied from one firm to another and in which initial negotiations took place informally between managers and employees. Under these conditions grievances often had to be handled on the spot, and the shop steward system developed to defend the workers' interests from case to case.[20]

Trade unionism and industrial relations thus favored local organization in the conduct of craft protest. The character of local organization, in turn, ensured that factory politics would be defensive in goals and exclusive in action. Skilled engineers dominated the district committees, which determined trade policy, making these bodies the "hard core of workers' resistance to technological change."[21] Shop stewards carried district committee authority inside the factory gates, bearing responsibility for defending local work rules. District committees, moreover, were organized along the same sectional lines as national trade unions, and shop stewards represented only members of their own unions. Engineers also organized on the job far more effectively than did less skilled workers. This collective advantage reinforced as well as reflected engineers' strategic position in the labor process. Technical and organizational advantages together enabled them, acting alone, to pursue goals that divided their interests from workers of other skills.

Despite their autonomy in handling industrial conflict, district

committees and shop steward representation thus reproduced the
defensive priorities and exclusive organization of craft unionism at
the local level. This institutional context inhibited innovative
demands and broader solidarities in the mobilization of craft grievances. Joint committees did occasionally appear at work, and
members of different unions did cooperate locally. Yet these movements—for the nine-hour day on the Tyne in 1871, for wage increases in London and Lancashire during 1873–1875, and for the
eight-hour day in the 1890s–did not concern issues of craft privilege or workshop control.[22] For the latter purposes local struggles
remained defensive and exclusive.

The absence of radical factory politics among engineers by no
means ensured harmony between local unionists and the ASE national executive. The Executive Council had no wish to see union
funds and reputation dissipated by ill-considered strikes and resented the reluctance of districts to submit trade decisions and
strike plans for executive approval, as required by the constitution.
For their part, rank-and-file engineers chafed under the executive's
moderation and the protracted constitutional procedures for reviewing disputes and approving strikes. Improved local organization gave engineers the means to take matters into their own
hands. The results were friction over unconstitutional strikes and
frequent criticism of national leaders for their excessive caution
and insufficient support of local struggles.[23] A lack of union discipline created problems for employers as well as for ASE executive
officials.

The 1897–1898 Lockout
and the Terms of Settlement

In the spring of 1897, a joint committee of engineering trade
unions in London initiated a movement for the eight-hour day, and
by the end of May more than one hundred firms had conceded.[24]
On June 5, however, a number of London employers (hitherto unorganized) announced the formation of a London branch of the
Employers' Federation of Engineering Associations (soon renamed
the Engineering Employers' Federation [EEF]). The joint committee refused to recognize the London association and served notice on individual recalcitrants that if they did not grant the forty-

eight-hour week by July 3 members would be withdrawn from their shops. The EEF responded in kind: if a strike took place, 25 percent of union members in federated firms throughout the country would be locked out each week, beginning July 13. This threat was carried out, prompting about seventeen thousand ASE members, along with several thousand from other unions, to leave work. By October the EEF led 579 firms in the lockout, with forty-five thousand craftsmen (twenty-two thousand from the ASE) out of work. After government intervention to bring the two sides together, and the rejection in December of two successive employer proposals, union executives withdrew the demand for an eight-hour day and recommended that their members accept the Terms of Settlement worked out between the Federation and the unions. In January 1898, unionists approved that recommendation by a vote of 28,588 to 13,927. By this time more than seven hundred firms had enforced the lockout against 47,500 skilled engineers.

The lockout clearly expressed the basic tendencies of factory politics during the 1890s, except in one respect: the conflict took place on a national scale. Engineers aimed to preserve customary craft controls at the expense of less skilled workers, and during the lockout cooperation among craft unions remained fragile. The disputes over workshop control that led to the lockout were conducted locally, and only the organization and tactics of the EEF shifted the battle to a national terrain. Finally, the lockout revealed tensions between a relatively accommodating union leadership and members committed to the defense of craft control at the expense of managerial prerogatives.

The lockout was the culmination of a period of intensifying friction over work practices, particularly dilution and piecework. In February 1897, for example, the EEF complained to the ASE of strikes over the manning of machines in Sunderland, Barrow, and Elswick and restrictions on overtime in Sunderland, Hartlepools, Clydebank, Belfast, and Barrow.[25] These disputes sought to prevent employers from substituting less skilled workers on certain machines or to secure the craft rate for new machines regardless of the skill required to run them. The conduct of the dispute was no less exclusive. At the outset the Boilermakers' and Patternmakers' unions refused to take part. In Barrow initial cooperation among unions of craftsmen and laborers broke down during the lockout.[26]

Local autonomy also played an important role. The strikes that precipitated the EEF's formation did not reflect any coherent national policy. Instead, they aimed to defend local work rules, which varied from one district to another. These strikes, like the demands in London, also continued the strategy of concentrating union resources on individual districts or employers. Such local independence highlighted a divergence in the priorities of national officials and union members. From the start of the lockout, ASE leaders sought to focus the dispute on the question of the eight-hour day rather than on issues of craft control. They did so in part with an eye to public relations. Yet, as the lockout wore on, union officials appeared more willing than the rank and file to trade workshop control for a shorter workweek. Unionists rejected the first settlement proposed by the EEF (declaring the employers' unfettered right to manage their shops without union interference and limiting even the right of unions to bargain collectively over wages) by 68,966 votes to 752. Shortly thereafter, union leaders, on their own initiative, placed before their members two ballot proposals. One offered the original terms, slightly modified in the union's favor; the other added to these terms a fifty-one-hour week (something never offered by employers). The proposals imply that union leaders were willing to accept management control over production in exchange for concessions on working hours and hoped that the ballot results would persuade employers to make that exchange. The union rank and file, however, rejected both proposals by huge majorities—thus demonstrating their own priorities.

Similar conclusions emerge from considering the employers' side of the dispute. The formation of local employers' associations in the north from 1894 on, and of the national federation in 1896, represented responses to the union strategy of picking off employers one by one or district by district. With the consolidation of local bodies in 1896, the EEF national treasury could be pitted against that of the ASE in any single dispute. Through national organization employers also sought to replace local autonomy in work rule formulation with industrywide standards.

Employer policies also demonstrate that craft control, not hours of work, was at stake. From the beginning of negotiations to the conclusion of the lockout, the EEF insisted on a basic principle: "The Federated employers . . . will admit no interference with the management of their business, and reserve to themselves the right to introduce into any federated workshop, at the option of the employer concerned, any condition of labour under which any of the trade unions here represented were working at the commencement of the dispute in any of the workshops of the federated employers."[27] Although employers hardly expected unionists to accept this principle gracefully, their strategy and demands imply a recognition that union leaders would be more accommodating than their constituents. Authority to remove craft restrictions on production practices was sought not on the shop or local level but through an agreement with national union officials. And the Terms of Settlement make it clear that the EEF expected union leaders to enforce this agreement on their members.

The EEF's objectives, then, were to establish management's right to change production practices as it saw fit; to do so on an industrywide basis, free from diverse local restrictions and unpredictable local action; and to commit national unions to enforcing these principles on their often unruly members. The Terms of Settlement (later renamed the Terms of Agreement) imposed on defeated unions in January 1898 were designed to realize these goals.

The agreement formally abrogated the union work rules developed to defend craft control. According to the Terms, "there shall be no limitation on the number of apprentices." As against work rules governing assignment of workers to machines, the Terms gave employers "full discretion to appoint the men they consider suitable to work [machines]. . . . The employers consider it their duty to encourage ability wherever they find it, and shall have the right to select, train, and employ those whom they consider best adapted to the various operations carried on in their workshops, and will pay them according to their ability as workmen." The Terms also asserted that "the right to work piecework at present exercised by many of the federated employers shall be extended to all members of the Federation, and to all their union workmen."

For many unionists the lockout and settlement were nothing less than an effort to destroy trade unionism in the industry. Such a prospect did find some enthusiasts among employers, who regarded unions and restrictive practices as two sides of the same coin. "Trade unionism as now practised in the British engineering trade has to go, or else the British engineering industry has to go. One or the other must be smashed. . . . It is not only to the interest but the duty of employers to 'smash the union.'"[28] Yet the EEF did not lump craft unions and craft control together, and the Terms presumed national unions with effective control over their members in the shops. The Terms, after all, represented a national agreement between union leaders and the employers' association. The desired solution to control conflicts was a centralized one, to be enforced by union executives on recalcitrant members. More important, the existence of well-organized national unions was required by the industrywide "Provisions for Avoiding Disputes" set forth in the Terms. Under this procedure, management in any federated firm agreed to meet deputations from their workers if a grievance arose. If the dispute could not be settled, it passed into the hands of the local employers' association and the union district committee. If, finally, the local conference "failed to agree," a central conference between national officials took up the question. Without a union this procedure would be unworkable, as would another stipulation of the Terms: that no strikes occur until the entire procedure had been completed. Preventing workers from walking out unconstitutionally required unions to keep their members in check.

Employers hoped—ultimately in vain—that the Terms would counter the most obnoxious features of engineering factory politics during the 1890s. Conflict produced by management's offensive in the workplace, combined with the peculiarities of union policies and industrial relations, would be contained through a national agreement. In place of craft restrictions the Terms prescribed not just management discretion but also a union obligation to uphold those prerogatives. For local autonomy in the formulation of work rules, the Terms substituted national standards. Indeed, although wages and hours could safely be left to district negotiation, control issues were taken out of rank-and-file hands altogether. Finally, union-management grievance procedures would replace unofficial and unpredictable strikes led by shop stewards or local leaders— and make unions responsible for keeping engineers at work. In addition, employers expected that full-time union officials would be more accommodating than rank-and-file leaders, and the procedure, by centralizing negotiations, was intended to make their moderate views prevail. A year after urging employers to smash the union, a leading trade journal argued that "it is immeasurably preferable in discussing matters of policy with the workmen to have a responsible agency to deal with, because, after all, the funds of a trade organisation have a balancing influence on its officers. . . . If a manager compromises with an irresponsible [unofficial] leader, the men may disown such a leader and replace him by a worse, if more talkative demagogue, whereas the unionist is more or less of a capitalist, with the steadying effect which financial expectations bring."[29]

The United States

Factory Politics up to 1900

Factory politics among machinists of the 1890s were typically defensive in goals, sectional in tactics, and conducted on a basis of local self-reliance. The strategic role of skilled men at work, the nature of craft unionism, and the character of industrial relations favored these responses to management offensives. Differences between the United States and Britain are found largely in the specific organization and tactics of craft struggles and may be attributed to the weaker position of machinists in the typical American shop.

Machinists attempted to block dilution with work rules limiting the number of apprentices and reserving essential machine shop tasks exclusively for duly apprenticed men. In this way they hoped to monopolize jobs and preserve their bargaining power at the expense of less skilled employees. If necessary, machinists fell back on the stipulation that "skilled" work (in effect, work that once required craftsmen, even if it no longer did) be paid at the standard union rate, thus reducing the competition from, if not the presence of, handymen in the shops. To further protect skilled jobs and wages, the IAM prohibited its members from working more than one machine at the same time.[30] The IAM's position on payment by results was just as uncompromising: the union's constitution simply forbade the introduction of piecework. Where piecework already existed, however, no national policy regulated its operation. Trade rules thus varied from one shop or district to another.

Strongly organized machinists often demanded that piecework systems be discontinued, with demands backed up by strikes and concessions written into formal agreements. But in most cases machinists had to rely on covert restriction of output to secure favorable piece prices, prevent cuts, and safeguard the earnings and effort levels of the average (or even less than average) machinist.[31]

Unionists did not consider these policies suitable topics for negotiation with employers. The IAM censured, fined, or expelled members who violated work rules, and it boycotted firms that refused to observe union conditions. Such unilateral strategies, to be sure, often failed. American employers were in a better position than their British counterparts to survive union boycotts because they relied less heavily on skilled labor and could readily find nonunion machinists. As a result the IAM was far more eager to confirm craft rules through formal contracts between employers and union locals.[32] Union contracts and formal work rules reflected the failure of traditional defenses. Before the 1890s, the strategic importance of machinists in metalworking, combined with a strong group ethos defining appropriate work behavior, usually sufficed to resist management encroachments. As employers became less dependent on craftsmen and piecework undermined work group solidarity, machinists had to resort to formal rules, formal organization, and formal controls over management.[33]

Whatever the tactics, machinists aimed to preserve workshop privileges for themselves alone. Like British engineers, machinists defended their jurisdictions from rival unions as vigilantly as they resisted the upgrading of less skilled workers.[34] Machinists backed up exclusive policies with sectional tactics. For example, they refused to instruct handymen or to give helpers the same guidance extended to bona fide apprentices. They took more drastic measures where needed. A Cleveland machinist reported the difficulties a handyman experienced in operating his machine: "The intense mental strain he underwent trying to locate the trouble caused him to stay away to-day and it will be to his interest to stay away for good. . . . I needn't add that the machine was o.k. before he took it and is o.k. now."[35] Other strategies, such as restricting output or simply boycotting obnoxious employers, relied on resources available only to skilled workers: their superior knowledge of production techniques and their indispensability for essential machine shop tasks. Striking machinists, moreover, received union benefits; the unskilled employees laid off during the dispute were left to shift for themselves.

An unsupportive national union and parochial industrial relations made machinists, like engineers, rely on local organization to defend craft interests. Responsibility for formulating and enforcing specific work rules lay primarily with local lodges, because in regulating piecework or shop discipline, for example, no national policies applied.[36] The variation and localism of industrial relations also favored local autonomy. Machinists employed in railroad shops faced quite different problems than those working for northeastern machine tool firms or midwestern agricultural implement factories. In the latter settings more advanced production methods and anti-union employers might require concessions on work rules to preserve even a toehold in the plant. With metal trades employers as yet unorganized, machinists faced few pressures to coordinate policy on a national basis.

Workshop organization played an important role in enforcing union rules. In many shops one or more machinists took responsibility for checking membership cards, notifying lodge secretaries of vacancies, and monitoring working conditions on behalf of the union. Whether or not they were formally recognized as a shop committee, such workers would be regularly involved in deputations to management (the IAM's usual first step in dealing with grievances), in calling shop meetings, and in leading strike committees.[37] It is less clear how tightly shop committees were linked to local lodges. Committeemen were union activists and often worked with local officials in formulating demands and planning shop meetings, but they were not usually formal union stewards. IAM lodges did, however, try to secure formal recognition for shop committees and protection against victimization of men doing "committee work."[38]

The role of shop committees in policing the works corresponded to an industrial relations system in which conditions varied from one firm to another, negotiations were in the first instance conducted informally, and many managers preferred to deal only with their own employees. Shop committees also overcame certain obstacles to the defense of craft rights created by formal union procedures. These bodies allowed machinists to act more quickly against encroachments than IAM procedures allowed. Shop committees also offered a means for united action by members otherwise divided among different lodges. Committeemen, finally, were more familiar with specific plant conditions than were local officials, much less executives in Washington. Machinists, like engineers, called in union officials only after the failure of their first line of defense: direct action.

Local autonomy was less strongly developed in the United States than in Britain. The IAM had some consistent policies governing dilution and incentive pay (including a ban on the two-machine system and the introduction of piecework), and union lodges incorporated these rules into contracts with employers whenever possible. The narrower discretion of American locals may be traced in part to the delayed development of unionism relative to changes at work. Machinists, unlike engineers, could not rely on custom and strong workshop organization to support craft rights. More standardized work rules, backed by the IAM Executive, represented a second line of defense.

Machinists also were less effectively organized on the job. Outside of the best-organized districts, shop committees appear to have been ad hoc affairs, forming to present demands or prepare for strikes, vanishing (or being discharged) once the crisis had passed. The fragility of workshop organization among machinists, compared to engineers, reflects the lesser importance of skill in U.S. manufacturing and the weaker position of craft unions on the job. American workers were also more nomadic than British ones.[39] Frequent job changes—in search of high wages, in response to grievances, or to evade blacklists—undercut work group cohesion and stable shop organization. Given the relative weakness of shop committees, demands and disputes that in Britain might have been initiated by shop stewards were instead the responsibilities of IAM lodge officials.

The weakness of workshop organization is also evident in the strategies adopted for defending craft standards. The IAM resorted more often than did the ASE to sympathy strikes and boycotts rather than unilateral action, and these strategies typically relied more on cooperation among local union leaders than on rank-and-file activism within the shops.[40] The relative importance of official cooperation again suggests the weakness of union organization on the shop floor and the inability of local work rules alone to hold the line. Indeed, Montgomery suggests that where work rules remained secure and union defenses intact craftsmen less often participated in sympathetic action.[41]

Trade unions and industrial relations, then, favored local autonomy in struggles to preserve craft control. In comparative perspective the different character of American production methods and craft union development did weaken local organization, especially within the plants. Yet even if IAM shop committees and lodges were less effective in resisting employer offensives, their organizational features ensured that protest would be defensive and exclusive. These bodies, like their British counterparts, extended the sectionalism of national unions to the local and workshop levels: shop committees represented only IAM members, and they relayed national and local policies to the rank and file. Shop organization, whatever its comparative weaknesses, also enhanced craftsmen's power relative to less skilled employees. These factors combined to inhibit joint action on widely shared grievances and progressive demands. Machinists instead typically acted alone and in defense of their traditional privileges.

Machinists' local self-reliance had one further consequence: endemic friction between the IAM Executive (the Grand Lodge) and the members over unconstitutional strikes. Union leaders in the United States, as in Britain, were more cautious in resorting to strikes and more conciliatory in their defense of craft privileges than were rank-and-file machinists.[42] Those in the shops had no wish to let encroachments stand or to see favorable opportunities to press demands slip by while constitutional procedures ran their course. Local organization provided an agency for prompt action. IAM lodges also retained the majority of each member's dues, lessening the need for Grand Lodge aid in conducting strikes.[43] As a result, between June 1899 and June 1901, national officers sanctioned 66 strikes involving approximately 9,650 machinists; over the same period local lodge reports (which would not have been exhaustive) showed them engaged in 246 strikes involving 12,912 machinists.[44] IAM leaders could only lament unofficial strikes and make ritualistic pleas for stronger Grand Lodge control over strikes and strike benefits. "Our Constitution prescribes the proper steps to be taken if there is a prospect of a strike resulting from an effort to settle a grievance, but of what use is it? How many of our past strikes have been undertaken in accordance with the provisions of our law . . . ? What is to prevent a dozen or more strikes at the same time?—each one of them inaugurated in the same way by the irresponsible authority of a Local or District Lodge?"[45] In 1900, the answer—for the IAM Executive and leading employers—appeared to be a national trade agreement.

The 1900 Strikes, the Murray Hill Agreement, and the Open Shop

Early in 1900, IAM District Lodge 8, representing all Chicago locals, presented 150 employers with a number of demands, of which the ostensible centerpiece was the nine-hour day. Most firms refused even to meet with District 8 representatives. A strike began on March 1; at its peak it involved some five thousand machinists. Following Chicago's example, four hundred more struck in Columbus, Ohio; three hundred in Paterson, New Jersey; and similar numbers in Cleveland, Detroit, and Philadelphia.[46]

When Chicago machinists first presented their demands, local employers were largely unorganized, and a number of smaller firms signed the union agreement. Larger employers soon banded together, however, under the auspices of the National Metal Trades Association (NMTA). Founded in New York City in 1899 to resist demands by patternmakers, the NMTA had eight members in Chicago by the beginning of 1900. The threat posed by Chicago machinists brought the NMTA additional members and inspired some seventy employers to form the Chicago Association of Machine Manufacturers. From the outset, local and national NMTA representatives took the lead in managing the strike and negotiating with union officials.[47] After some unsuccessful efforts to break the strike,[48] NMTA leaders informally pledged to accept the principle of collective bargaining, to grant the nine-hour day in installments over the coming year, and to refrain from discriminating against unionists or strikers. In exchange the IAM called off its strikes throughout the country, with all outstanding issues to be taken up in a national conference.[49] The Chicago Agreement, approved by local employers and IAM members in March, settled the strike on these terms. It established a board of arbitration, which, meeting in New York's Murray Hill Hotel, reached a national pact (the Murray Hill Agreement) on May 18.

The details of the dispute reveal basic characteristics of factory politics up to 1900, with conflict focused on craft privileges, local autonomy, and union discipline. The 1900 strikes continued struggles over craft control that had been accelerating since 1897. Between May 1897 and June 1899, for example, the IAM General Executive Board had received requests for assistance in fifteen wage disputes. Over the same period, locals sought support in twenty disputes over piecework, twelve over dilution, and eighteen over abuses in the hiring and firing of machinists.[50] Although IAM leaders claimed a shorter workday as the machinists' key goal,[51] proposed agreements put forward by local lodges emphasized instead issues of workshop control. IAM locals asked employers to recognize certain tasks as machinists' work, for which minimum wage rates must be paid. Machinists also demanded that employers observe the apprenticeship regulations laid down in the IAM constitution, and Columbus locals added a ban on the two-machine system. To check victimization and arbitrary employment policies, proposed agreements stipulated that in the event of layoffs employers give preference to those discharged when rehiring workers, "seniority and proficiency to govern." Finally, in a more general check on arbitrary authority at work, machinists demanded that shop committees be recognized for the purpose of negotiating grievances, with unresolved disputes to be referred to joint conferences between local union officials and the company. Failing agreement, a board of arbitration would be established, with two members selected by the union *local*, two by the firm, and a fifth chosen by those four. This board's decision would be binding.

These were traditional, exclusive goals. Machinists sought to protect their monopoly of basic machine shop tasks. Apprenticeship restrictions aimed to block the promotion of handymen at the expense of machinists. Minimum wage rates assigned to machinists' work prevented employers from substituting cheaper labor. In each strike the workers demanded not only that employers accept their definition of a machinist, but also that only IAM members be employed for that work. Those in other trades as well as those of lesser skills were to be denied access to machine shop jobs. Nor in the actual conduct of the strike were machinists inclined to cooperate with other crafts or with semiskilled workers.

The 1900 strikes also demonstrate tensions between local autonomy and national leadership. For the IAM Executive the 1900
strikes were to achieve the nine-hour day; but local lodges took the
initiative of adding their own demands, which varied from one city
to another. Referring to Chicago, IAM's Vice-President Wilson lamented that, although the union's key goal was the shorter workday, "the men were in that frame of mind that they thought they
could win anything, that they had only to make a demand and it
would be granted."[52] In the pursuit of local concerns, machinists
also lacked respect for executive authority and IAM constitutional
procedures. When President O'Connell and organizer Stuart Reid
arrived in Chicago, three thousand members had already walked
out. Convinced that this was enough, O'Connell and Reid urged
the rest to remain on the job. "Our request was ignored, and 1,500
more walked out. . . . All our energies have been exhausted trying
to keep men at work."[53] Nor was O'Connell sure that the strikers
would accept the Chicago Agreement and return to work. The decisive meeting was held at a Salvation Army hall, which conveniently contained a large bass drum. The drum was brought on
stage and "played a very important part, for it was beaten with
tremendous effect when speeches were being made favorable to
the agreement and was always silent when they were unfavor-
able."[54]

O'Connell had good reason for concern, for in his pursuit of the
nine-hour day and formal bargaining status he had agreed to drop
many of the control demands made by local machinists. The closed
shop, the formal recognition of shop committees, and the restrictions on the two-machine system and on management prerogatives
in hiring and firing were all abandoned by IAM leaders in the
course of negotiations.[55] Indeed, under the Murray Hill Agreement IAM officials promised that union members would "place no
restrictions upon the management or production of the shop, and
will give a fair day's work for a fair day's wage."[56] This clause, together with the Agreement's guarantee of employers' freedom to
hire nonunion labor, was apparently omitted from copies of the
pact circulated to IAM locals.[57] Clearly, IAM leaders were more
willing than their constituents to trade control for a shorter workday and formal bargaining rights, and they were aware that these
different priorities could create difficulties.

For employers, as for rank-and-file machinists, the problem of control dominated the 1900 strikes. Employers had no objection to the nine-hour day so long as it was widely granted and Chicago firms were not put at a competitive disadvantage. The minimum wages machinists requested caused no alarm because most Chicago employers already paid their workers at least that much.[58] What manufacturers could not accept were restrictions on their rights to hire nonunion labor, to assign workers to machines as they pleased, and to judge for themselves whom to retain and whom to discharge. Nor would they formally recognize a shop committee to contest their decisions and enforce union work rules. So long as union leaders agreed with these priorities, the NMTA would accept them as responsible bargaining partners. Union recognition and the nine-hour day were prices employers were willing to pay to consolidate their control of the shops.

NMTA strategies during the 1900 strikes also demonstrate employers' concern with two other features of factory politics in the late 1890s: local autonomy and irregular strikes. NMTA negotiators refused to settle the strikes on a purely local basis. Although wages were a legitimate subject for local bargaining,[59] local autonomy in the area of work rules and management practices was unacceptable. NMTA representatives in Chicago declined to deal with the local union because it "does not have a correct knowledge of conditions as they affect the industry at large. . . . But we will recognize your national union through our national association"[60] and thus ensure that "practically the same conditions of labor shall prevail in all the different sections."[61]

A national agreement would have the further virtue of protecting employers from irregular local disputes. The NMTA had been founded to present a united front against local labor demands. By recognizing national union leaders, employers hoped to enlist their aid in checking local (and often unofficial) strikes. The importance of this for NMTA leaders is indicated by their refusal to negotiate until IAM officers called off outstanding strikes. If President O'Connell could not do so, employers reasoned, there was no guarantee that he could enforce any subsequent agreement or prevent strikes pending arbitration.[62] Union officials evidently shared the NMTA's hopes for a national solution to local unrest. "If this idea— the board of arbitration—is carried out in a spirit of fairness and equity, mutual concessions being made . . . there need never be any more strikes or lockouts, as far as the machinists are concerned."[63]

The Murray Hill Agreement of May 1900 embodied the goals of NMTA and IAM leaders. Employers conceded the nine-hour day, to be introduced in two installments at six-month intervals, and granted enhanced pay rates for overtime work. NMTA members agreed to employ no more than one apprentice for every five machinists—a concession of little value to craftsmen because employers no longer relied on apprenticeship to train workers.[64] Employers also largely accepted the union's definition of a machinist as a worker competent to perform specified tasks. But no minimum wages were guaranteed for those tasks, and employers explicitly retained the right to decide which men were "competent to perform the work and to determine the conditions under which it shall be prosecuted." In return the union abandoned local demands for the closed shop, seniority rights, and shop committee recognition and pledged not to place any "restrictions upon the management or production of the shop."

The Agreement also reaffirmed the procedure that had been established in Chicago for dealing with disputes. Any grievance not settled informally within the shops had to be referred to the national board of arbitration, consisting of three representatives each of the NMTA and IAM. In November both sides agreed to add an intermediate layer of negotiations, involving representatives chosen by the local branch of the NMTA and by the aggrieved employees. No strikes or lockouts were permitted until the completion of national conferences, and NMTA and IAM leaders promised to discipline unruly members.

Confronted with many of the same obstacles as their British counterparts, NMTA firms thus adopted a similar solution: a national trade agreement affirming management control and enlisting union leaders to check rank-and-file workers.[65] IAM officials eager for recognition and organizing opportunities willingly obliged. Yet for all the apparent advantages of Murray Hill to employers and union executives, the Agreement collapsed within a year, with the breakdown in large measure engineered by the NMTA.

The reduction of hours to nine a day was to take place in two steps—the first half-hour in November and the second in May

1901. In November it became clear that employers did not assume that the cut in working hours would be compensated by an increase in wage rates. For the most part employers, with business ample and labor scarce, did raise wages. Machinists, however, demanded that their leaders secure a blanket pay hike corresponding to the nine-hour day, and here the NMTA balked.[66] Sticking to the letter of the Murray Hill Agreement, employers insisted that wage negotiations were a local matter, subject to national arbitration only upon local failure to agree, with each case decided on its individual merits. Although NMTA leaders refused to deal with wages on a national basis, they also advised local members faced with IAM proposals "that no individual action on said document be taken."[67] Having already committed itself to a national strike to win the nine-hour day at non-NMTA firms, the IAM chose to fight as well those NMTA firms that refused to grant wage increases. On May 20, 1901, some forty thousand machinists went out as planned. Strikes persisted at least into October, but except in Chicago and in small, non-NMTA shops elsewhere, the IAM failed to secure shorter hours, wage increases, or union agreements.[68]

The strikes against NMTA firms were nominally a breach of the Murray Hill Agreement, from which the NMTA, deploring the IAM's irresponsible behavior, withdrew. But employers' disenchantment with Murray Hill had deeper roots. NMTA representatives complained that the union's pledge to leave management to employers alone was not being honored in the shops. "In numerous cases and through widely separated localities the union machinists have flagrantly restricted the production of the shops, denied flatly the right of the employer to govern his own affairs, and have interfered with the management and methods of our shops, and it is this point which we declare to be the issue which we defend in this contest."[69] Nor did the Murray Hill Agreement succeed in preventing unauthorized strikes.[70] These were two sides of a single problem: national IAM leaders could not, after all, control their own members. Indeed, for many employers the Murray Hill Agreement had effects quite contrary to those intended by the NMTA. Union recognition helped spur dramatic increases in IAM membership, from 22,500 in 1900 to 32,500 a year later.[71] Rather than respecting the terms of agreement, machinists used their added power to repudiate those terms—refusing to work "harmoniously" with nonunion workmen, insisting on craft restrictions, and taking advantage of the business boom to stage quick strikes. Discussions among manufacturers at an NMTA conference late in May concluded that "the foothold gained in the shops by the union, under the operation of the New York agreement, had resulted in the introduction of practices by workmen which were subversive of discipline and detrimental to the interests of employers. . . . These facts being made clear at the conference, a determination to free themselves absolutely from union control grew with irresistible strength."[72]

The employers articulated their determination in the NMTA's "Declaration of Principles," adopted May 28, 1901. Management's prerogatives were once more asserted, combined not with a national system of union-employer arbitration but with the open shop. "Since we, as employers, are fully responsible for the work turned out by our workmen, we must, therefore, have full discretion to designate the men we consider competent to perform the work and to determine the conditions under which that work shall be prosecuted. . . . The number of Apprentices, Helpers and Handymen to be employed will be determined solely by the employer," and "employees will be paid by the hourly rate, by premium system, piece work or contract as the employer may elect." In the event of a dispute over some other issue, firms were advised to meet with representatives from their own employees, but no negotiations would be entertained if the workers went on strike.[73] This declaration brought the NMTA new recruits,[74] and beginning with the 1901 strikes the association's full resources were committed to defending the principles of managerial rights and the open shop—principles now defined as synonymous.

Comparative Conclusions

Engineers and machinists of the 1890s aimed to preserve customary prerogatives and privileges at the expense of both management and other workers. Craft protest rarely involved cooperation with members of other trades or with less skilled workers. The continued strength of craftsmen in late-nineteenth-century manufacturing favored mobilization behind such conservative goals and along sectional lines. The institutional environment for protest similarly promoted exclusive action. Unsupportive unions and localistic industrial relations led metalworkers to rely most heavily on district and shop organizations to defend their interests—a strategy that frequently put national leaders and the rank and file at odds. These same organizations, however, reproduced the exclusiveness of craft unions at the local level and made it unnecessary for machinists and engineers to seek the support and take into account the interests of other work groups.

The relatively tenuous position of skilled workers and craft unions in the United States did weaken workshop organization. Machinists often had to resort to sympathy strikes and were more dependent on local union officials to coordinate the defense of craft standards. Yet these differences in tactics and leadership had little effect on the goals and alliances of craft protest. Machinists still enjoyed a stronger bargaining position than less skilled workers, and they remained organized locally along sectional lines.

This picture of factory politics in the 1890s might suggest that engineers and machinists were uniformly conservative. They were not. Distinct minorities in both the ASE and the IAM endorsed socialism and supported the organization of less skilled metalworkers. Industrial unionist sentiments reflected the impact of Britain's "New Unionism" and America's Knights of Labor and the American Railway Union during the late 1880s and early 1890s, along with a growing recognition that changes in industrial organization required alternatives to traditional craft strategies.[75] Socialist and industrial unionist commitments, moreover, had some effect in both unions: ASE members elected a socialist General Secretary (George Barnes) in 1896, and IAM delegates in 1895 and 1897 expanded direct membership control over national officers through the use of the referendum. In neither union, however, did radicals influence the formulation of trade policies or the conduct of disputes. The conditions that would enable progressives to gain broader support among engineers and machinists did not develop until after 1900. During the 1890s, practical factory politics remained defensive in goals and exclusive in strategy.

For employers, craft control meant impediments to their right to manage. Local autonomy, with work rules varying in character and stringency from one shop or district to another, placed manufacturers on an unequal competitive footing, and rank-and-file initiative exposed them to unpredictable disruptions in production. The 1897–1898 and 1900 disputes typified these dilemmas for metal trades employers and at the same time seemed to offer an opportunity to solve them once and for all. The solutions represented by the Terms of Settlement and the Murray Hill Agreement were the same: formal union guarantees to respect management rights and to discipline union members, and to do so on a uniform, national scale.

The key comparative problem is to explain the subsequent divergence in employer strategies. Why did employers abandon the Murray Hill Agreement in favor of the open shop, while the Terms endured? Certainly the Murray Hill Agreement did not live up to employer expectations. Craft restrictions continued, as did unofficial strikes in violation of the arbitration procedure. Montgomery concludes that this inability of IAM leaders to hold their constituents to the terms of Murray Hill accounts for employers' recourse to the open shop.[76] But ASE national officials were perhaps even less successful in this regard, and still the EEF clung to the Terms. The most important reasons for this divergence involve, once again, contrasts in the modernization of the labor process and the timing of craft union development. Differences in production practices and the strength of trade unions had two important consequences for management strategy. First, NMTA employers had less to gain from collaborating with union leaders and less to lose in fighting them. Second, these differences in manufacturing techniques and craft unionism contributed to broader industrial traditions—traditions that made open shops especially attractive to U.S. employers and trade agreements congenial to British ones.

In the United States dilution had made greater headway, and had done so more rapidly, than in Britain. This progress made union restrictions more irksome to U.S. employers and simultaneously reduced their reliance on craft unionists to get the work done. NMTA members thus had both greater interest and greater resources to attack craft standards. Because the erosion of craft control was under way before the IAM's consolidation, U.S. employers had another advantage: relatively feeble union opposition. The NMTA faced a union much weaker than the ASE, and employers quickly found that the Murray Hill Agreement served to strengthen the IAM. The IAM enrolled only 11 percent of American machinists in 1900, compared to perhaps 50 percent of engi-

neers enrolled in the ASE and other craft unions.[77] Fighting the
IAM was a far more realistic option than taking on the ASE, and an
option that might have been foreclosed by union organization
under the protection of the Murray Hill Agreement. By the same
token the IAM was thus of less potential value in controlling ma
chine shop employees. In any case U.S. firms had less need for
unions to standardize labor costs and conditions among shops and
cities, for the concentration of capital and specialization of firms
eased competitive pressures by other means.

Given these conditions, one might reasonably ask why the
NMTA resorted to the Murray Hill Agreement for even a single
year. Although some NMTA leaders sincerely supported an experiment in national arbitration, for many members in 1900 (and many
more who accepted the NMTA's leadership in the dispute but
joined only in 1901), the Murray Hill Agreement was probably a
temporary expedient. The Agreement was affordable, and it provided some stability in labor costs when business was exceptionally
prosperous and skilled workers scarce. It also offered breathing
space for the fledgling NMTA to expand its organization and prepare for future battles. With increasing pressure on profit margins
in 1901 and after, employers had fewer incentives to abide by the
Murray Hill Agreement,[78] and they were in a stronger position to
insist instead on the open shop. It is also significant that the Agreement emerged from confrontations in Chicago, the nation's most
strongly unionized city.[79] Here collective bargaining survived even
after the demise of Murray Hill. Elsewhere the IAM was rarely in
a position to force collective bargaining on unwilling employers.

The British engineering industry, by contrast, experienced a
major boom for several years following the conclusion of the 1897–
1898 lockout, thanks to the Boer War. Although national collaboration rewarded the hopes of the EEF no more than those of the
NMTA, under prosperous conditions British employers were reluctant to risk a general confrontation with engineering craft
unions. For the remainder of the prewar years, there was no business slump so serious or prolonged as to tempt the EEF with the
prospects of abandoning the Terms. Indeed, the industry's procedures may have helped delay and limit wage advances relative to
prices, compared to what engineers might have secured if given a
free hand.

Industrial traditions as well as immediate practical considerations influenced employer policies. These traditions demonstrate the influence of the timing of changes at work relative to industrial relations. By 1897, British engineering had a tradition of collective bargaining between employers and skilled workers that stretched back over forty years. That tradition had been consolidated during a period of relative stability in manufacturing techniques and slow but steady growth in exports. Most progressive employers in the 1890s assumed that disputes should be resolved through negotiation and agreement.[80] Although some managers were tempted by the prospects of a union-free environment in the midst of the 1897–1898 lockout, manufacturers' continued reliance on skilled workers made open-shop policies unrealistic. EEF leaders saw the crisis instead as an opportunity to secure formal union compliance with managerial initiatives and a formal union role in shop discipline. A representative of the General Electric Company in London could justifiably claim in 1909 that "our attitude towards the Trades Unions has always been to support them so long as they give us a guarantee that their members are efficient workers."[81]

No such breathing space for the consolidation of collective bargaining existed in the U.S. metal trades. Even before the 1890s, U.S. employers had begun meeting new product markets and a scarcity of skilled labor with strategies of dilution and shop reorganization, rather than through a slow expansion of employment within the technical status quo. By the time the IAM gained its footing in the mid-1890s, rapid changes at work were already under way, and management had secured some freedom from dependence on machinists. Under these conditions union recognition and collective bargaining seemed to endanger employers' right to manage and appeared incompatible with business success.[82] Particularly in the northeast—where union organization was weakest and production methods most progressive—industrial relations traditions involved informal negotiation with the firm's own employees, if possible on an individual basis. No legacy of collective bargaining existed to help the Murray Hill Agreement survive the 1901 dispute.

Broader national traditions reinforced the choices made in each case. There is some validity in the stereotyped contrast between turn-of-the-century British and American employers—one civil, tactful, and conservative; the other rough, unyielding, intolerant of obstacles. The same conservatism that made most British engineering employers reluctant to seize new technical opportunities and revamp traditional workshop practices[83] made them unwilling to break with customary industrial relations. Given traditional manufacturing practices, they were in any case unable to dispense with engineers and their unions. U.S. employers, eager to overcome technical obstacles to more efficient and profitable production, were similarly impatient with the human obstacles presented by craft unions. A more advanced labor process put them in a better position to rid their shops of union interference. Moreover, they had at their disposal alternatives to bargaining with union leaders that were less available to British manufacturers—particularly judges willing to virtually ban strikes and boycotts and state and local governments willing to apply force on their behalf. Heavy-handed repression of union activity, in turn, received greater support from the press and the middle class in the name of property rights and American individualism.[84] Thus U.S. employers had not only the inclination to drive unions from their shops but also the means to do so.

The contrasting outcomes of the 1897–1898 and 1901 disputes should not be overdrawn. There remained British shops (particularly in new branches and centers of the industry) in which managers declined to deal with "outside" interference and employees risked discharge if they advertised their union affiliations or insisted on union conditions. Although most U.S. employers (and all NMTA members) refused to negotiate with union representatives, skilled machinists remained valuable. Unless they made trouble, their union ties were not too closely monitored. To keep the peace, employers met deputations to discuss grievances, even if these were in effect shop committees acting under local union instructions. Despite these qualifications, the conflicts of the 1890s had starkly different outcomes: in Britain the Terms of Agreement, in the United States the open shop. This contrast in particular accounts for the subsequent divergence in British and American factory politics.

Chapter Four

The Transformation of Craft Militancy, 1900–1914

Skilled metalworkers faced continued challenges to their occupational position and privileges during the fifteen years before World War I, and a growing minority rejected craft union policies as appropriate means to meet those challenges. Yet neither shop-floor grievances nor the simple number of syndicalists and industrial unionists account for changes in factory politics after 1900. Rank-and-file interests could be expressed in different ways, and radicals were not necessarily in a position to lead industrial unrest. Changing conditions, rather than ideological commitments, mobilized protest in new directions. From the turn of the century, trade unions and industrial relations impeded traditional strategies for defending craft control. Engineers and machinists, accordingly, developed new forms of local organization to promote their interests.

Citywide joint trade councils and increasingly active and autonomous shop committees provided useful vehicles for conducting day-to-day battles with employers. Pragmatism, not principle, encouraged most craftsmen to rely on local alternatives to established trade unionism. Innovations in rank-and-file organization reshaped factory politics. Trade councils and shop committees began to bypass union authority and bridge divisions of craft and skill. Such bodies gave radicalized engineers and machinists—still in the minority—opportunities for leadership in defiance of national union policies. Conditions after 1900 also enhanced radicals' prospects for popular support, even among conservative skilled workers. The mobilization of craft traditions through new institutions and under new circumstances favored alliances between rank-and-file militants and progressive leaders and programs. Faced with novel obstacles as well as new channels for protest, the frustrations of craft conservatives lent support to innovative goals and tactics, including cooperation among workers of various unions in negotiations and strikes.

Departures from defensive and sectional factory politics occurred in both Britain and the United States, and in each case those initiatives grew out of organizational developments at the local level. The context of protest differed, however. British engineers operated in an industrial relations environment that limited official channels for control struggles yet helped protect their shopfloor power and privileges. Among machinists, by contrast, open shops and more advanced manufacturing methods incited progressive movements but denied them an effective organizational base inside the factory gates. Unofficial organization and leadership took root more in metal trades councils and rebellious union locals than within the shops. The divergent institutional foundations for rank-and-file insurgency led to different patterns of factory politics. These causal links are clear not only when the British and U.S. experiences are juxtaposed; they emerge as well from comparisons within each national industry.

The Development of
Factory Politics in Britain

Engineering craft unions faced mounting criticism from their members during the fifteen years before World War I. For a significant portion of the ASE rank and file, the problems faced by engineers required a clear break with craft exclusiveness. The power demonstrated by federated employers in 1897–1898 suggested to many engineers the need for amalgamation among craft unions, as did continuing technological change, which blurred traditional trade boundaries and rendered obsolete the continuing demarcations among unions.[1] For similar reasons some engineers went further and advocated organizing less skilled engineering workers. Dilution increased the number of specialists and narrowed the gap between skilled and unskilled hands. Unorganized, less skilled workers might be recruited as blacklegs during strikes; standing together, engineering workers would have a stronger bargaining position and be better able to prevent employers from playing one grade off against another. Radicals, often connected with local Amalgamation Committees, accordingly called for "One Big Union for Metal, Engineering and Shipbuilding Workers."[2]

Such endorsements had minimal impact on ASE structure or policies. Joint consultation among union executives through the General Federation of Trade Unions or the Federation of Engineering and Shipbuilding Trades, for example, scarcely contributed to united action at the local level. Regular petitions from district committees requesting the ASE Executive Council to pursue more complete amalgamation achieved little before 1920. Similarly, support for industrial unionism was substantial but ineffective.[3] Running on a platform of "one union for engineering, working class solidarity and direct action," Tom Mann received 25 percent of the vote for ASE General Secretary in 1913. Delegate meetings in 1902 and 1912 created new membership sections for specialists and unskilled workers. But conservatives retained control in most districts, and local and national officials alike remained content to leave the new sections empty.

The Development of Local Organization

Unable to win significant reforms at the national level, militant engineers increasingly turned to joint local committees and, above all, to organization within the shops to coordinate policy, conduct negotiations, and manage strikes. Through Joint Engineering Trades Committees (JCs), representatives of craft union district committees could plan common local policies and bargain with employers' associations on a more equal footing. If engineers made little progress toward amalgamation at the national level, JCs provided one base for cooperation among crafts. And as unrest and unionization among less skilled workers mounted after 1910, engineers had in JCs a local alternative to exclusive organization: a body through which representatives of craft and general unions could work together. Because JCs were not subject to the direct authority of individual unions' executives, they also offered local engineers a base for action independent of sectional union constraints. Such independence led to frequent conflict between union leaders and district officials over the powers of JCs.[4] Although not active in day-to-day industrial relations and devoted largely to propaganda, local Amalgamation Committees in London, Birmingham, Coventry, Manchester, Tyneside, Sheffield, and Liverpool offered similar opportunities for workers of different unions and skills to discuss shared problems, develop joint strategies, and overcome sectional identities.[5]

The more important developments in local organization took place within the factories. After 1898, shop stewards and works committees gained new powers and exercised greater independence from formal union policies and leaders. Changes in the character of workshop organization reflected, in part, continuing efforts to combat management encroachments and to defend district work rules. Engineers relied on shop stewards to contest infractions of work rules and negotiate such idiosyncratic workshop issues as abusive supervision or compensating pieceworkers for faulty materials—issues for which union officials were too distant to be of timely and knowledgeable assistance.[6]

The crucial stimulus to expanded shop organization, however, came from the new industrial relations setting established in 1898. Engineers fighting dilution and piecework confronted not merely the encroachments of individual employers but also the management rights formally conferred on EEF members by the Terms of Settlement (called the Terms of Agreement after 1907). Under these conditions strong workshop organization became crucial to prevent employers from realizing the full benefits of their new entitlements. The Terms, for example, gave employers full authority to select, train, and assign workers to machines. Engineers responded by refusing to instruct green hands or rectify their work and by striking against the two-machine system.[7] Such strategies were usually organized within the shops, and they were often successful despite their illegality under the Terms.

According to the 1898 settlement, employers also enjoyed the right to introduce incentive pay. The ASE reaffirmed this right in the 1902 Carlisle Agreement, dropping all objections to premium bonus systems so long as management guaranteed overtime and minimum wage rates and did not cut prices unless "the methods or means of production" changed. Here, too, shop-floor organization became crucial for safeguarding rank-and-file interests. Shop stewards fought price cuts disguised as changes in manufacturing methods, and they ensured that piece rates and bonus times were set by collective rather than individual bargaining.[8] And if the workers in the shops could not prevent the introduction of obnoxious incentive schemes, they could at least make sure those systems did not pay. Following complaints that engineers could rarely make more than their time wages under a bonus scheme at the Humber automobile plant, the Coventry District Committee conceded the legality of the system but called on "the Intelligence of the men as to what speed they go at for only Dayrate pay."[9] Shop stewards helped make output quotas known—and they helped make them stick.

Shop organization thus acquired a new strategic value in combating employers' prerogatives under the Terms and the Carlisle Agreement. Perhaps more important, these Agreements committed the ASE to upholding management rights. The union thus became much less supportive of rank-and-file control struggles and in many cases openly opposed them. The result was greater self-reliance at the district and shop levels. Only rank-and-file vigilance could deny employers their right to introduce premium bonus schemes—a lesson emphasized in 1907 when engineers at Vickers struck against a new bonus scheme, only to be ordered back to work by the ASE Executive Council.[10]

Strong organization in the shops also proved necessary to overcome the constraints of the Terms' Procedure for Avoiding Disputes. The Procedure passed grievances not resolved at the workplace to local conferences between union and employer association representatives and, failing agreement, to a central conference between national leaders. The original disputants were to remain at work under the "current conditions," pending a final decision. This system encouraged workshop organization in two ways. Despite the Terms, engineers often refused to let grievances stand while the Procedure took its leisurely course—especially under favorable business conditions, when immediate strikes promised prompt rewards.[11] Engineers striking unconstitutionally were usually ordered back to work and the Procedure set in motion, but shop-floor vigilance remained essential for a second reason: to remove the bias in the "current conditions" clause. If engineers could prevent an employer from initiating an obnoxious change in work practices, forcing the employer to invoke the Procedure, then the benefits of the status quo lay with the employees, pending a decision at a local or central conference.[12]

In these responses to the Procedure, rank-and-file engineers once again found themselves at odds with their own union officials as well as with organized employers. ASE leaders were committed to the Procedure as the only legitimate means for dealing with shop-floor disputes.[13] Under the Procedure centralized negotiation not only took grievances out of local hands, but excluded local representatives as well.[14] ASE officials also assumed responsibility for enforcing the Procedure's ban on strikes while conferences were under way.[15] Workshop organization and activism offered a means for retaining local control and some freedom of action. Work slowdowns, overtime bans, and strikes initiated by the rank and file often succeeded in imposing domestic settlements on employers in violation of the Procedure and in defiance of ASE constitutional requirements that local action receive prior approval from the Executive Council.[16]

From 1909, the problem of long-term wage contracts at once reinforced and illustrated these dynamics. In 1908, Newcastle engineers struck to resist a wage reduction, bitterly attacking the Executive Council for its recommendation to accept the cut. To avoid similar antagonisms in the future, as well as to forestall wage reductions elsewhere, the Executive Council increasingly negotiated agreements for individual districts, fixing pay rates for periods of three to five years. Although these agreements appeared to safeguard members' interests during the trade slump of 1908–1909, after 1910 they became clear liabilities. Engineers found their pay frozen while the cost of living increased rapidly, and they saw their revived bargaining strength fettered by long-term contracts.

Under these conditions the agreements appeared to exemplify the pitfalls of centralized bargaining. The contracts had been negotiated in central conference, without proper account given to local participation and interests; and they deprived the rank and file of the freedom to exploit temporary advantages for immediate gain. Long-term agreements thus helped shift the terrain of struggle to the shops. Given strong organization at work and a willingness to defy procedural and union constraints, engineers could force wages above the agreed district rates. In some cases they did so by informally abrogating the agreements, in others by securing compensating concessions on piece rates and bonus times. Even where economic gains remained limited, militancy contained in wage matters found expression in other forms of self-defense, including battles for closed shops and restrictions on the manning of machines.[17]

Consequences for Factory Politics

For a significant minority of ASE members, changes at work demanded radical changes in the union's constitution and policy. Conservative views prevailed, and progressive energies turned to local alternatives to established craft unionism. Under new conditions, pragmatism required greater reliance on unofficial leaders and action, even among skilled workers firmly committed to traditional goals. New forms of protest followed. The effect of industrial relations and union constraints was to make rank-and-file organization both more independent and more antagonistic to ASE officials and the Terms. This outcome played an important role in a broader shift in factory politics. Traditional craft interests mobilized through new organizations and under new circumstances began to converge with radical programs, making possible tacit alliances between progressive leaders and militant conservatives.

Before 1898, shop stewards represented the authority of district committees in the plants. They were generally appointed by these committees and charged with monitoring union membership and work rules. In the years before World War I, stewards were more likely to be elected by the workers in the shops; they were also more actively involved in negotiations with management, and they more frequently exercised leadership in calling shop meetings and walkouts. The Terms and Procedure encouraged engineers to develop within the shops a capacity for independent action.[18] Industrial relations arrangements, however, also placed workshop organization and action in an increasingly adversarial relation to official unions. Craftsmen resented the prerogatives employers claimed under the Terms. ASE leaders had accepted those Terms. They had failed to improve upon them significantly in subsequent negotiations. They had no answer to the usual "failure to agree" at central conferences when local disputes over machine manning or piecework were discussed. Inevitably, the struggle against managerial encroachments directed rank-and-file hostilities against their own union executive. ASE officials appeared spineless at best, at worst they appeared to take the employers' side in conflicts over craft privileges and management rights.[19]

Under the Procedure the ASE also undertook responsibility to enforce centralized bargaining and to keep members at work. Here, too, union leaders appeared to side with employers in depriving engineers of control over local negotiations and tactics. Because district officials acquired a formal role under the Procedure and corresponding obligations to restrain unofficial action, they too became objects for the rank and file's resentment. A 1914 complaint by an Organizing District Delegate is symptomatic: "In Coventry there have been [in the last month] two strikes. . . . In both cases the local Committee had been ignored until after members had downed tools, and as this has happened on several occasions the Committee naturally resented what appeared to have become a policy. . . . However faulty the present methods of negotiation may be we are scarcely likely to find salvation in ignoring the rules we make for ourselves, and the D.C. cannot do otherwise in the interests of the society than insist on being consulted."[20]

Organizational developments had a broader significance, laying the groundwork for a break with traditional craft politics. Engineering craftsmen valued their control of workshop practices and their autonomy in regulating the trade. But these traditions had an exclusive dimension. Under attack by employers in the 1890s, the craftsmen characteristically responded with sectional goals and tactics. After 1898, new conditions for the mobilization of craft traditions produced a shift in factory politics. Two of these traditions— local autonomy and craft control—adopted a new political complexion and created a common terrain for craft conservatives and radicals. The third—exclusiveness—was significantly eroded.[21]

Craft conservatives and radicals shared a commitment to local autonomy in trade policy and action. Their motives differed. Conservatives upheld local authority to offset an overly cautious and compromising defense of craft rights by national leaders; radicals did so to safeguard their strongholds from interference by an executive in which they had as yet little voice.[22] Under the Terms and Procedure, however, the preservation of local autonomy acquired a distinctly insurgent quality. Conservatives and radicals alike asserted their rights of local control and freedom of action against a distant union officialdom and a bureaucratized system of collective bargaining. One such assertion of local autonomy—the 1908 North East Coast strike in defiance of Executive Council recommendations—led ASE General Secretary George Barnes to resign, citing "an undemocratic feeling in the Trade Unions which had worked itself out in the direction of mistrust of officials and officialdom."[23]

The growing strength and independence of shop committees reflected this repudiation of bureaucratic control. Shop committees also offered conservatives and radicals a common base from which to fight back. An explosion of unofficial and "spontaneous" action followed under the favorable economic conditions after 1910. In 1913, for example, ASE members struck twenty firms covered by the Procedure. Sixteen of the stoppages were unconstitutional.[24] Other forms of unofficial action (e.g., overtime bans) and cases of shop stewards "exceeding their authority" became increasingly common. These trends—ideological hostility to trade union controls and to centralized union-management collaboration, organizational independence, and what might be termed direct action— have been described as "presyndicalist,"[25] a suitably cautious formulation. The majority of engineers did not become convinced syndicalists. But there was a convergence between syndicalist ideology and rank-and-file action and a greater willingness of engineers to follow syndicalist agitators rather than official union leaders. In the exercise and organization of local autonomy, even industrial conservatives echoed syndicalist ideas.[26]

A similar coincidence of practical factory politics and radical ideology characterizes workers' control. Amid the nationwide surge of labor unrest from 1910 to 1914, engineers exploited economic boom and labor scarcity to pursue old goals with new vigor. Disputes and conferences over the manning of machines, premium bonus systems, and the closed shop increased dramatically.[27] Such challenges to management control differed from those before 1898. Traditional goals acquired an insurgent tone as rank-and-file engineers repudiated not only management's formal rights under the Terms but also union complicity in those rights. Engineers had

developed the organizational means to contest employer prerogatives despite the restrictions of the Terms and an overly compliant
union. New constraints and organizational weapons thus mobilized
traditional commitments to the craft status quo into more contentious and militant struggles. Nor did prewar factory politics merely
advance old ends in new ways. Engineers in many districts, for
example, no longer defended the status quo against the introduction of payment by results. Instead, they conceded this innovation
but demanded participation in regulating incentive systems. Here,
too, engineers won new controls at work through unofficial organization. Shop stewards and pricing committees gained de facto employer (if not necessarily union) recognition to negotiate the administration of piecework schemes.[28]

These changes did not transform craft conservatives into advocates of workers' ownership and control of the means of production. Despite persisting differences in their ultimate goals, however, the practical politics of conservatives and radicals converged.
Syndicalists and Amalgamation Committee movement activists in
engineering, as in coal and transport, aimed to secure worker control of industry. In practice their propaganda and strike leadership
overlapped with newly militant demands for job control on the part
of craftsmen. For both groups, moreover, the factory was the necessary terrain of struggle, and shop committees were a common
base for action. In the syndicalist scheme, organization within the
shops was to form the basic unit for workers' control and for industrial government; for craft conservatives it offered the means to
retain control over workshop practices and have a voice in management decisions, despite employer and union encroachments on
their autonomy. By emphasizing its support for local and craft autonomy, the Engineering and Shipbuilding Amalgamation Committee further bridged the gap between radicals and militant conservatives.[29]

There remained a third craft tradition, exclusiveness, that divided the two groups. For partisans of syndicalism, amalgamation,
and industrial unionism, changes in manufacturing practice rendered traditional divisions of craft and skill obsolete. All-grades
organization seemed imperative to keep pace with technological
change. The tactical weaknesses of a trade union structure splin-
tered into hundreds of craft societies and general unions (as against

increasingly concentrated capital and closely associated employers) also demanded more encompassing labor organization. Such views received considerable support among ASE members, as Tom Mann's 25 percent share of the vote for General Secretary in 1913 indicates.[30] Yet most engineers remained committed to sectional privileges and more disposed to close ranks against the advance of semiskilled workers than to join with them in "One Big Union."[31] This view prevailed in the union's constitution and national policy.

Still, convergence between the practical interests of skilled workers and the more ambitious aims of radicals did occur inside the factory gates. Even for conservatives the divisions among craft unions represented a strategic liability. The workers in the shops could act with greater knowledge and dispatch through their stewards than by reporting grievances to separate branches and district committee officials at some future union meeting. Because the Procedure covered most major engineering unions, members of different craft societies could best retain local control through cooperation on the job. United action assumed further importance given employers' willingness to exploit craft divisions for their own advantage.[32] Although most shop stewards represented the members of their own unions exclusively, stewards of separate crafts gradually formed works committees to handle common affairs. In some cases different craftsmen in a department elected a common steward.[33] Day-to-day conflicts at work, combined with the peculiarities of trade union structure and industrial relations, thus favored joint organization on the shop floor. Such organization did not in itself convert craft conservatives into class-conscious militants. But it did afford them needed opportunities to pursue interests shared with members of other trade unions and with radicals—specifically, the defense of local autonomy and workplace control. As engineering workers of different trades worked together—selecting common representatives, devising collective demands, and coordinating strikes—craft boundaries were eroded.

Skill boundaries, by contrast, remained intact. Shop stewards and works committees rarely included less skilled men and women in their constituencies before the war.[34] Few less skilled engineering workers were unionized before 1910, and they lacked the traditions of local autonomy, the strategic position in production, and the interests in fighting dilution and piecework that contributed to shop-floor organization among craftsmen. The very success of unofficial action by engineers also preserved exclusiveness. Because organization on the job protected the position and power of skilled workers, most engineers had little need to reevaluate sectional identities.[35] Exclusive shop committees, in turn, provided few opportunities for employees of different skill levels to develop common policies or act together in day-to-day grievances. Here, then, radicals and conservatives found no common ground. Only outside the shops, in local Amalgamation Committees, did there exist established institutions through which militants from trade and general unions could discuss common problems and plot collective strategies.[36]

The development of joint organization among craftsmen—and only craftsmen—had clear consequences for factory politics. During the prewar years members of different craft unions acted together in industrial disputes with growing frequency. They did so not only in wage movements but also in control struggles, contesting management authority in matters of dilution, piecework, objectionable supervision, and the closed shop. Unofficial workshop organization provided the underpinning for these trends. Joint action among Coventry engineering workers appears earliest at the two firms with the strongest shop organization: the Coventry Ordnance Works (COW) and Daimler.[37] These disputes were explicitly concerned with control issues. At COW in 1907, workers went out over victimization, task work, job cards, and dilution, as well as over overtime pay and the district rate. Daimler engineers struck in 1908 against the premium bonus system, bonus cards, incompetent rate fixers, and unjust dismissals. Both strikes were initiated without union sanction.[38]

Craftsmen and less skilled workers, by contrast, remained divided. Although engineering workers of different skills did occasionally undertake joint action during the wave of labor unrest after 1910, cooperation in negotiations and strikes rarely extended beyond economic issues. Given the continued strength of craftsmen and the absence of solidary organization on the job, the basic conflicts of interest between skill grades over dilution and piecework prevented common policies and action in matters of workplace control. Even in joint wage movements engineers proved willing to break ranks with less skilled workers, accepting settlements for themselves alone.[39]

Persisting cleavages between craftsmen and less skilled workers should not obscure the fundamental changes in factory politics between 1898 and World War I. New forms of organization gave radicals a foothold they were unable to achieve through formal union channels. The alternatives they offered—syndicalism, workers' control, solidary organization—had some appeal to workers with different political outlooks who nevertheless all chafed under union and bureaucratic constraints, employer offensives on the job, and the tactical liabilities of established craft unionism. There was a dilemma, however, in the status of workshop organization before the war. Strong unions and the Terms and Procedure provided both a protective and a restrictive shell for shop-floor activism. Despite rank-and-file hostility to union policies and the Terms, engineers clearly benefited from both. The ASE successfully defended union activists from victimization and made a special provision of a year's wage to any steward discharged for "executing his duties."[40] The Terms and Procedure, in turn, rendered certain grievances legitimate and established ground rules for handling them. The price was union discipline and procedural constraint. It was not always paid, especially during prosperous times when engineers could win disputes quickly, without benefit of union strike funds or fear of being fired. But ordinarily, the prospects of union censure, denial of financial support, and loss of the opportunity to invoke a binding grievance procedure were powerful obstacles to unconstitutional action. The weight of such considerations is indicated by ASE members' willingness, even in the militant year of 1914, to approve (by a two to one margin) a revised procedure for avoiding disputes following their vote to withdraw from the Terms.[41]

Dependence brings constraints. To the extent that engineers agreed to play by the rules of the game, factory politics remained relatively routine and circumscribed by sectional union priorities. The prospects of union sanctions made shop-floor leaders cautious in advocating unofficial action, especially when such action seemed certain to elicit union censure—as in walkouts in support of less skilled workers. An employer might, of course, decline to invoke the Procedure if acquiescence to shop-floor pressures seemed prudent. But usually, works committees and stewards eventually forwarded disputes to regular union officials, who would drop demands at odds with craft policies. Thus progressive initiatives were limited by restrictions on the freedom of action enjoyed by rank-and-file organization. Indeed, including plant conferences as a formal stage in the revised grievance procedure of 1914 suggests an effort by employers and union leaders to restrict workshop organization to official union business. Continued dependence on formal union structures also confined unofficial organization and movements to individual shops or, at most, to localities. Militants who might have coordinated insurgence or secured a broader following as yet had no effective institutional alternative to the district committees of sectional craft unions.

These limitations are clear in the period of labor unrest during the four years before World War I. Engineers shared the general enthusiasm for strikes and turned favorable business conditions to their own advantage. Historians have viewed industrial conflict in engineering during this period as limited compared to the conflicts involving coal, railway, and dock workers and less skilled men and women. Engineers' moderation has been attributed to the success of industrial relations procedures and the maturity of craft unions in the trade.[42] Yet the number of small, brief strikes increased dramatically, as did the use of such tactics as overtime bans.

That these disputes were so often initiated by unofficial leaders demonstrates the extent to which engineers had developed alternative forms of organization to advance their interests. Unofficial organization, moreover, often combined workers of diverse crafts (if not skills) in opposition to union policies and industrial relations rules. It is clear, though, that unrest remained localized and limited in scope. Unconstitutional action continued to rely on craftsmen's strategic workplace position and sectional interests. The absence of large-scale disputes involving skilled workers in the industry also reflects the accomplishments of union-management collaboration through the Procedure. Any large or protracted conflict would have required formal union sanction and risked a lockout by the EEF. Rank-and-file activists had yet to surmount union and industrial relations constraints on broadly based movements for workers' control.

The Development of Factory Politics
in the United States

After 1900, growing numbers of machinists recognized that technological change, the concentration of capital, and employer bel-
ligerence made unity among workers a strategic necessity. As
in Britain, however, increased enthusiasm for labor solidarity
achieved few national union reforms. Delegates to the 1903 IAM
convention narrowly approved the admission of specialists to the
union, but the complacence (or hostility) of national and most local
leaders ensured that few were recruited. In a far more contentious
move, delegates at the 1911 convention overcame Executive
Council objections and admitted machinists' helpers and female
machinists. Less skilled workers had little reason to join; they received fewer benefits, were consigned to separate locals, and could
organize such locals and strike only with the approval of the regular
craft lodge in the district.[43]

Unity among craft unions proved equally elusive. In one respect
the problem was less pressing than in Britain: with minor exceptions only one national union organized metalworkers in each craft.
From the early 1900s, proposals accordingly focused on the formation of metal trades federations with power to regulate joint trade
policies and strikes. At the national level such proposals failed. The
AFL's Metal Trades Department (founded in 1909) in effect institutionalized the authority of individual union executives, and resolutions threatening that authority were consistently defeated.[44]

The Development of Local Organization

Frustrated in their efforts to win national union reforms, progressive machinists increasingly sought to develop local organizations
suited to new industrial conditions. Rank-and-file metal trades
craftsmen and local officials, beginning in the early 1900s, took the
lead in forming citywide metal trades councils (MTCs) with representatives from the various craft union lodges. Shop employees of
individual railroad companies went one step further: "system federations" established after 1910 combined not only skilled workers
but also many clerks and laborers. The MTCs and system federations allowed local unionists from different craft societies to discuss

common problems and strategies, and these organizations could serve as springboards for sympathy strikes and boycotts. Because system federations joined workers of specific railway firms, they also became involved in direct negotiations and, in many cases, gained de facto employer recognition. Such departures from the sectional organization and executive authority of individual unions and the AFL's Metal Trades Department created considerable friction between national leaders and local union activists.[45]

Organization within the shops also appears to have become more common after 1900. Union agreements secured by the IAM normally provided for shop committees to monitor conditions and negotiate grievances and to protect committeemen from victimization.[46] Such agreements were few. Still, even in the absence of formal union recognition, shop committees would present complaints and demands to management, recruit new members, keep workers apprised of output quotas, and coordinate shop and strike meetings—often without reference to union officials or constitutional procedures.[47] Except in strongly organized shops and during business booms, however, shop committees were ad hoc ventures—forming to deal with a pressing grievance and dissolving once the crisis had passed.[48]

Some of the same factors that stimulated local organization in Britain operated among machinists. Other conditions peculiar to the United States favored local organization different in character and limited in strength compared to British engineering. Machinists, like engineers, needed shop committees to defend customary work practices. Institutionalized vigilance at work allowed craftsmen to act more promptly than union procedures permitted, guided by their close knowledge of shop customs and local trade conditions rather than by distant national concerns.[49] As in Britain, novel systems of payment by results spread rapidly after 1900. Through rank-and-file organization machinists hoped to protect craft rates, collective bargaining, and workplace solidarity against incentive schemes that rewarded workers according to their individual merits and encouraged competition for desirable jobs and high earnings.[50] The rise of system federations of railway shop crafts was closely connected with the battle against incentive pay schemes,[51] and whenever conditions seemed favorable (as during the economic revival of 1907–1908) or organization was strong, machinists took action to secure regular negotiations on piecework rates and conditions or to abolish the system altogether. They typically did so through their shop committees.[52]

New industrial relations conditions and union policies gave local organization both an added impetus and a shape quite different from that found in Britain. Even before 1901, IAM leaders displayed less enthusiasm for control struggles than did the rank and file; the defense of craft standards, accordingly, required local self-reliance. Conditions after 1901 led Grand Lodge officials to approach such issues with even greater caution. The open-shop drive forced the IAM to devote enormous resources simply to preserve recognition in its strongholds and defend members against victimization. Shaky finances and a stagnant membership seemed to demand that the union concentrate on the most tangible goals with the widest appeal—wage increases and the nine-hour day. Strikes over control issues had less obvious benefits and presented a less compelling advertisement for IAM membership. They were also likely to fail. The National Metal Trades Association offered its support to any firm (even nonmembers) fighting union encroachments on management prerogatives. IAM strikes that focused on workshop control thus could confront the full resources of the NMTA—financial aid, legal counsel, "special contract operatives" (spies), strikebreakers, and private guards. By contrast, "the Association warns its members that it does not extend its protection against ordinary wage strikes."[53] Consequently, IAM leaders often treated strikes against dilution, piecework, or obnoxious foremen as a hopeless waste of the union's limited means compared to disputes over wages and hours.[54]

Rank-and-file organization received ambiguous encouragement from open-shop conditions. Anti-union employers refused to recognize the IAM, insisting that they would deal only with their own employees. Shop committees thus assumed a greater importance as a means of collective bargaining. This was hardly a freely chosen alternative. Most machinists had no other opportunity to defend their interests on a day-to-day basis. In practice, shop committees often had close ties to local union officials. They might, for example, be appointed by the local lodge, arrange shop meetings on union instructions, and convey to employers what were in fact union demands. They also sought to enforce IAM rules and to recruit members. Such ties were clearest during organization drives and local movements for wage increases or shorter hours. At the very least, however, shop committees had to maintain the fiction of independence from "outside" influences. For example, after the nationwide strikes of 1901, several Bridgeport manufacturers suggested that the workers would have done better had they made suggestions through shop committees rather than through the IAM. Local machinists obliged by organizing within the shops, and in 1903 "every manufacturer in Bridgeport was waited upon by a committee representing his own employees and requested to give the men a nine-hour day without lowering the wages."[55]

Ironically, the same circumstances that encouraged workshop organization among machinists also eroded shop committee influence and security. Craftsmen rallied within the shops to confront changes in manufacturing techniques, but in the most progressive (and fastest growing) sectors of the industry, employers depended less and less on skilled workers. Where the labor process made it easy to replace machinists or required their services only in small numbers, firing an activist caused management little inconvenience. More developed production methods, in turn, supported the open shops which distinguished American from British industrial relations. Few agreements protected union militants or provided formal opportunities to appeal management decisions to union negotiators, and the IAM was unable to defend most members from victimization. U.S. shop committees were thus weaker and more vulnerable to employer reprisals than were British stewards. In the face of belligerent anti-union practices, shop committees had to keep their ties with formal union organization clandestine and infrequent. Open shops thus encouraged rank-and-file organization within the works and contributed to its independence from union authority. But the independence of shop committees usually amounted to a position of isolation from union affiliation and protection.[56]

Consequences for Factory Politics

New industrial relations and workshop conditions, together with the failure to achieve union reform, led many machinists to develop new types of local organization after 1901. Contrasts in the labor process and industrial relations practices account for divergent patterns of local organization among machinists and engineers. Differing contexts for the mobilization of protest, in turn, produced distinctive forms of factory politics. In Britain the frustrations of craft conservatives and the ambitions of radicalized engineers found common ground in unofficial organization and action. A similar convergence occurred in the U.S. machine trades. However, rank-and-file insurgence achieved neither the shop-floor power nor the independence from union authority found in British engineering.

Machinists of varied political inclination shared with engineers a commitment to local autonomy. Craft conservatives sought to retain their freedom of action despite the constraints of a Grand Lodge dedicated to centralized authority, rank-and-file discipline, and cautious trade policies. Socialists defended grass-roots autonomy so long as the union executive remained in conservative hands. But this convergence had greater ideological and practical limitations in the United States than in Britain. The IAM was not bound by industry agreements to prevent unsanctioned strikes or to accept management rights. National leaders regularly denounced unofficial strikes and often refused to pay benefits, but these actions did not fulfill obligations to employers. Machinists could thus fault union officials for their caution and lack of support, but they could not accuse them of complicity with capital to deprive workers of their rights and freedoms. In the absence of centralized collaboration between the IAM and employers, conservative and progressive machinists did not find common ground in a political critique of union authority or an endorsement of direct action. Accordingly, the exercise of local autonomy lacked the "presyndicalist" qualities visible among engineers. Local action also lacked firm roots in workshop organization. Shop committees—weakened by deskilling and open-shop policies and deprived of strong union ties and support—were not effective bases for either the defense of craft standards or unofficial radical leadership. Relatively feeble shop committees and limited rank-and-file hostility toward union leadership thus narrowed both the organizational and the ideological terrain for alliances between conservative and radical machinists.

The defense of local control was rooted primarily in organizations outside the factory gates. Challenges to national union authority and leadership in many unsanctioned strikes came from militant IAM lodges and MTCs rather than from any clearly defined shop-floor institutions. Here local activists—both defenders of the craft status quo and progressive critics of trade unionism—could defy national policies yet avoid direct employer reprisals. IAM President James O'Connell complained in 1910 of "a growing evil and persistent custom . . . of assuming responsibility [for] involving our members in a strike or quitting work without first securing permission from the General Executive Board, or even consulting the Grand Lodge. If benefits are refused in such cases in accordance with the constitution, the Grand Lodge officers are subjected to all sorts of unjust abuse and criticism."[57]

Metal trades councils similarly offered a common base for conservatives who found AFL rules governing sympathy strikes too cumbersome and restrictive and for radicals dedicated to industrial unionism. In 1911, Metal Trades Department President O'Connell had to warn against the "tendency on the part of the various local Metal Trades Councils to strike out for themselves without due regard for our laws or without even consulting the officers of the Department." Metal Trades Department conventions witnessed annual battles between local delegates and national union executives, with MTC representatives demanding greater authority to coordinate trade policies and initiate strikes.[58]

Relatively independent union lodges and MTCs occasionally gave radicals opportunities to lead industrial unrest. Industrial Workers of the World (IWW) activists, for example, gained positions in a number of IAM lodges and MTCs between 1905 and 1910 and led strikes involving machinists and less skilled workers.[59] Before World War I, however, neither union locals nor MTCs succeeded in fusing conservative and radical machinists' support for local autonomy into an effective insurgent movement. The IAM's freedom from compromising relations with employers moderated rank-and-file hostilities and minimized the influence of syndicalist appeals. Local union activists thus could not usually rally craftsmen—however dissatisfied with cautious national policies—behind movements explicitly challenging trade union authority. Machinists regularly defied union rules but rarely saw in local lodges and MTCs a principled alternative to union bureaucracy.

Citywide organization also had a strategic liability. The weakness of machinists on the job and their enforced isolation from unions denied local officials (of all political persuasions) strong shop-floor support. Without an effective base within the shops, local lodge and MTC leaders were especially vulnerable to IAM and AFL controls. Although IAM leaders learned to live with unsanctioned strikes, they acted quickly and effectively against the most politically charged challenges to their authority—disciplining rebellious locals (e.g., Schenectady in 1906 and New York City in 1909) and securing a constitutional amendment in 1909 expelling IWW sympathizers from the union.[60] Metal Trades Department leaders, similarly, blocked all proposed reforms that would have increased MTC powers relative to the national leadership of individual trade unions.[61] Local activists could not counter executive authority with well-organized popular insurgence to the extent that their British counterparts did.

Machinists also moved away from traditional, defensive craft goals and tactics during the prewar period. A majority of IAM members approved a 1903 addition to the union constitution expressing their ideal of using "the natural resources, means of production and distribution for the benefit of all the people." Between 1904 and 1910, local IAM lodges were increasingly involved in electoral activity on behalf of the Socialist Party, and in 1911, the socialist William Johnston won the IAM presidency.[62]

Radical rhetoric and electoral activity are not incompatible with the defense of exclusive occupational privileges. However, the development of socialist commitments among machinists was echoed in factory politics. In Britain, traditional commitments to job control converged with progressive goals as the Terms forced conservatives to assert their workshop rights against craft union complacence; strong workshop organization, moreover, gave conservative and radical engineers a common base for defying union policies. The IAM's cautious trade policies and inadequate support for craft struggles did encourage machinists to turn to local leaders and unconstitutional action. But the IAM did not lend its weight to management prerogatives, and unofficial organization was weak. It was above all the impact of scientific management on the workplace and on the ideological terrain of control conflicts—and not, as in Britain, new industrial relations conditions and rank-and-file organization—that mobilized broader support for progressive demands.

Faced with scientific management, craft conservatives had to reevaluate traditional strategies and goals. Eventually, they proved willing to ally with more radical machinists in the fight against new management techniques. The break with defensive policies reflected, in part, the *weakness* of skilled workers in the United States. The erosion of craft standards had proceeded further and more rapidly in America. As a result, by the 1910s the defense of customary apprenticeship regulations, machine assignment rules, or standard union day rates was (in contrast to Britain) no longer a realistic proposition in most metalworking establishments. The intense and well-publicized controversies over scientific management also helped shift the terrain of debate over control. Advocates of "efficiency" schemes seem to have been successful in characterizing customary craft practices as restrictive and unscientific. IAM spokesmen rarely denied management the right to study machine shop tasks or claimed that only qualified workers should be allowed to operate certain machines.

Once the unilateral insistence on craft rules had been abandoned, debate inevitably moved to the question of what role workers should have in shop management. The polemics of efficiency engineers themselves highlighted this question. On one side they called for a more cooperative mental attitude between management and workers; on the other they argued that only experts could determine the best ways of performing shop tasks. Such arguments forced the question of who benefited from management "science" and what form workshop "cooperation" should take. The conclusion reached by the IAM business agent for machinists in government employment had considerable appeal to the rank and file: "Harmony of feeling can not exist between employer and employee in a plant where the desire for profits [prevails]. . . . Neither does cooperation exist where everything is decided by the management and the workers have no voice, but all questions which are ordinarily decided by conference with the workmen are to be decided by the expert time-student."[63]

Scientific management not only challenged craft controls; it also imposed forms of supervision regarded as demeaning and tyrannical. If class-conscious opponents of management rights remained a minority within the IAM, populist standards of individual rights and democratic participation had a much broader base. Many machinists might have been unwilling to go as far as Roy Kelly, a metal polisher at Rock Island Arsenal, when he charged that Taylorism was "a scientific scheme to exploit labor" or when he argued that "a workman should be allowed to share to the greatest extent the wealth he creates." But his claim that "it is un-American to time any man as you would a racehorse or a machine"[64] was widely applauded. Craft conservatives did not come to advocate workers' ownership and control of the means of production. But within the populist tradition they could join radicals in denouncing the tyranny of scientific management and in asserting the democratic entitlements of workers in industrial government. In the words of a Charlestown Navy Yard machinist, scientific management "is despotic management. . . . That is, the men are forced to do as they are told. Orders come down absolutely from above. We believe that the men should have definite rights, and that they should be allowed to express their rights through their committees and through their organization."[65]

If craft conservatives and radicals could hardly be expected to agree on the need to overthrow capitalism, behind what progressive response to scientific management could they ally? Machinists united in fighting the introduction of efficiency schemes and supported union efforts to eliminate the worst abuses of scientific management—notably the stopwatch—through legislative action.[66] Yet they could not prevent the installation of the key components of scientific management, particularly dilution and bonus schemes, and with them the erosion of craft practices and union rates. Progressives thus increasingly advocated not a return to the craft status quo but the imposition of alternative standards for classifying employees and involving workers in shop decisions.[67] Such alternatives would not be widely advanced until World War I. In the meantime, experience with scientific management made some conservatives more sympathetic to radical criticisms of capitalist control of production. William Johnston received disproportionate electoral support in 1911 from midwestern and western railroad workers and industrial lodges in New England. The latter included machinists working in plants where scientific management had made the greatest advance; the former included craftsmen facing incentive pay and time study for the first time. Both favored a socialist for the union presidency.[68]

Scientific management's assault on craft traditions thus played a key role in rallying machinists behind demands for workers' standards and participation in industrial government. But in the absence of strong organization on the shop floor, support for alternative standards appeared more in rhetoric than in practical action. Where machinists were able to organize effectively at the plant level—as in many government arsenals and navy yards—their responses to scientific management often took the form of unofficial strikes and a critique of capitalist control that few IAM officials were willing to endorse. Through such organization, whether in the shops or in system federations, traditional craft grievances and demands for workers' control converged. Yet in most plants shop committees were too weak to give machinists the opportunity to challenge management rights—or to overcome executive restraints.[69] With machinists isolated and vulnerable at work, the elaboration of progressive programs for workers' control fell to local militants. System federations, MTCs, and union lodges offered radicals platforms from which to denounce IAM and AFL solutions to workplace grievances and to present their alternatives to the rank and file. All too often, weak organization in the shops deprived them of any significant following.

Traditions of local autonomy and shop control contributed to some changes in factory politics before the war. Craft traditions also included exclusiveness—a preoccupation with occupational turf and a contempt for mere laborers and handymen. Signs of an emerging consensus in favor of lowering the boundaries dividing crafts did begin to appear, however. Machinists who rejected full amalgamation still had good reasons to endorse common action and joint organization. The division of skilled metalworkers into separate societies was recognized as a strategic liability. Specialization and deskilling at work, the concentration of capital, and strong employers' associations all appeared to weaken the bargaining position of individual craft unions. Even conservative machinists realized the need for some compensating changes in labor organization. They also found impractical the constitutional obligation of each union's members to secure executive approval before acting with other craftsmen. The prompt and united defense of shared interests demanded institutions through which craftsmen of different unions could discuss grievances, negotiate with employers, and initiate disputes.

There is little evidence that organization within the shops facilitated joint action among members of different trades, much less different skill grades. Shop committees lacked the power and the permanence of Britain's shop steward system. Among the reasons for relatively weak workshop organization were manufacturing practices that undercut the leverage of skilled workers. At the same time, more advanced production methods that eroded the position of craftsmen might be expected to blur occupational distinctions and favor broader solidarity on the job. Instead, new management techniques heightened divisions among craftsmen and between grades. For example, incentive pay favored competition between machinists over lucrative jobs, discouraged camaraderie as employees hustled to make their quotas, and created shop-floor frictions as workers opted to run two machines (contrary to union rules) in hopes of increasing their wages. By replacing standard union scales with individualized pay, scientific management also contributed to mutual suspicion and jealousy over earnings.[70] Nor did the diminishing gulf between craftsmen and unskilled workers favor solidarity across grades. Instead, systematic procedures for upgrading less skilled men and women at the expense of craft monopolies and union apprenticeship rules tended to emphasize the conflicts of interest between grades.[71] The sight of piece-working specialists and semiskilled operatives earning as much on repetitive tasks as highly trained tool room machinists aggravated craft resentments against less qualified employees.[72]

Such divisions were often reinforced by ethnic cleavages. Isaac Cowen, an ASE organizer in the United States, noted in 1902 the "common practice" among American employers "to quietly pit one nationality against the other in the workshop. German[s] were ever ready to race the Irish, the Irish the Polander, Sweed [*sic*], or any other nationality."[73] The foreign born composed one-third of Bridgeport's 1907 population, and when local manufacturers faced shortages of unskilled help in 1912, they arranged for the Immigration Bureau to send new arrivals to the city.[74] National differences divided workers by craft and plant as well as by skill. Foundry workers at the Bridgeport Malleable Iron Works were mostly Hungarian; Swedes predominated among machinists at Coulter and McKenzie and the Nilson Machine Company.[75]

Regular works committees or broadly representative shop stewards might have compensated for divisions rooted at work and in ethnic identities. But in the absence of stronger unions and industrial relations protections such common organization could not survive. Cooperation was more ad hoc, appearing in occasional joint deputations and strike committees. For example, sympathetic action among rank-and-file craftsmen occurred with some frequency, often emerging from mass meetings and taking place without union sanction. American ASE officials complained in 1910, "We have already suffered through our men coming out with others on sentiment and not submitting their grievances to the District Committee. [American and Canadian] Council hereby instruct[s] our members that under no circumstances must our members come out on strike without first consulting the A. and C. Council or their District Committee."[76] But solidary action lacked a firm institutional base within the shops from which to achieve effective independence from sectional union authority or security from management hostility.

Further removed from employer reprisals, joint organization in local MTCs was more secure. Through such bodies, craft union representatives could plan common strategies, resolve jurisdictional disputes, and at least attempt to enter into collective negotiations with employers and employers' associations. The MTCs had little formal authority to call strikes or conclude agreements without prior approval from the executive of each constituent union. Yet they did at times become vehicles for sympathy strikes and boycotts, thus helping overcome the tactical weakness of craft union structures and hierarchies.[77] MTCs also led the battle within the AFL's Metal Trades Department for amalgamation and greater autonomy in initiating joint action locally.[78] Although MTCs provided a forum for discussion and helped erode craft barriers for local activists, their educational role was not matched by practical power. Open shops deprived MTCs of an organized base within the shops and gave them little opportunity to assume a role in collective bargaining. Without an organized workplace constituency, in turn, MTC militants' proposals for amalgamation and local autonomy in trade policy carried little weight with AFL leaders.[79]

The often rebellious IAM lodges shared the same dilemma. Local officials occasionally extended strike benefits to nonunionized metal craftsmen, contrary to IAM rules, and cooperated with the leaders of other local unions without proper executive approval.[80] Nevertheless, they faced the same obstacles to effective organization in the shops as did MTC representatives and, like the MTCs, offered militants no secure base from which to challenge the authority of union officials.

If local joint organization among craftsmen was weak, organization combining skilled and less skilled workers scarcely existed at all. A narrow majority of IAM members endorsed the principle of industrial unionism as early as 1903,[81] and machinists at times joined less skilled workers in industrial disputes, in some cases under IWW leadership.[82] No structural basis existed through which industrial unionist sentiments or temporary enthusiasm for all-grades action could be consolidated and trade union policies overcome. Solidary action among machinists and less skilled workers was infrequent and short-lived; and IAM members cooperating with the IWW in particular faced expulsion by their national executive. This was the fate of two lodges in Schenectady, one in Cleveland, and three in New York City.[83]

The development of independent and solidary organization among U.S. metalworkers, then, was blocked from within by the labor process and from without by trade unions. Divisions at work restricted the membership of shop committees to machinists. Manufacturing techniques and industrial relations practices kept the committees relatively weak and isolated from local union leadership. These organizational conditions shaped the goals of factory politics. Under favorable economic conditions local officials often led citywide offensives for wage increases or shorter hours, simultaneously presenting individual firms with identical demands but through committees of their own employees. It was much more difficult for union officials to support machinists in routine disputes over machine assignment, piecework, or obnoxious supervision. Control struggles tended to remain isolated within the plants, lacking citywide coordination by union locals or MTCs. By contrast, progressive initiatives—demands for amalgamation, local autonomy, systematic checks on management authority—tended to remain isolated *outside* the plants. MTCs and local lodges might have helped machinists bridge craft and skill divisions and develop alternatives to conservative union policies. Although they offered radicals sanctuary from employer reprisals, however, they were cut off from the shops by anti-union labor policies. Lacking an autonomously organized constituency among the rank and file, in turn, radicals were in no position to defy national IAM and AFL leaders. Thus joint organization at the local level was little more effective than shop committees as a foundation for independent, solidary action in support of workers' control.

Patterns of factory politics in the prewar years confirm these conclusions. In Bridgeport, struggles over workshop control between 1901 and 1915 were typically confined to individual crafts, in single departments or firms, and had little continuity over time. When broader alliances appeared among craftsmen or among workers of different skill levels, they were not only short-lived, but they also concerned more readily shared, economistic interests— higher wages, shorter hours. Concerted action over such issues took place among machinists at different plants on two occasions, among different grades at a single firm in one instance, among different grades and crafts once, and among different tradesmen on a widespread basis in 1915. In contrast, during the same period eleven strikes involved issues of control (piecework, work rules, foremanship, etc.). Of these, only the 1901 citywide strike (part of a national dispute) involved more than one firm, and in only one dispute did machinists and less skilled workers act together.[84] A similar pattern of strike activity has been identified in Detroit.[85]

These characteristics of Bridgeport factory politics reflect, in part, ethnic cleavages that separated workers of different skills, trades, and plants. They also correspond to conditions in which divisions at work and in trade union structure had not been offset by joint organization, and shop committees remained isolated from citywide leadership.

Conclusions: The Prewar Status Quo

Departures from defensive and exclusive factory politics before World War I developed on the basis of new forms of local organization. Relatively independent and more broadly representative institutions for rank-and-file protest allowed engineers and machinists to defy conservative trade union policies and overcome conflicting workplace interests and competing craft union affiliations. The organizational conditions for progressive factory politics emerged more fully in Britain. Shop stewards and works committees gained significant power in plant-level labor relations and often exercised that power with little regard for official union procedures. Increasingly, their constituents also included craftsmen from separate trade unions. Shop committees in the U.S. machine trades had less influence over shop affairs, were more isolated from local unionism, and represented machinists alone. In neither case did workshop organization involve the interests or participation of less skilled employees.

The comparative development of the labor process contributed to these contrasting outcomes. Advanced production and management techniques diminished machinists' strategic power and reinforced divisions among craftsmen and between grades of labor. This explanation for the weakness of rank-and-file insurgency among machinists is consistent with common interpretations of American labor politics.[86] It is also incomplete because it understates the role of industrial relations conditions. Strong unions and established trade agreements gave British shop-floor militants protection for organizing and recognized procedures for pursuing grievances. Such safeguards did not exist for most machinists. The IAM was too weak to prevent victimization, and employers were too committed to the open shop to allow union interference with their decisions and their employees. The strength and permanence of workshop organization suffered accordingly. Union policies and industrial relations agreements in Britain gave engineers additional incentives to organize on the job. If they were to defend customary rights and retain their freedom of action, they had to combine at work, independent of official union structures. Because engineers of different unions shared similar grievances and similar union and industrial relations obstacles to effective action, they increasingly acted jointly through works committees and common shop stewards. Shared frustrations of this kind were absent in the United States. Union leaders appeared cautious and conservative, but they were not bound by trade agreements to hold their members in check.

Differences in the organization and setting of protest shaped factory politics. By World War I engineers had achieved substantial independence from their unions in formulating demands, negotiating with employers, and calling strikes. Yet unions were committed to agreements that declared some demands illegitimate, centralized collective bargaining, and proscribed strikes during the course of grievance procedures. The result was an increasingly adversarial relation between the unofficial movement and trade unions. Machinists and IAM leaders had their differences. But weaker unofficial organization offered the rank and file less of an independent base from which to challenge union policies. More important, the IAM had no obligation to enforce trade agreements on its members. Relations between the IAM Executive and the rank and file, accordingly, were less contentious; and popular opposition rarely assumed the form of a political critique of trade union bureaucracy or articulate demands for rank-and-file control and direct action—views that found increasing support among engineers.

Union recognition and formal trade agreements encouraged unofficial action in Britain but also restricted its scope. Rank-and-file organization developed most fully on the shop floor. Even during business booms, when engineers could afford to ignore constitutional procedures, disputes not resolved on the spot generally passed into the hands of union officials in negotiation with employer representatives. Outside any individual shop, collective bargaining arrangements thus reinforced the national union leaders' authority and policies. Engineers certainly waged control struggles in violation of their union and its commitments to employers. Industrial relations rules confined those battles to small-scale, plant-based conflicts, however; and once confrontations moved beyond the factory gates, sectional craft priorities were reasserted.

But union leaders and trade agreements should not be condemned unequivocally for their conservative influence on rank-and-file control struggles.[87] The absence of union discipline and industrial relations procedures in the United States hardly paved the way for radical factory politics. Instead, feeble unions and open shops helped produce weak, isolated, and exclusive workplace organization among skilled workers. Under these conditions divisions at work and in trade union structure inhibited solidary action with respect to control issues. Battles over piecework or dilution were generally confined to individual crafts and departments; they were also more likely to assume the form of sporadic outbursts than to become a sustained, coordinated movement on behalf of craft rights. With rare exceptions, unity among machinists at different plants or skilled workers of different trades within a shop could develop only around common economic interests.

The relative importance of craft control and economistic goals in British and American factory politics was reinforced by the labor process. Engineers' success in defending craft privileges through strong workshop organization helped maintain their capacity for effective sectional strategies—and thus minimized the practical need for broader coalitions and novel demands. Craft protest under new conditions did involve growing insurgency and solidarity among skilled workers, but it continued to exclude the interests and participation of less skilled workers. Dilution in the American machine trades undermined the ability of machinists, acting alone, to defend craft standards. Yet on issues of deskilling and piecework, production practices also accentuated conflicts among individual workers and occupational groups. Concerted action could generally be mobilized only in support of shared economic grievances; control struggles remained fragmented.

In the broader view the strength, solidarity, and autonomy of workshop organization in Britain promised radical engineers the opportunity to expand their grass-roots constituencies. Particularly in the turbulent four years before World War I, proponents of workers' control, amalgamation, and direct action appeared to have the backing of growing numbers of engineers. They secured such support not through union offices but by assuming or influencing the leadership of unofficial plant organization. The weakness and isolation of shop committees in the U.S. effectively forced militants out of the workplace and channeled progressive energies into union and Metal Trades Department reform. By the same token, however, militants lacked the grass-roots support needed to achieve reforms in the face of conservative union opposition.

Perhaps the different weight of various radical doctrines is related to these organizational contrasts. Syndicalism, with its emphasis on workers' control, direct action, and the factory as the proper unit of industrial government, paralleled rank-and-file practice among British workers (in coal and transport as well as in engineering). Actively involved in contesting management authority, committed to local autonomy in industrial disputes, and often hostile to trade union bureaucrats, even engineers politically unsympathetic to syndicalist doctrine seemed to practice what syndicalists preached. U.S. machinists were among the strongest supporters of industrial unionism and socialism in the AFL. They were not generally associated with syndicalism, however. One reason may be that industrial unionism and socialism—doctrines that in the American labor movement, particularly, involved union reform and *political* action by the working class—corresponded to the dilemmas of radical machinists. An independent, solidary industrial movement, constructed from the shop floor up, simply was not feasible. Constitutional change and electoral action appeared more promising. The IAM's organizational weakness in the shops, moreover, left progressive movements least developed at the point where issues of control and direct action were paramount: at work. Under these conditions, with radicals condemned to silence at work or confined to the sanctuary of the local union office, syndicalism had little practical relevance. Metal trades amalgamation (or even one big union) and working-class political strength, by contrast, might compensate for the power of capital at work. Such goals were in any case the ones radical machinists were in a position to pursue.

Internal comparisons confirm this analysis and suggest that contrasting patterns of factory politics do not simply reflect differences in national traditions. The experience of railroad shop craftsmen was in many respects closer to the British than to the American norm. Occupied primarily with repair work, railroad shop practices remained relatively traditional. Skilled labor was essential, piecework less widely used, and detailed production planning inappropriate.[88] Railroad shop crafts were also more strongly unionized, and collective bargaining more common, than in most other sections of the trade. As in Britain, in fact, many employers preferred to deal with union leaders rather than shop-floor representatives, and agreements typically provided for the arbitration of local disputes by national officials.[89]

A more traditional labor process, combined with some union and industrial relations safeguards, produced stronger local and shop-floor organization. Dissatisfied with grievance procedures and the lack of union support for disputes over work practices, craftsmen formed system federations that combined members of different unions and permitted joint action independent of sectional union officials. The consequences for factory politics mirror those in Britain. Railroad craftsmen appear to have contested management practices (incentive pay, dilution, the use of stopwatches) more effectively than skilled metalworkers elsewhere in the United States. More important, they did so through large-scale, solidary action mobilized through "unofficial" joint bodies (the system federations)—unofficial action and organization that developed in opposition to the national authority and craft structures of American trade unions. In the most dramatic example, system federations on the Illinois Central and Harriman lines initiated a strike in 1911 involving close to forty thousand workers of different trades and skills. They did so without the approval of several union executives (including the IAM Grand Lodge) and demanded that management negotiate directly with the shop crafts federation. Finally, it was among railroad shop craftsmen—actively involved in control struggles, jointly organized on an autonomous basis, and hostile to union executives and union-management collaboration— that syndicalism had the widest appeal for skilled metalworkers.[90]

If railroad shops reveal a "British" exception to the U.S. rules, Coventry suggests a pocket of American conditions in England. As a center for cycle and automobile manufacture, Coventry firms featured unusually advanced production techniques, with a high proportion of semiskilled workers, widespread use of incentive pay, and more methodical management practices.[91] Working-class organization and the engineering industry itself were also relatively new to Coventry. For much of the prewar period, craft unions were weak by British standards. Before joining the EEF in 1907, leading employers recognized unions reluctantly, if at all.[92] Thus Coventry, more than other British engineering centers, shared with most American metalworking an advanced labor process, weak unions, and open shops.

The organizational consequences of these characteristics correspond to the U.S. pattern. Shop stewards were unevenly and sparsely distributed throughout the city's engineering works for much of the prewar period (with some concentration at the Coventry Ordnance Works, where the production of heavy armaments in small numbers gave engineers a stronger bargaining position and permitted more thorough unionization). Efforts by the Coventry ASE District Committee to increase the number of stewards in 1907 had little effect,[93] and shop representatives could not assert independence from union officialdom. Stewards, in fact, did not act openly as delegates of the workers; they were appointed secretly by the Coventry District Committee. Local ASE officials explained in 1911 that "this is done owing to the difficulty of getting Members willing to Stand as Shop Stewards[;] also to Safeguard our Members against Victimization."[94] Coventry's shop committees, like their U.S. counterparts, were thus relatively weak and isolated, offering an inadequate base for action independent of union district committees. For most of the prewar years, joint organization seems to have been confined to bodies outside the factories—notably the Coventry Engineering Joint Committee and the local Amalgamation Committee.

The outcomes for factory politics resemble those in America. Local engineers appeared willing to trade craft standards for economic concessions, showing more concern that employers observe minimum wage rates than manning regulations and more interest in their piecework earnings than in abolishing the system altogether. The Coventry District Committee, in fact, often found it necessary to censure members for violating work rules (rules that barred the two-machine system or limited overtime, for example) in their pursuit of higher pay.[95] Conflicts between ASE members and leaders, common in better organized districts, were also muted in Coventry until after 1910, when rank-and-file organization at work became stronger, and the Terms and Procedure applied to most local firms. Finally, strike data reveal a pattern of conflict similar to that in Bridgeport, with control struggles fragmented and cooperation among different crafts and skills focusing on economistic issues. Between 1900 and 1914, twenty local strikes by ASE members raised questions of workshop control. None included more than one firm, only one involved the less skilled Workers' Union, and only five featured joint action with other craft unions. By contrast, of six disputes involving purely economic issues, two affected more than one firm, and four entailed cooperation with other unions (including three in which the Workers' Union took part).[96]

The foundations of the prewar status quo were fragile. In Britain, union and industrial relations constraints and the persistence of craft privileges at work limited departures from defensive and sectional policies. Yet these constraints were already tenuous and craft privileges hardly assured. Struggles for workers' control in the United States remained less developed than in Britain, checked by vulnerable and isolated shop committees (i.e., weak unions and open shops). In both countries World War I would topple these pillars of the prewar order.

Chapter Five

The Impact of World War I

World War I has often been called the first "war of machines." Each belligerent nation also had its own domestic front where the key combatants were not machines but those who made them. In a war of machines, munitions had to be manufactured in large numbers and without interruption. Efforts to meet these requirements heightened the discontent and the militancy of skilled metalworkers.

At work, war production increased the grievances of engineers and machinists. It also increased their power. The scale and techniques of wartime manufacture, combined with the shortage of skilled men, encouraged the wholesale recruitment of "unqualified" men, women, and youths. Such changes threatened the status but not the jobs of craftsmen. Engineers and machinists were at a premium, especially for the greatly expanded tasks of setting up machines for less skilled operatives and making the jigs, gauges, and tools on which repetition production relied. Skilled workers' bargaining position and their capacity to disrupt production on a large scale increased accordingly.

Labor unrest was compounded and shaped by trade union policies and government intervention in the industry. The principal craft societies agreed to compromise work rules and forgo strikes in the interests of war production. The British and U.S. governments sanctioned changes in manufacturing techniques and added legal authority to the patriotic concessions made by unions. State regulation of industrial relations added bureaucratic distance and delay to negotiations and settlements. Both governments appeared to favor employer interests through espionage legislation, military courts, restrictions on labor mobility, and a punitive use of the draft. In many of these policies, skilled men felt themselves singled out for unjust treatment. The hardships of scarce food and housing at exorbitant prices were more widely distributed, and workers of different trades, skills, and plants could unite in opposition to profiteering and incompetent government regulation.

The war accelerated trends at work and reinforced union policies already evident before 1914. Case studies of Coventry and Bridgeport, however, show how wartime developments altered the terrain of struggle over workshop control. Changes in the labor process were more abrupt and union and government policies more restrictive in Britain than in the United States. Conditions after 1914 nevertheless favored the mobilization of radical factory politics, in different ways, among engineers and machinists alike.

Coventry

The 1890s brought Coventry to industrial prominence as a center for the booming bicycle trade. That trade's stagnation at the end of the decade encouraged local manufacturers to convert to motorcycle and automobile production. By 1910, the city's employment and output in these industries led the country, with local car firms alone engaging seven thousand workers in 1911.[1] Coventry also featured substantial machine tool production, including one of Britain's biggest and most progressive firms, Alfred Herbert, and a major private armaments company, the Coventry Ordnance Works. These factories tended to be quite large by British standards: in 1908, Daimler (motor cars) employed twenty-three hundred engineering workers, Humber (motorcycles and autos) and COW nearly seventeen hundred each, and Herbert's more than a thousand.[2]

With local industry unusually advanced in terms of standardized and repetitive production, and firms already specialized in the manufacture of machine tools, engines, and motor vehicles, Coventry was well equipped to become a leading munitions center. During the war the city produced a quarter of the nation's airplanes and huge quantities of heavy armaments, army vehicles, and lighter munitions; and machine tool output increased ninefold.[3] Industrial expansion brought a corresponding boom in the local work force. Employment at Daimler and Herbert's doubled, and by the end of 1917, some thirty-two thousand men and women had been imported to meet the city's labor needs. Between 1914 and 1918, Coventry's total population increased from over 115,000 to more than 151,000.[4] As a result transportation facilities and schools were overwhelmed, food was scarce and costly, and in housing "the grossest forms of overcrowding and profiteering" prevailed.[5]

Unions shared in Coventry's boom. Local ASE membership increased 50 percent, to 4,000 by the end of 1916, with the Amalgamated Toolmakers' Society reaching about the same size and smaller craft societies enjoying similar growth rates. When the Amalgamated Engineering Union consolidated most of these unions in July 1920, it claimed 14,000 members in Coventry. The city's principal organization for less skilled engineering employees, the Workers' Union, experienced even more spectacular growth, swelling from less than 3,000 members before the war to 8,590 in late 1916.[6]

The Labor Process

War production dramatically accelerated dilution and the spread of payment by results.[7] Materials had to be manufactured quickly, in enormous quantities, and to standardized specifications. Dilution to meet these requirements had three main components: the introduction of new machinery, the subdivision of tasks, and the recruitment and upgrading of workers. Automatic machinery designed for repetitive production of specialized materials, combined with equipment to ease the handling of heavy pieces, enabled men and women with little prior engineering experience to enter munitions factories. Jobs customarily performed by craftsmen were divided into more and less skilled components. On the one side qualified engineers specialized in fabricating jigs and gauges and instructed and set up machines for less experienced operatives. On the other side green hands performed most routine production work. New machinery and the division of labor thus made it possible to use "dilutees" in large numbers.

Early in the war new employees—particularly women—were largely confined to new work (e.g., in the manufacture and filling of shells) instead of replacing engineers directly. As the army's manpower needs increased, however, women as well as less skilled men were upgraded to skilled, "male" jobs. In Britain as a whole, female employment in private metalworking firms grew from 9.4 percent in July 1914 to 24.6 percent four years later; in government establishments (arsenals, dockyards, national shell factories) it grew from 2.6 percent to 46.7 percent over the same period. In July 1916, 22.7 percent of women in private concerns were reported as "directly replacing males"; two years later 32.7 percent were.[8] Even where not directly replacing males, women moved into work traditionally done by men alone. In January 1918, for example, females in government-controlled firms represented 21.4 percent of employees in machine tool manufacture and 21.9 percent in ordnance.[9]

Mechanization and subdivision of labor came less abruptly in Coventry than in more traditional engineering centers. These principles of manufacture were already well established in the city. But even here twenty thousand women were imported during the first three years of the war, while the recruitment and upgrading of unskilled men or the assignment of two or more machines to one man took place on an unprecedented scale. The character of war production also permitted a wide extension of payment by results, and increasing numbers of skilled men faced piecework and premium bonus systems by the war's end—even in such traditional bastions of craftsmanship as repair departments and tool rooms.[10]

Occupational standards that engineers had successfully defended before 1914 now seemed at risk. New machines and reorganization appeared to threaten their craft, and the mass of dilutees threatened their jobs.[11] Together, dilution and piecework also undermined traditional pay differentials. Dilution split off from skilled occupations those tasks requiring the least experience (and which, for engineers on piecework, allowed the highest earnings), assigning them to new hands working with modern equipment. These men and women were generally paid by output, with the government guaranteeing piece rates in the interests of maximum production. As a result many engineers earned less than the semi-skilled operatives—"till lately 'gardners and coachmen'"—who depended on them for instruction, assistance, and provision of proper tools.[12] Dilution and piecework thus offered considerable benefits to less skilled workers at the expense of engineering craftsmen. And if Coventry's skilled workers faced a less radical assault on their customary status and privileges, they shared with engineers in Glasgow and elsewhere the experience of their unions and their government sanctioning workshop changes and limiting their opportunities to redress consequent grievances.

Unions

The ASE and other craft societies agreed to abandon strikes and restrictive work rules on munitions production at the beginning of 1915. The March 4 "Shells and Fuses Agreement," signed (with government prodding) by the EEF and major craft unions, allowed women and semiskilled workers to perform operations customarily done by fully qualified men but not requiring their skill. The agreement applied only to shell and fuse production, was explicitly confined to the war period, and forbade employers from "making such arrangement in the shops as will effect a permanent restriction of employment of any trade in favour of semi-skilled men or female labour." The Treasury Agreement of March 17 extended these principles to all war production, adding further guarantees for customary skilled wage rates and the restoration of trade union customs after the war. Unions also agreed to suspend demarcation rules for the duration. All parties to the Treasury Agreement, finally, renounced strikes in favor of union-employer negotiations and (in the event of a deadlock) government arbitration. During separate conferences with government representatives, the ASE secured some further safeguards and a promise to limit war profits before accepting the Treasury Agreement on March 25. The Munitions of War Act made these undertakings legally binding in June.[13]

In a small turnout ASE members approved the Shells and Fuses Agreement by a vote of 14,137 to 9,817, but many engineers felt that officials had not sufficiently protected the status of skilled men either during or after the war. The Treasury Agreement, which not only extended the scope of union concessions but also added the no-strike commitment, inspired much harsher criticism, and it confirmed the popular suspicion of trade union bureaucrats that had been evident before the war. A Sheffield shop steward noted of union leaders, *"They* are not likely to be subject to the schemes they have introduced, hence they can talk glibly about safeguards." Coventry officials denounced the agreement and its successors as "contrary to the interests of our members" and "not a course that is democratic."[14] Trade union renunciation of strikes, however, did more than heighten rank-and-file antagonism to union leaders. The Treasury Agreement and the Munitions of War Act ensured that unions would be neither useful instruments for nor effective sanctions against local militancy. Members had little use for unions that had conceded important rank-and-file claims at work and abandoned the right to strike. Union strike pay became unnecessary, for disputes did not last long; union unemployment benefits became superfluous, because jobs were easily found; union leaders' goodwill and negotiating acumen became dispensable, because the government ultimately settled disputes. Unofficial organization would fill the gap left by trade union impotence as engineers worked through shop stewards to negotiate with employers and organize strikes.

Government Intervention

World War I brought an unprecedented involvement by the British government in engineering shop conditions and industrial relations. Concessions on work rules made (more or less) voluntarily by trade unions in the Shells and Fuses and the Treasury Agreements received legal mandate in the Munitions of War Act of June 1915. Section 3 of the act required that "any rule, practice, or custom not having the force of law which tends to restrict production or employment shall be suspended." Those supporting restrictive practices risked government prosecution. By suspending trade union restraints on the manning of machines, government officials hoped to use less skilled men and women on operations previously monopolized by engineers. Government tribunals also encouraged the spread of payment by results, construing union opposition to incentive pay as "restricting production."[15] In order to overcome employers' reluctance to antagonize their irreplaceable skilled men, the Ministry of Munitions dispatched "Dilution Commissioners" to devise plans (in consultation with employees and union representatives) for introducing new machinery, subdividing operations, and recruiting and upgrading workers. Although the details of these plans remained subject to workshop negotiation and conflict, the government also made available local Munitions Tribunals through which employers could ensure recalcitrant workers' conformity to government rules.[16]

Government intervention extended to engineering industrial relations as well. The first stage in resolving disputes remained negotiation within the plant, followed in most cases by local conferences. Persisting disagreements went not to national bargaining between union and EEF leaders, however, but to compulsory arbitration by one or another government agency. Even when employers and labor representatives agreed on wage increases, these increases had to be approved by the Ministry of Munitions. A wide range of state regulations governed the rates paid to dilutees, and in fixing wages the general trend was to replace collective bargaining with periodic increases, awarded by the government, to compensate for inflation.[17] Whatever the deficiencies of the prewar Procedure, at least the steps in pursuing a demand had been clear. Now engineers confronted a baffling array of government boards, tribunals, and committees with overlapping responsibilities and heavy schedules. Confusion and bureaucratic delay in hearings and decisions resulted, followed by frequent difficulties in enforcing awards.[18] In the meantime engineers were denied recourse to strikes by the Munitions of War Act.

The government sought to manage the labor market as well as to resolve labor disputes. Skilled engineers were deemed more valuable in the shops than in the trenches and were freed from military service. As the army's need for fresh troops increased, however, the circle of exemption gradually closed, and the precise grounds for exemption and the degree of authority delegated to craft unions in protecting their members were among the most contentious issues of the war.[19] The government further sought to ensure that scarce skilled labor would be equitably distributed and reasonably paid. To prevent large firms from bidding up the price of labor and monopolizing skilled employees, Section 7 of the Munitions of War Act prohibited giving "employment to a workman who has within the last previous six weeks . . . been employed on or in connection with munitions work . . . unless he holds a certificate from the employer by whom he was last so employed that he

left work with the consent of his employer." These "leaving certificates" limited both the personal freedom and the economic leverage of engineers. Skilled workers wishing to "better themselves"
had to either secure their employer's permission or forgo six weeks'
wages. Given the scarcity of labor, manufacturers naturally exercised restraint in issuing certificates and occasionally refused them
for punitive purposes. Even when January 1916 amendments to
the Munitions Act proscribed the system's worst abuses, leaving
certificates remained a cause of great resentment among engineers
until 1917, when the certificates were abolished.[20]

Not all engineering workers opposed these policies. The imposition of dilution threatened skilled men, the more so because the
government appeared insufficiently vigilant in protecting dilutees'
wages. The suppression of union work rules naturally affected
those most strongly organized and those with the most elaborate
defenses before the war—craftsmen. Restrictions on the mobility
of labor imposed the greatest hardships on those with the most
valuable skills. Less skilled workers had no such investment in the
prewar industrial status quo, and they welcomed the opportunity
to do work and earn wages formerly reserved for qualified men.
Less skilled workers and their union representatives also resented
the preferential exemption of craftsmen from conscription, particularly after November 1916. At that time craft societies won the
privilege of protecting their own members from the draft under
the Trade Card scheme—a privilege subsequently denied to
unions organizing less skilled workers. Exemptions were not only
reserved for engineers under the Trade Card system; in addition
they seemed to be based more on union membership than on any
legitimate criteria of skill.[21]

Yet government policies also imposed hardships that transcended the specific conflicts of interest among labor. Engineering
workers of varied skills resented state intervention in workshop
discipline. Under the Munitions of War and the Defense of the
Realm Acts, behavior hindering production became a criminal offense. Employers could now take legal action in disciplinary problems for which they would otherwise have had no effective sanction. Workers faced prosecution and fines not only for opposing
dilution and inciting strikes but also for failing to obey orders, poor
timekeeping, gambling, reading newspapers, or possessing liquor

while at work. Between August and December of 1915, 4,166 workers were prosecuted in Munitions Tribunals, mostly for breaches of work rules.[22] The Coventry ASE District Committee frequently denounced "the attitude of employers in using the Munitions Act to tyrannise our members in the Workshops."[23] Together with the use of leaving certificates, government intervention was widely felt to buttress employers' authority at workers' expense—the more so because labor interests were inadequately represented on Munitions Tribunals.[24] This feeling crossed skill and craft boundaries. Late in 1916, George Morris was sentenced to three months at hard labor for initiating a strike in Coventry. Morris, local secretary of the Workers' Union, had acted to secure the proper wage rate for three semiskilled workers at COW—hardly an issue of immediate concern to skilled engineers. Yet the sight of a trade union official being tried in criminal court for performing legitimate union business led a mass meeting of ASE members in November to vote "to down tools immediately the conviction of G. Morris is confirmed at Quarter Sessions."[25]

Engineering workers generally resented the government's apparent inability to spread the burdens of war evenly and equitably. Regardless of trade or skill, many considered that patriotic sacrifices were all on one side. Wages lagged behind the cost of living, yet landlords and food merchants prospered; wage increases were meager and delayed, yet manufacturers' profits were large and assured. There existed as well a widespread sense that collaboration between the government and national union leaders took place at the expense of the rank and file and their chosen representatives, leaving workers with nothing but a string of broken promises. The Ministry of Munitions offered a somewhat condescending retrospective of the situation by early 1917:

The workpeople, men and women, were tired. Long hours of continuous strain in the factory, overcrowded houses and lodgings devoid of every comfort, dear unpalatable food, hardly to be got by dreary waiting in the queues, the absence of amusement and recreation, bereavement . . . produced a nervous irritability. . . . Men in such a mood distorted out of all proportion the grievances which arose from the administration of the Munitions of War and the Military Services Acts. . . . Nor were the grievances few. The irksomeness of the leaving certificate, the inequalities of exemption from military service, the delay in securing arbitration, the

ponderous working of the departmental machinery, the disproportion between the earnings of piece-workers and the highly skilled time-workers,
who supplied their tools and maintained their machines, the rapid rise of
prices and the slow increment of wages . . . produced abundant material
for discontent. . . . The suspension of the right to strike by the Munitions
of War Act, depriving as it did the union executive of the one effective
sanction of their will, had undermined their authority over their members. . . . The closer their relations with the Government, the more were
they suspected of having sold their cause. . . . In these circumstances,
power passed into the hands of the shop-stewards. . . .[26]

Bridgeport

The principal industrial base of Bridgeport, Connecticut's leading
manufacturing city, was metalworking of all kinds: electrical products, machine tools, phonographs, sewing machines, automobiles
and trucks, submarines, brass goods, and arms and ammunition.
War orders from abroad, and later from the U.S. government,
made Bridgeport a boom city. In the vast expansion of plant, employment, and output, Remington Arms and the Union Metallic
Cartridge Company (UMC) (under common ownership) led the
way. UMC employed twenty-five hundred men and women and
turned out forty-eight thousand cartridges a day in August 1914.
At the war's peak UMC's plant had doubled in physical size and
boasted twelve thousand employees and a daily output of six million cartridges for the Springfield rifle alone. Remington Arms
built what was claimed to be the country's largest factory under
one roof in 1915, with three hundred guards, seven hundred tool
room machinists, messengers on bicycles and roller skates, and a
work force that eventually reached nine thousand. By the middle
of 1915, the city accounted for two-thirds of all small arms and
ammunition shipped to allies. Remington-UMC produced most of
these munitions, but many smaller firms adapted to fill orders and
many more to supply Remington-UMC with the requisite tools
and jigs. Elsewhere in the city the American and British Company
and Bridgeport Projectile (renamed Liberty Ordnance in 1917)
turned out heavier armaments, Lake Torpedo Boat's 1914 capacity
of five submarines a year grew to twenty by the war's end, and the
Locomobile Company operated twenty-four hours a day to fill British demands for trucks—and Russian orders for touring cars.[27]

Bridgeport's boom attracted workers from all over the country. The local population jumped from one hundred thousand to one hundred fifty thousand between 1914 and October 1916 and reached one hundred seventy-three thousand a year later. The industrial work force grew by similar proportions, to fifty-four thousand (including twelve thousand women) by the middle of 1918.[28] Despite Remington's construction of a "subcity" of accommodations for its employees, workers faced soaring rents and overcrowding, if they were able to find lodging at all. Landlords happily evicted tenants if someone offered a few dollars more a month. Three men would divide a single bed in shifts, and the desperate could rent mattresses spread under beds "for a few cents less."[29]

Local employers, organized since 1901 in the Bridgeport Manufacturers' Association, had long enforced the open shop, but wartime demand for labor finally gave machinists the security to organize. Local IAM membership stood at about four hundred fifty early in 1915; it reached nineteen hundred at the end of that year. IAM lodges probably achieved a peak strength of four thousand members by 1917, representing roughly half the city's machinists and 10 percent of all local metalworkers.[30] Many of the new recruits were "boomers": machinists who migrated according to employment opportunities (among them strikers and blacklist victims) and brought with them traditions of union activism uncommon in prewar Bridgeport.[31] The IAM organized most successfully in the smaller subcontract shops, which required highly skilled workers, and in the munitions factories, where war profits made employers more conciliatory.[32] The organization of machinists was never as strong as that of Coventry engineers; and although a few less skilled workers belonged to AFL Federal Unions, they had no union representation akin to Coventry's Workers' Union. In terms of both numbers and strike power, however, the position of Bridgeport's unionized machinists improved dramatically after 1914, for which they could thank not only the labor market but also wartime production conditions and government intervention.

The Labor Process

Deskilling accelerated in Bridgeport factories during the war. By mid-1918, roughly 13 percent of the city's metal trades employees were women, a figure typical of the country as a whole.[33] This represents perhaps half the British norm: the military made much lighter demands on U.S. males. At least until 1917, moreover, most women worked at UMC, where female labor had been common even before the war. Far more important was the enlarged recruitment, training, and upgrading of less skilled men for repetitive work—work equipped and set up by skilled machinists. UMC's 1914 work force of twenty-five hundred increased to twelve thousand by 1918, a jump of 380 percent. From January 1916 to June 1918, the growth in a sample of skilled metalworking occupations, excluding machine setup men, was barely half as great. The category of machine setup men, by contrast, expanded 744 percent.[34]

These numbers reflect a basic reorganization within the factories. Machinists in large firms were withdrawn from production departments, their varied tasks parceled out to semiskilled workers operating special-purpose machines with "foolproof" jigs and fixtures. Inexperienced workers from all trades could be trained for such jobs in a matter of days.[35] Machinists took responsibility for setting up and equipping the machines and were increasingly confined to the tool room. Even there the enormous demand for tools, gauges, and fixtures led to factory methods of production, and many skilled men found themselves assigned to single machines, "working continuously, week after week, upon the same part of the same tool."[36]

War production did not bring a marked expansion of payment by results for most skilled machinists. But there was an accelerated fragmentation of day rates in favor of multiple occupational categories, each with a finely graded scale of rates. These categories were generally defined by machine: firms hired boring mill hands, planer operators, or precision grinders more often than "general machinists" and "toolmakers." Each classification in turn offered a hierarchy of grades and wage rates. Most firms had three or four grades for each job, and as little as one-half cent per hour might separate one rung on the ladder from the next.[37] In principle, workers were assigned a rate when they started, and they moved up the scale in accordance with their output, skill, and loyalty. With this scheme, employers claimed, they could efficiently train and upgrade new employees and reward individual merit. In practice "job reassignment" often became a pretext for pay cuts or a means to evade wage awards. But even if employers strictly and sincerely followed the system, it undermined both union pay standards and the basic notion of an "all-around" machinist. Like their British counterparts, machinists paid by the hour also faced a decline in wages relative to the semiskilled pieceworkers whose machines were set up and repaired by skilled workers.[38]

Deskilling and new employment policies could be divisive. Less skilled munitions workers stood to gain from the upgrading and piecework earnings that created so much resentment among machinists. Fragmented job categories and wage rates and competition for promotion also threatened workshop solidarity among skilled operators. Nor did machinists at different plants share identical grievances, for deskilling proceeded unevenly. Remington-UMC, where the manufacture of tools and gauges on a factory basis undermined craft standards among even the most highly skilled machinists, represented one extreme. More traditional craft production persisted in subcontract shops making relatively small numbers of precise jigs and fixtures. In between were large plants such as American and British, Liberty Ordnance, Bullard Engineering, and Locomobile. The heavier armaments and vehicles these firms turned out in limited batches still required some of the skill and versatility of old-time machinists.[39] Other employer policies antagonized machinists and specialists throughout the city. A notable example is the continued reliance on victimization to deal with rebellious workers and a continued refusal to recognize unions or to engage in collective bargaining.

Bridgeport machinists thus shared with Coventry engineers enhanced power and heightened discontent. The demand for craftsmen to set up and repair machines and produce tools increased enormously. The reorganization of production also put machinists and toolmakers in a strategic position, from which they could have disrupted munitions production on a massive scale. At the same time, machinists faced diminished earnings compared to less skilled operatives (and relative to the cost of living), large-scale displacement from production work by quickly trained and upgraded recruits, and a systematic assault on craft standards through the subdivision of work and fragmentation of occupations. In contrast to British engineering, however, challenges at work and the

benefits of the economic boom at first came without significant
union or government constraints on action.

Unions

Until the United States entered World War I in 1917, the IAM had
a free hand. Its leaders used that freedom to advance familiar goals
(especially wage increases and the eight-hour day) and to recruit
new members after long years of employers' union-busting. Union
policies came to approximate Britain's more closely, once mobilization efforts began early in 1917. In April the AFL's Metal Trades
Department resolved that "there shall be no cessation of work in
any Government plant or in any private plant engaged in the manufacture of war materials for the Government of the United States
during the period of the conflict, provided a plan is adopted
whereby all grievances of employees . . . may be taken up for adjustment within a reasonable time." AFL unions also agreed not to
use their wartime powers to impose any *new* restrictions on production or to secure the closed shop.[40] Finally, unions accepted the
introduction of women in war production if men could not be
found for the same work, providing those women enjoyed pay and
conditions equal to the men they replaced.[41]

   In return for these concessions, the IAM (and the AFL generally) received significant government support for union activities
and some influence over war policies (including the appointment
of IAM President William Johnston to the National War Labor
Board [NWLB]). Even after U.S. entry into the war, the IAM remained free to defend such prewar customs and advantages as it
had achieved. Although union officials had considerable incentives
to observe them, AFL pledges were also voluntary—largely followed in practice but enforced as far as possible by union discipline
rather than by legal mandate.

Government Intervention

The U.S. government maintained its traditional laissez-faire approach to industrial relations until 1917. After America's declaration of war, government officials laid many plans; had the war
lasted another year, state policies would have more closely re-

sembled those of the Ministry of Munitions. The armistice cut short these plans, and intervention remained less direct and less prolonged than in Britain. This contrast is particularly clear in workshop practices. Direct intervention in plant management was minimal, partly because U.S. manufacturing techniques were already suited to war production and partly because employers resisted government meddling.[42] The War Labor Policies Board, for example, developed a scheme to allocate skilled labor more systematically and to train and place women in men's work where possible.[43] Such plans were unpopular: proposals to help train unskilled men and women for shipbuilding work drew denunciations from the Boilermakers' Union and the Seattle Metal Trades Council.[44] But war agencies never involved themselves in the details of dilution, going little further than to facilitate the recruitment of new hands through the U.S. Employment Service and to include among NWLB principles the general guideline that in war industries "methods of work and operation on the part of employers or workers which operate to delay or limit production, or which have a tendency to artificially increase the cost thereof, should be discouraged."[45] By the same token, machinists received no guarantees that privileges abandoned during the war would be restored in peacetime. And although the government accepted the principle that women should receive equal pay for equal service, this was never rigorously enforced.[46]

Outside of the details of work practices and management policies, industrial relations were more closely regulated. Beginning in the summer of 1917, the Secretary of War insisted that all ordnance contracts include a "labor disputes clause" requiring that controversies affecting war production be submitted to the War Department for settlement. Contractors would be compensated for any increase in labor costs incurred by these settlements. In effect, employers and employees working on government orders were subject to mandatory arbitration. Because most employers still did not formally recognize unions, the usual procedure was for union officials to call on the appropriate government adjustment board or mediation service (these varied by industry and over time), whose staff would then shuttle back and forth between employer and labor representatives in search of agreement. Official agencies took up disputes in munitions production on a case-by-case basis and issued awards for individual firms or, at most, cities. Consequent delays and inequities between one firm, city, or industrial branch and another caused machinists considerable frustration. The National War Labor Board, established in March 1918, assumed ultimate authority over labor disputes in munitions.[47]

Government regulation of industrial relations was in other respects considerably less exacting than in Britain. Strikes remained legal. The AFL did agree not to strike, and the first principle of the NWLB was that labor disputes should not be allowed to interrupt war output. However, government action to enforce these sanctions consisted only of informal pressure on union officials to order their members back to work and refusal to arbitrate grievances during a strike.[48] Government manpower policy also remained limited in scope. No significant restrictions on labor mobility, akin to Britain's leaving certificate, applied in the United States, although the War Department may have encouraged major suppliers not to hire workers away from other firms.[49] Skilled men could, if they wished, claim exemption from the draft, but craft unions never gained the power to issue those exemptions. Nor did the government formally lend its authority to shop-floor discipline, nor did it establish any official tribunals to which employers could refer errant workers for punishment. Government officials did add their voices to employers' in branding strikes unpatriotic, and the efforts of the Department of Justice and local law enforcement agencies to defend the national interest did not always make fine distinctions between the labor militant and the traitor.[50] Officials also made few efforts to prevent employers, in cooperation with local draft boards, from withdrawing exemptions from recalcitrant workers and strikers, even though this "was repeatedly called to the attention of the authorities in Washington."[51] Workers strongly resented these abuses, but the fault seemed to lie more with despotic employers than with government policies systematically supporting management authority.

On balance, government intervention probably benefited organized labor. The eight-hour day, which unions had rarely won through their own efforts, became law in all factories on government work. More important, state regulations afforded some protection for unionists, organizing, and collective bargaining. The NWLB barred discrimination against union members, and although employers often continued to discriminate, union officials could call on the government to order reinstatement. Workers' rights to organize and bargain collectively received state backing. These rights were not easily or uniformly enforced, and "collective bargaining" did not require union recognition. But here, too, the opportunity to invoke government protection for organizing gave unions an important new weapon against open-shop employers. Even though direct union-management bargaining remained elusive, the IAM enjoyed an unprecedented degree of informal recognition. If it could organize a plant thoroughly, employee deputations were in fact union shop committees. And if supervisors and employees failed to settle a dispute, the case could be referred to government arbitration, with union officials acting as the representatives of the workers in the shops.[52]

Yet for all the apparent evenhandedness of state intervention, rank-and-file machinists shared with Coventry engineers a strong sense of the inequities of war policy. Government agencies typically required that grievances be presented by national union officers. Centralized arbitration and the enhanced power of union executives, in turn, sacrificed the particular concerns of local machinists and the authority of their direct representatives.[53] Variations in wage awards from one locality to another or between machinists under the jurisdiction of different adjustment boards (e.g., on munitions work and shipbuilding) caused further frustration. Finally, wartime sacrifices seemed to fall disproportionately on the working class. Patriotism for workers meant tighter budgets, more crowded housing, longer hours on the job, and delays in grievance settlements. For manufacturers it meant lucrative munitions contracts.[54] Although laborers heard often enough that the war would make the world safe for democracy, little seemed to be done to curb despotism at home. "While our members and the wage-earners in general are sacrificing their lives on the battlefields of Europe, we who comprise Uncle Sam's industrial army can not stand idly by and see the 'Kaisers' of American industry continue their un-American practices in the workshop. . . . We want to be able to show our brother members when they . . . again pick up their tools to reenter the shop . . . that they now can enjoy the freedom and democracy they were fighting for."[55] The same applied outside the shops. In Bridgeport, municipal curbs on free speech, orders to "work or fight," and the conspicuous presence of the local militia proclaimed a double standard: a national commitment to world democracy and a heavyhanded defense of employer interests at home.[56]

Comparative Conclusions

Many of the problems and opportunities facing engineers and machinists during World War I extended trends under way before 1914 rather than breaking sharply with the prewar status quo. The war brought labor-saving machinery, an increased division of labor, and a greater reliance on semiskilled workers for production tasks. Yet these challenges to the position of skilled metalworkers were entirely familiar in character, if not in degree, from prewar years. Dilution was clearly more abrupt in Britain and involved a distinct invasion of the shops by women. But in both countries the war did not so much create new workplace grievances as intensify old ones. The novelty lay more in how war production enhanced the power of engineers and machinists to fight back—a situation offering powerful temptations for skilled men to use their exclusive influence for sectional benefits.

For all the rhetoric of national emergency and sacrifice attending union concessions, these too had ample precedent. Since 1898, ASE members had seen their union opposing strikes and conceding customary work rules on their behalf. During the war, however, concessions made on paper took effect in practice. The IAM's acceptance of the no-strike pledge, similarly, may not have appeared a dramatic change to machinists, accustomed as they were to the IAM Executive's caution and condemnation of unofficial strikes. Nor did the IAM's agreement not to impose restrictions on war production represent a sacrifice of long-established privileges, for the union had few prewar privileges to abandon. But this policy took effect when, for the first time in many years, conditions gave machinists extraordinary bargaining advantages. What sets the two cases apart is that the IAM retained greater freedom of action, and for a longer period, than did the ASE, especially at the local level. The important similarity—one that significantly extended rather than broke with prewar trends—was the diminished value of union executives for rank-and-file protest.

British industrial relations, finally, proceeded in the same direction as before the war. The Terms had already removed formal bargaining from local hands, delayed settlements, and restricted the right to strike. The war made these procedures legally enforceable. At least until 1917, open-shop employers in the United States remained little more disposed to deal with unions than in any prewar business boom. Thereafter a tight labor market and government intervention did make a difference. Employers had to make concessions to their employees and to negotiate indirectly with union officials even while they refused unions any formal recognition. This reversal of the open-shop drive narrowed the gap between American and British labor relations. And in both cases wartime industrial relations heightened rank-and-file resentments by further curtailing local autonomy and delaying settlements. This trend toward centralization was more extensive in Britain than in the United States.

The most decisive novelty of the war was government intervention. State backing for changes in the labor process (dilution), union policies (restraints on strikes), and industrial relations (centralized bargaining) was unprecedented and introduced a new element into factory politics by directing workers' frustrations against the state and reinforcing the appeal of local control over industrial policy. Other aspects of government intervention, including Britain's restrictions on labor mobility and efforts to prop up employers' authority on the job and the U.S. government's qualified support for unions, broke more sharply with the prewar status quo. State intervention in Britain was more far-reaching and long-lived than in the United States. Labor regulations in Britain also discriminated more clearly against engineers, particularly by using manpower policies and Ministry of Munitions authority to compensate for the shortage—and power—of skilled workers. But in each case state impositions and failures created both sectional grievances for craftsmen and frustrations more widely shared by metalworkers of different skills and trades. The character of factory politics during the war would be influenced by the relative salience, at particular times, of divisive or inclusive issues raised by state controls.

Chapter Six

Coventry: Workers' Control and Industrial Relations Reform

In both the United States and Britain the period from 1915 to 1919 saw the fullest development and final containment of craft radicalism. Prewar accomplishments and traditions—joint organization in defense of local autonomy and workshop control—formed the basis for wartime initiatives. These long-standing trends accelerated during the war in response to government intervention in labor relations and new assaults on craft standards. More important, war conditions lifted key restraints on popular militancy. In Britain union discipline and industrial relations constraints on unofficial organization and action were more easily evaded. In the United States strengthened unions and a moderation of open-shop policies allowed greater power for shop committees and closer coordination by local lodges. These changes expanded the institutional space within which broad alliances for workers' control could develop and increased local militants' opportunities for popular leadership. The defeat of workers' control movements involved restoring union authority and procedural restraints in Britain and isolating American shop committees from union support and direction. In each case the effect was to undercut independent, solidary organization and the influence of radicals among engineers and machinists.

Britain's Shop Stewards' Movement

Radical factory politics in the wartime engineering trades was synonymous with the Shop Stewards' Movement. Although the character of the movement varied from one time and place to another, its common denominator was a tremendous expansion in workshop organization and insurgence under the auspices of shop stewards rather than full-time union officials.[1]

Shop stewards were well placed to play a central role in war-time unrest. Long before 1914, shop delegates had assumed re-sponsibility for regulating work rules and piece rates. These tasks expanded greatly during the war with government-sponsored changes in production techniques. Stewards acted to defend work-ers' interests in dilution, bargaining with managers over specific manning arrangements, wage rates for upgraded workers, and other concrete applications of general government regulations.[2] The shop stewards' role in preserving direct control and freedom of action for rank-and-file engineers also assumed far greater im-portance amid compromises made by union leaders and central-ized union-government collaboration in handling grievances. Through shop organization engineers also reclaimed the right to strike, which had been abandoned by their union officials and pro-scribed by law—a right of considerable practical value in cutting red tape and forcing the government to consider local grievances.[3] The increased functions and power of workplace organization re-flected both the abdication of traditional union responsibilities and the greater freedom of unofficial action from national discipline. With jobs easily found, the government intervening to settle dis-putes, and union executives forgoing strikes, labor leaders had no effective sanctions to apply against unconstitutional behavior.[4] The forces that before the war had kept rank-and-file protest relatively routine and circumscribed were thus suspended.

Greatly expanded organization within the factories gave rank-and-file engineers a stronger base for autonomous action. The Shop Stewards' Movement further challenged union authority by extending independent organization beyond individual shops. Lo-cal Workers' Committees, combining delegates from different plants in an engineering center, entirely bypassed established trade unions. Some were little more than propagandist bodies, but others led large-scale strikes and secured grudging recognition from government officials. From 1917, a National Administrative Council (NAC) of the Shop Stewards' Movement sought to coordi-nate local policies on wartime issues. The NAC had limited control over individual stewards or works committees and little weight in decisions made by the government, unions, or employers. In the NAC and unofficial organization at the plant and local levels, however, the Shop Stewards' Movement offered an alternative to craft union structure and policies—one that repudiated the government's efforts to deal solely with official trade union representatives.[5]

The Shop Stewards' Movement also extended the prewar tendency for workplace organization to ignore craft divisions. In the interests of production efficiency, the Munitions of War Act suspended customary demarcation rules in the factories. Distinctions between craft societies remained intact, but because craft workers faced common problems on the job and could expect little help from their respective unions, they had their own interest in common organization at work. Such organization often involved members of different unions electing a common departmental steward to act on their behalf. In other cases stewards chosen by workers of given crafts formed joint works committees to deal collectively with management. Such stewards and committees thus had powers and constituencies that bypassed established trade societies.[6]

The inclusion of less skilled employees in plant organization marked a sharper break from the prewar status quo. Unionized semiskilled men and women frequently had their own representative on works committees. Occasionally, a member of a general union would act as the steward for an entire department, including its skilled employees. On a less formal basis elected stewards negotiated on behalf of all the workers in their department, regardless of grade. Frictions between men and women of different skill levels persisted, but for the first time all-grades workplace action attained an institutional base.[7]

The structure of the Shop Stewards' Movement, then, met two key prerequisites for radical factory politics—independence from trade union authority and cross-sectional organization. These characteristics paved the way for effective radical leadership and for broadly based alliances in support of workers' control.

The development of unofficial organization gave militants from Amalgamation Committees (ACs) (especially in England), the Socialist Labour Party (SLP) (particularly in Scotland), and the Industrial Workers of the World (IWW) exceptional opportunities for influence among engineers. Such partisans were willing to defy union and government restrictions, and they figured prominently among the local and shop-floor activists who assumed the initiative in bargaining and leading disputes once trade unions had abandoned those tasks.[8] Despite their differences, AC, SLP, and IWW militants shared syndicalist and industrial unionist commitments, and they viewed works committees as the necessary basis for all-grades organization, for the displacement of reactionary craft unionism, and above all for democratic control of industry.[9] Criticizing previous efforts to reconcile the interests of different craft unions and skill grades, a Sheffield Workers' Committee leader wrote, "Characteristic of them all . . . is the fact that always have they sought for a fusion of officialdom as a means to the fusion of the rank and file. We propose to reverse this procedure. Already we . . . are driven back to the workshops. With the workshops, then, as the new units of organisation . . . we can erect the structure of the Great Industrial Union [and] invigorate the labour movement with the real democratic spirit."[10]

Most shop stewards and rank-and-file engineering workers were not ideological radicals; rather, most were committed trade unionists concerned above all with defending traditional craft rights. Radical ideals had practical appeal for engineers under war conditions, however, and progressive programs could achieve mass support. Working-class solidarity made sense when sectional unions ceased to defend rank-and-file interests. The ideal of local control rooted in workplace organization had tactical value where national collaboration between unions and government deprived workers of their customary autonomy and industrial rights. Notions of workers' control found a sympathetic audience when distant authorities mandated changes in work practices—changes from which employers, not workers, profited. Such goals not only had broad appeal; in unofficial organization engineering workers also had the means to pursue them on a collective basis. As early as 1915, for example, Clydeside engineers, acting through the Clyde Workers' Committees rather than their district officials, gave mass support to an alternative approach to dilution: dilution could proceed only in consultation with local shop delegates and without lowering employers' *total* wage bill. Skilled workers, in other words, accepted the sacrifice of traditional privileges but insisted on local control, a voice in implementing dilution, and guarantees that the interests of all workers—including the less skilled—would receive equal consideration with those of capital.[11]

Radical factory politics were by no means an inevitable outgrowth of unofficial organization. Indeed, the Shop Stewards' Movement embodied a basic dilemma, as James Hinton has emphasized. Although many of its leaders proclaimed class goals, wartime struggles were based on craft power. The most important source of insurgence, moreover, was dilution, an area in which the interests of craftsmen and less skilled workers proved difficult to reconcile—especially as it came to be bound up with issues of military exemptions and postwar restoration of craft privileges. How these dilemmas were worked out in specific patterns of factory pol itics depended in large part on the alliances and goals favored for mobilization at given times. In the case of Coventry this selective mobilization turned on two general factors: first, the relative strength of competing organizations within the labor movement at various times (the Coventry Workers' Committee, the Joint Engineering Trades Committee, and individual district committees), and, second, the relative salience of different issues animating rank-and-file struggles. Certain general grievances regarding Munitions Tribunals, shop committee recognition, or local control of the allocation of labor favored broad alliances and progressive leadership. Sectional concerns over draft exemptions, dilution of private work, the mobility of skilled labor, or restoration of craft customs did not. As the organizational and ideological terrain changed, so did factory politics.

The Development of Radical
Factory Politics in Coventry

The Shop Stewards' Movement in Coventry developed relatively late in the war. The Amalgamated Society of Engineers' District Committee policies during 1915 and 1916 reflect the same sectional concerns as before 1914 and do not seem to have been disputed by most engineers. Coventry District Committee strategies aimed to minimize encroachments on the status and earnings of skilled men within the limits set by union compromises and government regulations. Firms seeking to extend premium bonus pay were informed that "our members were not allowed to work this system where it had not previously been in force."[12] The response to a Coventry Ordnance Works plan to train unskilled labor in November 1915 was typical of District Committee policy regarding dilution. "No objection would be raised to such procedure where skilled men *could not* be obtained provided the men concerned were paid at least the district rate, that the firm supply [the District Committee] with a list of such men and that the said men shall only work the machines for the period of the War."[13] The District Committee also sought to limit the two-machine system and opposed employment for women in tool rooms and machine tool manufacturing.[14]

Similarly exclusive preoccupations appear in District Committee relations with other unions. The ASE District Committee reaffiliated with the Coventry Engineering Joint Committee (CEJC) in April 1916 on the condition (among others) that "on questions of importance to any society or societies these may demand a card vote," a provision ensuring the ASE greater influence over CEJC decisions than smaller craft societies in the city possessed.[15] As for less skilled workers, local ASE officials frequently complained that the Workers' Union encroached on craft societies' jurisdiction and made the transfer of its skilled members to the "proper" trade union a precondition for the Workers' Union's admission to the CEJC (a condition the Workers' Union refused to accept).[16] District Committee leaders also assisted the National Federation of Women Workers in its local organizing efforts, viewing this body as a more tractable repository for "temporary" female labor than the Workers' Union.[17]

Local officials, however, ultimately accepted the rules laid down by their Executive and the government—that craft restrictions be suspended and strikes eschewed. Rank-and-file engineers thus turned to other agencies to defend their interests. Shop stewards and committees offered the most important and useful alternative to the District Committee leadership. The development of workshop organization in wartime Coventry consisted partly in a greatly increased role for stewards in negotiating with management and calling strikes. As in other engineering centers, general government mandates for new production techniques had to be adapted to particular conditions in each plant, a task that required constant bargaining between management and employee representatives. Because of trade union and Ministry of Munitions rules, only shop-floor vigilance (including the threat of a strike) could ensure that dilution or piecework operated on terms favorable to labor. Although shop stewards before the war had referred disputes to local officials, by October 1916 the Coventry District Committee found itself merely noting that "through the Shop Steward" Herbert's efforts to substitute laborers for ASE employees had been defeated.[18] Unconstitutional action before 1914 had typically divided local engineers from national officials. Wartime restrictions on union activity affected district officials, along with national ones, and created new tensions between engineers and their nominal local leaders. As early as August 1915, the District Committee secretary had to ask Herbert's shop stewards "why they had not notified DC of the recent strike" there.[19]

By the beginning of 1917, ASE Executive Council and District Committee officials alike voiced concerns over "irresponsible" stewards. One reason stewards seemed increasingly irresponsible was that, by mid-1916, they were elected from the shop floor rather than appointed by union branches (as they had been before the war). Departmental elections, moreover, often disregarded union affiliation. A delegate belonging to the Amalgamated Society of Toolmakers or even the Workers' Union might represent ASE members in negotiations with management. Stewards of different unions also formed works committees to handle common grievances. In neither case did any individual district committee have clear authority over shop leadership, and such stewards and committees had constituencies that ignored the boundaries of craft and skill laid down by engineering trade unions.[20]

The Coventry Workers' Committee (CWC) represented a more decisive challenge to craft unionism. Under the leadership of Workers' Union militants, AC activists, and SLP members, the CWC elevated joint organization to a citywide level, combining workshop delegates in a body entirely independent of, and hostile to, individual trade unions. The CWC had less influence than did Workers' Committees in such centers of wartime unrest as Glasgow or Sheffield. However, the extent of CWC activities called forth anxious inquiries from the ASE EC as early as April 1916[21] and led several district committees to embark on a spree of preemptive workshop organization. ASE officials noted "the formation of irresponsible Shop Committees" in April 1917 and urged "our Shop Stewards to secure full representation on such Committees." The previous month local ASE leaders had joined United Machine Workers', Toolmakers', and Steam Engine Makers' district committees in resolving to establish joint committees in the larger Coventry firms, reassuring their Executive Council that "our objects are to keep a responsible hold on such Stewards' Committees."[22] Despite these efforts, by April 1917, shop committees in some plants (including Hotchkiss-et-Cie, a machine gun manufacturer) were connected to the all-grades CWC rather than to individual craft unions.[23] Even without firm ties to specific workshop bodies, the CWC enjoyed considerable support from skilled and less skilled workers alike—as the events of 1917 would show.

The development of citywide joint organization was not confined to the CWC. The CEJC offered engineers a more respectable vehicle for concerted action. Fourteen craft unions, with a local membership totaling twenty-six thousand, had representatives on the CEJC by May 1917.[24] These delegates assumed a major role in negotiating with the local employers' association and formulating common policy, often at the expense of national and district officials of individual unions. CEJC representatives also consulted with the Workers' Union on local policy, even though the Coventry ASE District Committee continued to veto formal Joint Committee membership for the Workers' Union.[25]

Shop committees, the CWC, and the CEJC represented the principal alternatives to craft unions and the potential bases for control struggles. Each brought workers together despite divisions rooted in the labor process, and each did so independently of sectional trade union authority. If the different factions—craft union and Workers' Union stewards, progressive CEJC officials, CWC militants—could agree on anything, it was the demand, raised at the beginning of 1917, that employers recognize shop stewards as legitimate spokesmen for their employees. The issue of shop steward recognition overshadowed sectional concerns over dilution and military exemptions for most of 1917, creating common ground for engineering workers of varied skills and political commitments. Each group stood to benefit from victory. Shop stewards would gain formal standing and greater authority with respect to management. Insofar as the CEJC secured direct ties to shop committees, it could improve its leverage with the employers' association and prevent rank-and-file unrest from passing into the hands of the CWC. The latter hoped to expand its organized workshop constituency and, on that basis, gradually to displace individual craft unions in the local labor movement. Shop committees, finally, were crucial to the practical implementation of workers' control—as each group defined this goal. The evolution of factory politics in Coventry involves the shifting fortunes of these contending factions.

CWC partisans offered the most ambitious vision. Shop committees were to form the basic unit in building workers' control, beginning at the plant level and extending upward through the local Workers' Committee to the NAC of the Shop Stewards' Movement. This organization was designed to bypass reactionary craft unionism in two respects: it would unite workers regardless of skill or trade, and it would locate democratic control of the movement with the rank and file rather than delegating authority to distant bureaucrats. Shop committees would, in the short term, secure for labor a larger voice in "management" decisions; ultimately, they would become the democratic cell for workers' ownership as well as control of production. Members of the Workers' Union figured prominently among CWC activists. Most important was Tom Dingley, who was also the local Amalgamation Committee chairman and active in the SLP and the IWW.[26] CWC participation, however, crossed union lines: the Hotchkiss shop committee affiliated with the CWC included an ASE member along with Dingley. This committee first demonstrated the CWC's (limited) power in Coventry.[27]

On April 6, 1917, Hotchkiss stewards discovered tool room work being done in the production shop at less than the tool room wage rate and ordered a strike. Their demands soon included not only the proper pay but also management recognition of their committee. Members of craft societies and the Workers' Union came out despite efforts by the CEJC and ASE District Committee President Alf Doherty (a Hotchkiss employee) to keep the men at work. CEJC delegates declared themselves "unanimous in expressing their disapproval of the movement and its organisers, who are simply trying to usurp the powers of duly authorised local trade union officials. They united in encouraging the management to ignore absolutely the self-called Shop Committee."[28] For Hotchkiss managers and other local employers, this was gratuitous advice. Coventry's Engineering Employers' Association (EEA) warned the EEF secretary that "we view with great concern the recognition of Shop Committees of this nature, as they are generally controlled by extreme men."[29] The Ministry of Munitions proved responsive to these concerns and managed to appease employers and trade union officials at the expense of the CWC. On April 10, Alf Doherty called a meeting of Hotchkiss employees affiliated with the CEJC and assured them that the question of recognition would be taken up in conference, with Ministry of Munitions involvement. The workers agreed to return the following day.

Although CWC stewards at Hotchkiss agreed to this arrangement,[30] the eventual settlement proved less than satisfactory. Ministry of Munitions representatives persuaded employers and trade unions to accept a shop committee at Hotchkiss whose responsibilities "were not to encroach upon the powers either of the Management or of the union executives."[31] A Ministry official assured the EEF that "the functions of the Committee which it is proposed to set up are in the main for welfare purposes."[32] In addition, the constitution of the new Hotchkiss Works Committee required each steward to be "endorsed by their respective Union District Committees," directed unresolved plant grievances to local union officials, and affirmed that no strikes would occur.[33] Under these conditions CWC militants boycotted shop steward elections, making the new Hotchkiss Works Committee even more agreeable to employers and union leaders. Although the CWC maintained support at Hotchkiss, its organizational roots were henceforth confined to the fitting shop.[34]

Union and government officials succeeded in ending the Hotchkiss strike and in setting up a more docile works committee, but they failed to break the CWC's influence among the city's munitions workers. In need of more men for military service, the government announced at the end of April the abolition of the Trade Card scheme and the extension of dilution to private work.[35] A rumor that the restoration of trade union practices after the war would be delayed by as much as seven years compounded unrest in Coventry.[36] ASE members endorsed a resolution demanding the retention of the Trade Card and denouncing "the taking of any of our members into the army, so long as a single diluted unit remains in our trade."[37] But Coventry District Committee officials refused to sanction a walkout on the issue and on May 6 instructed all shop stewards to ignore strike orders issued by unofficial bodies.[38] Nevertheless, under the banner of local control over manpower, thirty thousand Coventry engineering workers answered the call for strike action issued by the Amalgamation Committee and the CWC on May 8.[39]

CEJC leaders now seized the initiative. Joint Committee Chairman Davis secured pledges from the Ministry of Labour on May 9 that skilled men would remain protected from the draft and that the Dilution Bill would apply solely to the war. On the strength of these assurances, the CEJC then ordered affiliated members back to work; most complied the next day. CWC activists could not stem the resumption of work, and their defeat was confirmed May 11 when CEJC officials called a mass meeting and persuaded the fifteen to twenty thousand in attendance to condemn the strike.[40]

The CEJC, rather than individual District Committee leaders, won the initiative from the CWC in May. They did so in part by reassuring skilled workers that their exclusive interests would be safeguarded. The nationwide May strikes forced the government to abandon plans to extend dilution to private work and to appease engineers by abolishing the leaving certificate system.[41] Yet there was no simple retreat to craft sectionalism after the May strikes. CEJC officials knew that the complacence of trade union leaders could restore the CWC's influence.[42] They also understood the general appeal of shop committee recognition and the weakness of traditional craft divisions. Accordingly, during the summer of 1917, CEJC officials developed a new shop steward system. They made their plans, which were based on discussions among Joint Committee representatives and (much to the annoyance of the ASE District Committee) the Workers' Union, without sanction from national trade union leaders.

The proposed scheme abandoned the direct democratic control from the shop floor that was central to Workers' Committees; instead it made the CEJC (whose delegates were elected on a residential basis) the executive committee over all shop stewards. Stewards were also denied authority to initiate industrial action, with strikes banned pending the outcome of a local grievance procedure. These principals made the proposal unacceptable to the CWC, which stood aloof from negotiations over the scheme and lost influence in the shops as the CEJC signed up stewards.[43] But the Joint Committee rules gave shop committees considerable power to negotiate with employers and provided that "any change in the Shop or Works must receive the consent of the Joint Engineering Committee before being accepted by the men concerned." Nor were sectional boundaries left intact. All members of a particular shop, regardless of union affiliation, elected stewards—a provision that allowed for Workers' Union participation despite a stipulation that stewards belong to CEJC-connected societies. The plan further provided for cooperation among stewards through works committees, and it made both responsible to the CEJC rather than to the district committees of individual unions. Grievances not resolved within the plant passed not to separate craft societies but to the CEJC as a whole.[44] In these respects the program was more radical than anything envisioned by District Committee, much less Executive Council, officials.

From September through November, the CEJC sought to gain acceptance of its shop stewards' scheme from both individual employees and the Coventry EEA as a whole.[45] The question was of considerable urgency. In attempting to negotiate grievances at such local firms as White and Poppe, Rudge, and Humber, stewards received "unsatisfactory treatment," and at least two were fired. Shop stewards responded by calling unofficial strikes.[46] Such unrest reinforced the CEJC's commitment to formal controls, in part to "prevent the interference of outside bodies."[47] The Coventry EEA, however, insisted that recognition was a question for conferences between the Employers' Federation and union executives (and urged individual firms not to accept the CEJC proposals).[48] ASE District Committee leaders found this plan agreeable.[49] The CEJC did not, for their scheme would hardly receive favorable attention from national officials of individual craft societies.

Matters came to a head at the end of November. On November 17 and 18, "unrecognized" stewards led ten thousand men and women in a citywide strike to protest severe food shortages.[50] The following day shop stewards at White and Poppe requested an interview to discuss the application of a government award regarding premium bonus pay. Management refused, and the stewards led employees on strike. When the secretaries of the ASE and the Toolmakers visited the firm, they asked that the stewards be admitted to negotiations, "but were immediately met with the retort that they had no Stewards here." The men "would accept nothing less than [the deputation] going as *Shop Stewards*," and the dispute was referred to the CEJC. The latter called a meeting of shop stewards on November 22; the outcome was a demand for a *local* conference on recognition of the CEJC plan. The Coventry EEA conceded only that deputations to member firms might include a spokesman, "not necessarily a party to the dispute." It would not formally recognize shop stewards until the issue had been resolved at the national level.[51]

This response satisfied neither the CEJC nor Coventry's shop stewards. Meeting together on November 24, they resolved to strike for immediate recognition of the CEJC plan. From November 26 to December 4, fifty thousand Coventry workers—including members of the Workers' Union—took a holiday.[52] Local union officials carefully emphasized the moderate aims of the strike and the importance of securing formal controls over shop stewards. "The main fact which we want the public to understand," ASE District Committee President Doherty told local newspapers, "is that the shop-steward movement here in Coventry is now an authorised branch of trade unionism, affiliated to the Joint Engineering Committee and under that body's control. It is no longer pulled all over the place by the small unofficial militant section."[53] In private conferences between the CEJC and the Coventry EEA immediately after the strike, "the unions stated that the Shop Stewards' Rules were prepared to enable them to deal with an outside movement which threatened to get out of their control."[54]

If local officials repudiated the Workers' Committee movement, however, their demands showed too little respect for either management or craft union authority to win national approval. The CEJC accordingly insisted that the strike "must be settled locally, and before a resumption of work takes place."[55] On December 3, shop stewards and the CEJC agreed to a compromise worked out by local labor and employer representatives and government officials. The strike would be called off immediately, but local negotiations would address the issue of recognition.[56] Under government pressure, however, national negotiations began ahead of schedule (on December 7), preempting local conferences.

Containment

The EEF and all major engineering unions—save the still wary ASE—signed the Shop Stewards' Agreement on December 20, 1917. Union leaders and employers were reluctant parties to the agreement. Employers felt their right to manage threatened and feared the connection of workshop representatives to the Shop Stewards' Movement. Trade union officials had long shown "great anxiety . . . that the Ministry should take no steps which might encourage [shop committees] to undermine the authority of trade union executives."[57] Coventry's strike (and the threat of sympathetic action in Birmingham),[58] however, demonstrated the need for positive measures to control unofficial organization. The Ministry of Munitions consequently pressed for an agreement that would buttress both trade union authority over the rank and file and managerial control at work. Ministry officials hoped "that the constitution of officially approved works committees, with functions more or less clearly defined, would help check the more revolutionary tendencies of the shop stewards' movement by bringing it into an ordered scheme."[59]

The document followed this agenda closely. In contrast to the CEJC scheme, the agreement restored authority over shop stewards to sectional trade unions. Stewards would be elected solely by members of their own union, and no recognition or facilities were granted for shop committees through which stewards of different unions or departments could cooperate. The agreement further denied stewards power to negotiate with management over dilution and piecework, as proposed by the CEJC. Indeed, far from granting the CEJC veto power over changes in workshop practices, it was stipulated that "Employers and Shop Stewards shall not be entitled to enter into any agreement inconsistent with agreements between the Engineering Employers' Federation or local Associations and the Trade Unions," including those respecting managerial rights. Finally, stewards were incorporated into an industrywide grievance procedure, with their functions closely regulated and circumscribed and with disputes quickly passing out of their hands to district and national union officials.[60] As a former Daimler steward recalled, "The principle of recognition once established put the shop steward in a position of authority, acceptable to management in accordance with the agreement. His duties were defined in relation to management functions and the rules were laid down to govern his own activities as the workpeople's representative. By recognition the national movement had become institutionalized."[61] Although the ASE did not sign this agreement until 1919, district officials of all major craft unions promptly endorsed it in practice.[62]

The Shop Stewards' Agreement aimed to reimpose sectional organization, restore trade union authority over the rank and file, and isolate radical leaders. In a sense, militants and employers cooperated to isolate the left. Shop stewards affiliated with the National Administrative Council resolved December 6 "not to recognize the findings of any conference on the status of shop stewards at which they were not represented," and Workers' Committee partisans refused to stand for office under the new system.[63] In Coventry, CEJC policies initiated in May 1917 had already isolated the most radical local leaders. After December the Joint Committee continued to press for recognition of its own scheme but now did so in opposition to local district committees.[64] Coventry employers ensured that neither the CEJC nor remaining radicals would regain lost ground. The EEA refused CEJC requests to incorporate its own shop stewards' rules in the national agreement, and during the early months of 1918, individual firms sacked militant employees—including Tom Dingley.[65]

The events of 1918 demonstrate the successful containment of radical factory politics in Coventry. In January the government again proposed extending dilution to private work and withdrawing its schedule of draft-exempt occupations (thus making certain skilled engineers eligible for military service). The appearance of some unemployment, in which skilled men seemed to be discharged while dilutees remained at work, added to local unrest.[66] In the ensuing crisis local ASE officials failed to secure cooperation from the CEJC to fight government measures. The Workers' Union's Coventry branch—members of which had no wish to restrict their entry into skilled jobs on private work or to see ASE men protected from the draft at their own expense—also resolved to stay at work if any dispute arose.[67] With the support of its stewards and many members, the Coventry ASE District Committee thus resorted to sectional action. Local resolutions at first reflected the antigovernment and antiwar direction in which engineering protest tended throughout Britain early in 1918.[68] Amid conflicts with the CEJC and the Workers' Union, however, less idealistic interests came to the fore. The Coventry District Committee never implemented strike plans made on January 27.[69] But their calls to create recruiting tribunals (composed equally of skilled workers and employers) to review military exemptions did receive rank-and-file support.[70] ASE stewards provided District Committee Secretary Walter Givens with lists of all dilutees in their shops to be forwarded to recruiting officers and used to ensure that dilutees would be drafted first and promptly removed at the war's end.[71] In the meantime ASE members insisted that they should not be laid off until employers discharged less skilled workers.[72] The District Committee also resurrected a policy of having its own stewards regularly meet apart from those of other local unions.[73]

These divisions within Coventry's labor movement hardened in July when, in its nationwide effort to distribute scarce skilled labor more equitably, the Ministry of Munitions applied to four Coventry firms an "Embargo" on hiring additional skilled men without Ministry approval. The measure appeared to restore restrictions on skilled workers' mobility (removed with the abolition of leaving certificates the previous year) while leaving dilutees free to move as they pleased. This hardship was all the more keenly felt given the high earnings of semiskilled pieceworkers compared to those of engineers paid by the hour. At Hotchkiss posted notices defining "skilled men" as those earning the district rate for qualified engineers (as many dilutees did) appeared to extend to less skilled workers government guarantees of postwar employment originally promised to craftsmen alone.[74]

The Workers' Union had no interest in defending the privileges of skilled men and declared itself against any strike.[75] The CEJC at first resolved to strike July 22 if the embargo was not removed—a decision supported by the district committees of local craft unions. But on July 21 the CEJC reversed itself, recommending that engineers remain at work while a national conference of Joint Allied Trades Committees considered the matter. Several developments convinced the CEJC to defer action. First, the Ministry of Munitions agreed to review the embargo with "properly accredited bodies both of employers and trade unions." Second, the government publicly declared the prospective walkout "an attempt to overthrow the policy of the State in a time of national danger" and threatened that "any person who is guilty of inciting others to leave work, or takes any part in organising the strike, renders himself liable to very serious penalties under the Defense of the Realm Act."[76] Finally, the CEJC received only lukewarm responses to its strike plans from other cities and from the National Administrative Council of the Shop Stewards' Movement.[77]

This decision produced a decisive split between the CEJC and individual unions. Twelve thousand members of the ASE, the Toolmakers, and the Steam Engine Makers struck July 23, explicitly declaring their confidence in their respective district committees.[78] CEJC appeals for a return to work were ignored, and a local union leader declared that "anything that emanates from the Engineering Joint Committee is quite unofficial."[79] The government eventually issued reassurances on the status of skilled men, agreed to establish a committee of inquiry to resolve the dispute, and announced its intention to draft strikers. Given these concessions and threats, Coventry engineers, acting through their individual unions, returned to work July 29.[80]

With these events Coventry's trade unions regained leadership of local craft militancy from the CEJC. The Joint Committee's demise as a force in the local labor movement would be consolidated after 1918. Constituent district committees withdrew the Joint Committee's authority to call strikes and, with the resumption of peacetime industrial relations procedures, passed disputes not to the CEJC but to the national officials of individual trade unions.[81] The secession of the Amalgamated Engineering Union (merging the ASE and numerous smaller craft societies in 1920) from the CEJC at the end of 1920[82] confirmed what had occurred two years earlier: the isolation of the CEJC from the local labor movement.

The 1918 disputes very much concerned issues of control—contesting dilution and asserting workers' right to have a voice in wartime manpower policy. But radical programs put forward in 1917 were no longer on the agenda. Engineers now aimed to preserve their privileges at the expense of less skilled workers. This outcome owed a good deal to the particular issues raised during 1918.

Military service, deskilling of private work, embargoes on skilled men, and doubts concerning the postwar restoration of craft rights all accentuated cleavages of skill at work and provided the ideological conditions for mobilizing exclusive factory politics. Perhaps more important was the reform of trade union structure and industrial relations sponsored by the government and embodied in the Shop Stewards' Agreement. The new structure of workshop organization completed the isolation of CWC radicals and began that of progressive CEJC leaders. It undermined cross-craft and cross-grade solidarities developed earlier in the war by restricting shop stewards' constituencies to individual unions and departments. And by reimposing union authority over stewards and incorporating them into formal union-management grievance procedures, the Shop Stewards' Agreement consolidated the priority of sectional craft interests in factory politics.

These outcomes would be reinforced after the armistice. The restoration of craft customs (which proceeded with remarkable smoothness)[83] and trade union rights eliminated the major grievances that had radicalized engineers and fed the unofficial movement. At the same time, insistence on removing or demoting wartime dilutees and reestablishing traditional privileges provided an outlet for—and confirmation of—sectional craft militancy. Wartime radicals throughout Britain moved into left-wing politics after 1918; the industrial action of their erstwhile constituents attended to narrow craft interests, with local union officials in control.[84]

In Coventry, as elsewhere in Britain, factory politics during the first two years after the armistice aimed to regain ground abandoned during the war. The unofficial movement returned for a final bow in 1922. During the national engineering dispute of that year, Coventry's Central Unemployed Committee—a body led by the Communist Party and including the familiar Tom Dingley, among other wartime radicals—challenged the AEU District Committee's control of the local Lockout Committee. By 1922, however, not only radicals but also conservative union leaders were becoming isolated from the shops. During the 1920s, rank-and-file engineers increasingly abandoned craft standards—and often craft unions—if these led to disputes or limited earnings. This diminished enthusiasm for strikes and the letter of district work rules sprang in part from an economic slump and high unemployment, but the trend had deeper roots. A fuller understanding of the city's factory politics requires a reexamination of Coventry in another light: in contrast not to the United States, but to the rest of Britain.

The Limits of Coventry Militancy

Coventry's factory politics departed from the British norm well before World War I. Like many American machinists, the city's engineers were willing to exchange craft standards for economic benefits; when strikes over issues of workshop control did occur, they rarely united workers of different trades, skills, and plants. This pattern of industrial conflict was linked to organizational conditions in which shop stewards were scarce, enjoyed little security from employers, and exercised little autonomy from the district committees. Conflicts between union officials and the rank and file, accordingly, remained limited. World War I did transform the local labor movement. Engineering workers developed far stronger organization at work and a greater capacity to act against management and apart from union leaders. In 1917, skilled and less skilled workers joined to demand more direct rank-and-file control over production practices and collective bargaining.

Even during the war, however, Coventry engineers did not pursue radical goals or organizational innovations with the enthusiasm of their counterparts in other centers of insurgence. Opposition to wartime manpower policies, which animated struggles elsewhere—the battle against dilution in Glasgow in 1915 or against the conscription of skilled men in Sheffield a year later—found only faint echoes in Coventry. When industrial unrest finally spread to the city at the end of 1916, engineers and semiskilled workers acted together less to enlarge workers' control than to ensure that dilution did not undermine wage standards—a goal of common concern to engineers and upgraded workers. By British norms Coventry displayed a curious combination of militant action for higher wages and an acceptance of new production techniques.

The comparative weakness of craft radicalism is also clear from the CWC's inability to secure a strong base among the city's rank and file. The CEJC represented a more significant challenge to established trade union control of local unrest. As the Shop Stewards' Agreement and the events of 1918 demonstrated, however, the split between unofficial organization and individual district committees in Coventry during (as before) the war was narrower than in other cities and was patched up with less difficulty.[85]

The immediate postwar years marked a return to and consolidation of the prewar status quo. Local activism centered on wage issues, and shop stewards lost the power and independence they had gained during the war. However, a new split developed between union officials and rank-and-file engineers. Well-entrenched, conservative union leaders, devoted to traditional craft rights, found themselves cut off from the shops—partly by the employers' counteroffensive, more significantly by workers' willingness to concede management rights and abandon craft unionism in favor of higher wages.[86]

Coventry workers, then, stand out among British engineers—before, during, and after the war—in their weak unofficial organization and their preoccupation with economic rewards rather than workshop control. These peculiarities may be traced first to three features of the labor process: the history of dilution in the city, the role of piecework, and the "chargehand" system. Characteristics of local unionism and industrial relations, in turn, both reflected and complemented the impact of the labor process on Coventry's factory politics.

By World War I, dilution was already well advanced in Coventry. Semiskilled workers accounted for 45 percent of local engineering employees in 1911 (compared to an industry average of 18 percent),[87] blurring the traditional division between all-around craftsmen and unskilled laborers. Nor had many engineers personally experienced dilution. Coventry's history as a metal trades center began with the cycle and auto industries in the 1890s. The relatively inexperienced workers required for cycle and auto production were secured not by downgrading skilled engineers but by recruiting unemployed craftsmen from older, depressed local trades and migrants from the countryside.[88] Thus the traditions, techniques, and representatives of engineering craftsmanship never enjoyed the prominence in Coventry that they did in older metal trades centers.

Coventry's industrial and labor history made wartime manufacturing less traumatic. Relatively modest changes had to be made in prevailing production practices, threatening fewer skilled workers and confronting more feeble craft traditions. The very weakness of craft traditions favored an unusual degree of solidarity between engineers and semiskilled workers, but that alliance centered on economistic concerns. The Coventry ASE District Committee had long demanded standard rates for occupations customarily filled by apprenticed engineers, regardless of who actually performed those tasks. This strategy conceded management control over production techniques in exchange for high wages—a position that dovetailed with the Workers' Union's insistence on the proper rate for upgraded men and women. The Shop Stewards' Movement's call for workers' control and autonomous organization, by contrast, found a less receptive audience. The national suspension of craft customs by unions and government did not antagonize rank-and-file interests in Coventry to the extent that it did where more traditional manufacturing practices prevailed. Local militancy was thus not forced to repudiate established trade unions and their leaders, and the challenges to union authority offered by the CWC and CEJC in 1917 were short-lived.[89]

Widespread payment by results further narrowed the base for radical factory politics, partly by removing basic questions of control from the agenda of workplace conflict and partly by fragmenting that conflict among departments and plants. The initial introduction of incentive pay often spurred bitter struggles and encouraged the development of workshop organization. Once established, however, payment by results gradually shifted the terrain of conflict within the shops. Even before the Terms of Settlement and the Carlisle Agreement permitted employers to implement incentive schemes, local ASE officials had concluded agreements with individual firms allowing piecework subject to union safeguards for earnings and collective bargaining.[90] Most disputes in Coventry did not challenge management's right to use piecework. Instead, they focused on the specific operations and periodic abuses of the system. When were price changes justified? How much were pieceworkers entitled to earn over their day rates? What was proper compensation for unavoidable delays in a job? Over time Coventry unions and employers developed standard agreements to resolve such questions and constitutional procedures to handle particular disputes.[91] Such arrangements established basic ground rules for conflict over payment by results that were endorsed by employers and workers alike.

The acceptance of piecework subject to the rule of law defused contentions over workshop control in another respect. Many of the resentments at the introduction of incentive schemes focused on intrusive rate fixers, closer scrutiny of workers, and unfair piece prices or bonus times. Gradually, however, production became more standardized and management accumulated records of rates for particular jobs. Effort levels and incentives became part of the shop routine, with less occasion for overt confrontation. There may accordingly have been a decline in close discipline and personal driving—the sort of obnoxious supervision that earlier had spurred angry protest and demands for checks on management authority. Disputes over such issues do indeed become rare in Coventry after 1914, and Amalgamated Engineering Union (AEU) members questioned in 1925 reported a "complete absence of bullying" at Triumph Cycle and "fairly easy" or "fairly comfortable" conditions at Maudslay, Rover, Lea and Francis, and other firms.[92]

Payment by results not only depoliticized questions of control and routinized many workplace conflicts in Coventry;[93] in addition, when disputes over incentive pay did occur, they tended to be highly idiosyncratic, concerning specific rates, bonuses, price fixers, and safeguards. Such struggles over payment by results accustomed Coventry engineers to fighting individual managements rather than joining workers in other plants in opposition to local capital as a whole.[94] These traditions in turn may have contributed to the relative weakness of the unofficial movement during World War I. CWC partisans aimed to unite workers irrespective of their workplace or union affiliation; to overstate the case, the most radical section of Coventry's Shop Stewards' Movement instead found itself limited to the Hotchkiss fitting department. The same pattern of isolated struggles over particularistic shop concerns may also help explain the unwillingness of Coventry engineers to come out in 1922 in support of generic principles of craft control.

A final feature of the labor process in Coventry that inhibited mobilization for control demands was the chargehand system. Under this system a skilled man took charge of a gang composed of a few other engineers and perhaps a half-dozen less skilled workers. The gang would be responsible for a particular job, with chargehands performing the most skilled tasks and supervising their subordinates (e.g., helping set up automatic machines for less experienced operatives). Employers paid the gang on a collective piecework basis, with chargehands negotiating a price for the job. If the price received for the completed work exceeded the time wages of the gang's members, they shared the surplus, usually in proportion to their day rates. The chargehand himself gained a bonus for his supervisory role, often an initial cut of the collective bonus, with the remainder then distributed throughout the gang. With variations from one firm to another, the system appears to have been exceptionally widespread in Coventry.[95]

The chargehand system undermined control struggles by creating conflicts among engineers (and obscuring conflicts between workers and employers) in the areas of dilution, incentive pay, and workshop authority. Chargehands profited from dilution: by replacing skilled gang members with cheaper workers, they increased both the total piecework bonus and their proportionate share of it. In 1901, the Coventry District Committee persuaded one firm to cease paying its chargehands a preferential percentage of the group piecework balance and to distribute wages through the office rather than through the leading hand. The District Committee cautioned a chargehand "that it was his duty as a member of this society, not to employ or encourage cheap labour on his job, as they as charge men would not receive any financial benefit."[96] As late as 1927, when a gang member at Maudslay reached the age of twenty-three and became entitled to the skilled rate, he "was told by his chargehand to seek a fresh job as the 'gang' could not afford the increase in his rate."[97]

Efforts to secure collective control over piecework also faced opposition from leading hands, especially when union officials—or even managers—sought to reform the chargehand system itself. Leading hands criticized the attempt by the ASE's Organizing District Delegate to eliminate the system at Swift in 1914 and sabotaged a new pay scheme at Rover under which their wages would not come out of group piecework earnings.[98] Even efforts to hold management to agreements regarding price cuts and mutuality could encroach on chargehands' earnings and discretion in arranging rates. Maudslay chargehands in 1927 would accept reductions without consulting their mates in the gang, and they kept prices secret from underhands.[99] The supervisory role chargehands assumed and their interest in maximizing the work pace of their gangs, finally, often made fellow workers (rather than management) the targets of rank-and-file hostility when driving and abusive discipline occurred.

The labor process thus favored economistic factory politics in Coventry. Deskilling weakened craft traditions; piecework directed individual interests toward higher pay. The collective pursuit of control demands, by contrast, faced considerable obstacles. Advanced dilution narrowed the constituency for control struggles in Coventry, chargehand arrangements created conflicts of interests between leading hands and gang members in matters of dilution and piecework, and incentive pay tended to quarantine individual shop-floor disputes. Payment by results also permitted employers to substitute constitutional procedures for the most abrasive and personal conflicts over shop discipline and work pace, while the chargehand system deflected some grievances from employers to leading hands.

Working conditions in Coventry, then, channeled rank-and-file militancy toward the pursuit of economistic interests. The national resolution of wartime conflicts and the reemergence of conventional industrial relations procedures after 1918 consolidated the position of craft conservatives in local union office and reinforced their authority over shop stewards. Coventry was no exception in this respect. Indeed, the very weakness of the city's unofficial movement in 1917 made craft leadership all the more secure. This peculiar combination of an advanced labor process and traditional leadership eventually split Coventry's labor movement—not, as in the war, between conservative district committees and more militant members, but between union officials dedicated to craft standards and engineering workers preoccupied with economic concerns.[100] The divergence became clear during the 1922 engineering lockout, when District Committee leaders proved far more committed than their constituents to the restrictive policies that (on a national scale) precipitated an industrywide lockout. By the mid-1920s, union leaders found themselves cut off from the shops, largely because their craft policies no longer corresponded to the experiences and interests of Coventry engineers.

The 1922 engineering lockout represented the EEF's most dramatic step to reverse union gains made during World War I and to reaffirm employers' right to manage.[101] Engineering workers retained a strong bargaining position for two years after the armistice as the industry prospered, and the ASE joined numerous smaller societies in 1920 to form the 450,000-member Amalgamated Engineering Union. With wartime restrictions lifted, engineers used their power to press old demands, including restrictions on manning machines, payment of apprentices, and overtime work. By the end of 1920, however, production began to slump, prices slide, and unemployment surge. Employers responded by imposing wage cuts (totaling 25 percent over the first half of 1921) and sacking and blacklisting militant shop stewards. The principal weapon in management's counterattack was the industrywide lockout of 1922.

Conflicting interpretations of the 1920 Overtime and Nightshift Agreement provided a convenient pretext for this dispute. The Agreement stipulated that overtime would be worked only when "necessary." In an effort to spread work amid heavy unemployment, the AEU insisted that under the Agreement unions as well as employers had to see the "necessity" of overtime before it could be accepted. Many district committees and individual shop committees simply banned overtime unilaterally. In April 1921, the EEF threatened to lock out AEU members unless the union withdrew all embargoes on overtime and allowed employers the right to overtime without prior approval. With roughly 25 percent of its members unemployed (and drawing benefits accordingly) and many more on short time, the union finally conceded employer demands in November 1921, including the familiar principle that "Trade Unions shall not interfere with the right of the Employers to exercise managerial functions."[102] AEU members, however, rejected the proposals in January 1922 and were locked out on March 11. They were joined on May 2 by members of forty-six other unions to whom the EEF—recognizing a favorable opportunity to settle accounts—extended its demands. Altogether the lockout involved 260,000 engineering workers (90,000 of them belonging to the AEU). Unions other than the AEU accepted the EEF's terms on June 2 and returned to work. The AEU followed June 13.

The Terms of Settlement reaffirmed the Procedure for Avoiding Disputes, including the stage of workshop negotiation added by the 1917 and 1919 Shop Stewards' Agreements. Only regarding general changes in wages and hours or departures from prior agreements, however, did employers have to respect the status quo pending conferences. Management decisions to alter working conditions or implement overtime had to be followed even while appeals were considered. Under the new agreement, if intended changes would "result in one class of workpeople being replaced by another," employers promised to give employee representatives at least ten days' advance notice, during which unionists could initiate discussions. Even in this case employers were entitled to "give a temporary decision" at the stipulated time.

The lockout's settlement placed more stringent limits on the rank and file than on union executives. Employers had never formally conceded to unions a right of prior approval in management decisions; this power had been won informally through workshop organization and vigilance, particularly during World War I. By both incorporating shop stewards in the procedure and exempting management control from certain procedural obstacles, the EEF undercut the independence and strength of workshop organization. In conjunction with heavy unemployment and victimization, the settlement thus consolidated union authority and the priority of official policies in engineering factory politics. EEF policy in 1922, as in 1898, was to use rather than eliminate the union. The claim made in a poster distributed in Coventry was not mere propaganda: "There is no justification for the statement that the Employers' policy is directed towards *smashing the Trade Unions:* on the contrary, the employers *have frequently taken steps to assist the unions* in maintaining their authority over their members, and they will continue to do so."[103]

Coventry's experience during and after the lockout departed from industrywide trends in two respects. First, rank-and-file engineers proved reluctant to join the battle over management prerogatives. Second, although the 1922 Terms of Settlement strengthened official controls over shop-floor activism, in Coventry the consolidation of trade union leadership helped undermine workplace unionism and cleared the way for rank-and-file economism in defiance of craft policies.

Overtime was a major source of contention in Coventry as elsewhere. With unemployment rising, the Coventry AEU District Committee (rather than works committees, as in some other districts) banned overtime in 1919. But many engineers continued to accept overtime, and the District Committee regularly fined errant members in an effort to enforce the ban.[104] As the lockout approached, District Committee officials anxiously warned members that union orders must be followed in stopping and restarting work.[105] Most AEU members did stay away from EEF-affiliated shops on March 11, the first day of the lockout. When EEF firms offered to take back former employees on the employers' terms, however, some returned; and after engineering unions other than the AEU capitulated on June 2, many AEU members resumed work even before their own society gave up the fight on June 13. The numbers of AEU members repudiating the orders of the District Committee and the extent of its alienation from the realities of local conditions are suggested in the lockout's aftermath. Over the next two months a subcommittee of the District Committee fined more than nineteen hundred members—about 20 percent of the local membership—who had returned to or applied for work at Federated establishments before June 13. Naturally, many dropped out of the union rather than pay their fines.[106]

The extent of defections confirms that the principles of craft control fought out in 1922 had limited appeal to Coventry engineers, at least as compared to holding a job. Coventry District Committee officials, by contrast, clung to traditional craft union virtues even at the cost of their own credibility and authority on the shop floor. They admitted, for example, that "by their activities on this [Complaints] Committee [they] have become ostracised by both Employers and Members."[107] Rank-and-file attitudes are also suggested by the precipitous decline in local union membership—a decline more rapid and devastating than in other engineering centers. Coventry AEU membership dropped 57 percent between July 1920 and February 1923. Nationally, AEU losses amounted to 30 percent over the same period.[108] This collapse had many sources, but among them were the unrealistic prosecution of AEU members by District Committee officials and the irrelevance of craft policies to Coventry engineering workers.

The weakness of craft militancy during the 1922 lockout anticipated a broader divergence between union leadership and policies and shop-floor realities in the 1920s. Relatively strong and independent shop committees had provided the foundations for radical factory politics in 1917. The Shop Stewards' Agreement and the 1922 Terms of Settlement restored the authority of District Committee officials, but the principles of craft unionism they followed had diminishing appeal for Coventry workers. As the influence of trade unions inside the factory gates receded and workshop organization atrophied, the problem of unofficial action returned in a new guise: engineers were increasingly free to pursue economistic interests at the expense of craft standards.

Local union leaders and employers in effect cooperated to undermine the position of shop stewards after 1918. Coventry District Committee officials maintained unyielding vigilance against unofficial action for several years following World War I. They did so, of course, when unofficial leadership came from the left: by cooperating as little as possible with the Coventry Unemployed Committee (headed by Communist Party members and several former CWC activists, including Tom Dingley) during the 1922 lockout, the District Committee succeeded in alienating many unemployed AEU members.[109] But District Committee leaders took an equally hard line against shop stewards and individual members who agreed to piecework cuts, running two machines, or overtime, contrary to district rules. In the early 1920s, many engineers had to either accept management orders or lose their jobs, with little hope of finding more work soon. When, after acting through their stewards, engineers chose employment, they found themselves summoned before the District Committee, reprimanded (if they bothered to go), and fined (if they bothered to remain unionists). As for errant stewards, the District Committee would remove them from office and advise their employers (as in a 1920 case) "that we do not recognize their Works Committee."[110] District Committee hostility toward unofficial bargaining within the shops ignored rank-and-file criticisms. One unionist, "questioned as to the temper of the men if Rule was enforced re: not getting conditions of the District, [said] he was afraid it would mean losing a lot of . . . members."[111]

District Committee leaders eventually realized that a diminished membership and weakened shop-floor organization benefited management more than union authority. In October 1922, the Coventry District Committee decided to "revert to the old system of Shop Stewards and appoint such from the membership in the various shops, without in any way notifying the employers upon the matter."[112] This move tacitly conceded both the need for shop stewards (if only to get information on working conditions) and members' reservations about standing up on behalf of union rules for fear of victimization. Secret shop stewards, however, could do little more than report on the sorry state of unionism inside the factory gates. When workers at Armstrong Siddeley agreed to piece price cuts in 1927, the District Committee could only bemoan their impotence. "As we unfortunately could not get the men at this firm to re-institute the Shop Steward System we were . . . in the dark as to what had actually happened. . . . We were more entitled to Cooperation than the Employers, from our members."[113]

Employers encouraged this state of affairs. Radical shop stewards had largely been driven from the shops in 1918. After the war, and especially after 1922, even loyal craft unionists demanding standard rates and adherence to craft rules faced the sack. But most EEA members did not insist on dealing only with individual, nonunion employees. If shop-floor representatives, union stewards or not, proved cooperative, management would meet them to discuss wage rates or piece prices. Such bargaining was not an empty formality. For men willing to abandon union restrictions and accommodate management's efforts to boost productivity, employers were ready with compensating wage increases.[114] Plant-level bargaining had another advantage for employers. The EEA continued to meet unions in local conferences and to abide by agreements concerning grievance procedures and piecework. If disputes did occur, the EEA was quick to support union authority and collective bargaining procedures (including the continuation of work during conferences). By negotiating directly with shop stewards, however, employers could often secure "voluntary" concessions on piece prices, consistent with the "mutuality" clause of national agreements. By insisting that all grievances be handled first between management and workers, as stipulated by the Procedure, the EEA could at once follow industrial relations rules and ensure the union's exclusion from shop affairs: so long as their earnings did not suffer, most engineers would accommodate management, and few would risk their jobs by referring a dispute to local conference.[115] From the District Committee's point of view, shop stewards were thus "doing the dirty work of the Management."[116]

Between unrealistic union policies and self-serving employer tactics, workshop organization lost the strength and independence acquired during the war. This development, combined with advanced dilution, piecework, and chargehand arrangements, produced Coventry's "unofficial" economism. The reform of union structure and industrial relations initiated in 1917 had reinforced craft authority and policies, but unusual characteristics of the labor process in Coventry favored rank-and-file economism. As the AEU lost its hold in the shops and was increasingly excluded from industrial relations procedures, the influence of the labor process proved decisive for factory politics. Engineers traded craft rights for economic concessions—concessions made possible by a highly profitable auto industry (from the mid-1920s) and employers' willingness to reward productivity on a domestic basis.

The rebirth of unionism in the 1930s, ironically, would confirm this two-sided defeat of radical factory politics. On the one hand, new shop stewards filled the long-vacant niches established in 1917, devoting their energies to rebuilding individual unions rather than to developing organizational alternatives on the shop floor. Sectionalism remained intact. On the other hand, resurgent militancy centered on bread-and-butter issues, especially piece prices and bonus times. Isolated from unions and employed under conditions that favored economistic interests, a new generation of workers—mainly semiskilled—had matured untouched by craft traditions. Labor's revival in the 1930s, then, challenged neither union nor management authority; and those authorities, in turn, left no room for workers' control.[117]

Chapter Seven

Bridgeport: Craft Radicalism and Management Control

World War I witnessed an explosion of rank-and-file insurgence in the United States, particularly in the industry most affected by war orders: the metal trades.[1] As in Britain, innovations in local organization and unofficial action laid the groundwork for progressive factory politics. War conditions enabled machinists to organize more successfully at work and to coordinate action with metalworkers of other trades, skills, and plants. Rank-and-file militancy defied union executives and craft boundaries, but unlike the Shop Stewards' Movement it did not develop through novel, unofficial organizations. American Federation of Labor and government policies left local lodge and Metal Trades Council officials sufficient discretion to support popular insurgence. The consequences for factory politics were much the same: local radicals overcame their prewar isolation and were able to lead broadly based rank-and-file action on behalf of progressive goals.

Wartime Militancy in the U.S. Metal Trades

Many of the wartime developments discussed in Chapter Five favored stronger workshop organization among machinists. Munitions production, by accelerating dilution, further eroding craft standards for job classification and pay rates, and speeding the influx of cheap labor, provided clear incentives to organize in self-defense. Had shops remained open and unions weak, such incentives would not have been decisive. After 1914, however, the balance of power between management and labor shifted. Manufacturing techniques gave skilled tool room workers far greater leverage to disrupt output, labor shortages made most employers reluctant to antagonize their employees, and the government provided some protection for collective bargaining and union activity on the job. War conditions reversed the prewar open-shop drive and greatly enhanced union power—especially on the shop floor.

Union and government policies encouraged organization on the job in other ways and ensured that rank-and-file power would be exercised unconstitutionally. National IAM leaders were slow to grasp new opportunities, warning members in 1915 not to "engage in strikes carelessly or thoughtlessly. . . . More lasting progress can be made by patient negotiation than by reckless stoppage of work."[2] Yet under war conditions a "reckless stoppage of work" often gained concessions. By organizing in the shops, machinists could win demands without having to wait for constitutional strike procedures—or, given the labor market, without worrying over strike benefits. In the heady year of 1915, 136 of the 179 strikes *recorded* for machinists were unsanctioned.[3] While IAM officials devoted their attention to extending the eight-hour day and raising wages, local action forced concessions on issues of more concern to the members (such as shop committee recognition, restrictions on piecework, or checks on obnoxious supervision). Autonomous organization provided the means to pursue these alternative goals.

Workshop vigilance became still more imperative with U.S. entry into World War I. Given the unprecedented opportunities to settle old scores with employers, machinists refused to be bound by the IAM Executive's no-strike pledge. Because machinists could not expect Grand Lodge support, they had to rely on shop committees and, in many cases, sympathetic local labor leaders to prepare demands, meet management, and conduct strikes. Machinists were also unwilling to accept the AFL's renunciation of demands for union recognition and the closed shop, goals long sought but now seemingly within reach. Here, too, strikes to win union shops had to be managed independently of national IAM officials. Despite the IAM's refusal to back and the government's refusal to enforce such demands, they were advanced frequently and often won de facto employer compliance (e.g., dismissing a nonunion worker in order to keep the peace).[4]

From 1917, government intervention further encouraged rank-and-file independence. In effect, adjustment boards and mediation agencies rewarded unofficial strikes, for with heavy schedules only the most pressing cases were dealt with quickly. Work stoppages satisfied government criteria for urgency, so walkouts often expedited settlements.[5] Even when strikes did not bring prompt government action, they sometimes forced concessions from employers and thus circumvented long and distant procedures for resolving disputes. Such direct action retained for machinists a measure of local control at a time when union leaders and government officials alike pressed for centralized bargaining.[6]

By bringing workers of different trades and skills together in joint action under common leadership, local organization challenged not only the IAM Executive's authority but also basic principles of craft unionism sanctified by the AFL. Solidary movements in Britain involved the formation of institutions separate from established unions, notably the Workers' Committees. In the United States, by contrast, existing local bodies extended their constituencies and assumed new powers in defiance of national policy. Before World War I, Metal Trades Councils (MTCs) had enjoyed little discretion under AFL rules, sparse support in the shops, and negligible influence with employers. From 1915, they became far more militant and effective agencies for joint action, leading the president of the Metal Trades Department to complain that "local Councils have assumed an authority that lies only with the international organization, thereby putting the Council in the position of being the supreme authority. . . . [This] has resulted in strikes being ordered without the constitutions of our affiliated organizations or of this Department being complied with. Such strikes have . . . created much friction between the local unions and the executive officers."[7]

On their own authority IAM lodges also cooperated with activists from other unions and allowed unorganized and less skilled workers to participate in local decisions. District meetings in 1918 to plan a spring offensive throughout New York City, for example, included representatives of machinists' helpers as well as craftsmen.[8] Machinists' shop committees did not generally include representatives from other crafts or grades. But as the strongest union voice in most munitions plants, they seem to have assumed leadership in factorywide disputes. The 1915 strike in East Pittsburgh is a dramatic example. Here forty thousand workers, ignoring AFL orders, followed toolmakers in a ten-day walkout, which shut down numerous firms affiliated with Westinghouse.[9]

These developments altered the terrain of conflict, overcoming prewar obstacles to workers' control struggles. Shop committees acquired a new independence from both employer and union constraints. At work, militants gained a measure of security from management reprisals, and shop committees secured some recognition in day-to-day negotiations. Within the labor movement, stronger workshop organization and resurgent unionism reinforced each other at the expense of national IAM authority. The increasing power of local lodges meant that shop committees could expect more outside backing in their battles with employers. Militant support from the shops, in turn, strengthened the position of MTC and lodge officials—officials often representing or willing to represent a broadened coalition of metalworkers—vis-à-vis Metal Trades Department and IAM leaders.

U.S. metalworkers never constructed organizational alternatives to craft unionism (equivalent to Workers' Committees or the National Administrative Council of the Shop Stewards' Movement) because local leaders were able to accommodate rank-and-file insurgence. Union and government policies placed no restrictions on local action before 1917 and comparatively mild ones thereafter. IAM lodges and MTCs, unlike their British counterparts, were thus free to pursue common policies and mount joint action on an informal basis. Their growing ties to shop committees allowed city officials to coordinate local strategy more effectively than before 1914.

Under these conditions union lodges and MTCs became effective vehicles for rank-and-file action and gave local militants (including members of socialist parties and the IWW) a promising base from which to recruit popular support. Progressive factory politics in both countries developed independently of and in opposition to national labor executives. Radical leadership in Britain, however, was of necessity rooted on the shop floor or in unofficial committees; in the United States it could be exercised through local union offices. By 1919, IAM representatives in New York, Newark, Buffalo, Chicago, and many northwestern shipbuilding centers were denouncing the infiltration of locals and the unofficial strikes instigated by advocates of "One Big Union."[10] AFL and IAM leaders responded to the challenge by revoking the charters of dissident unions (e.g., Detroit's Carriage, Wagon, and Auto Workers' Union) and lodges (e.g., in New York and Bridgeport), suspending One Big Union enthusiasts from membership, and passing laws prohibiting "outside organizations from taking a strike vote of the membership of international organizations connected with the American Federation of Labor."[11]

Ideological as well as institutional conditions favored a convergence of progressive leadership and rank-and-file insurgence. By 1917, demands formulated by left-wing activists had gained popular support among privileged and highly skilled machinists as well as semiskilled machine tenders. When unions repudiated strikes and collaborated with the government at the expense of local interests and representation, proposals for more democratic and accountable forms of industrial government had considerable appeal. As unions spurned unprecedented opportunities to win management concessions (for closed shops or work rules), metalworkers would tentatively endorse more ambitious programs for workers' control.

Metalworkers of varied skills and political orientations united behind two specific demands raised with growing frequency during the war's final year: shop committee recognition and occupational classification. For radicals, shop committees would lay the foundation for a democratic industrial unionism and workers' control of production.[12] For many metalworkers, the proposal was less ideologically charged but still compelling—a means to consolidate gains made in the shops, to restore a measure of direct control lost to union bureaucrats, and to have a greater voice in management decisions. The call to classify jobs into relatively broad categories, each with minimum wage rates, also facilitated alliances. As a matter of practical self-interest, classification would protect the status and income of skilled machinists against individualized pay and dilution. But proposals extending classification to specialists, semiskilled operatives, and helpers could forge all-grades coalitions against management control of the labor process. Proposals for classification and shop committee recognition reinforced each other; shop committees, it was hoped, would take responsibility for administering classification systems.[13]

Even where most fully developed, these were fragile accomplishments. Machinists and toolmakers always faced the temptation to use their sectional power for exclusive gains. They could, for example, abandon encompassing classification schemes in favor of wage increases benefiting only themselves. Shop committee recognition could also cut both ways, cementing alliances between rank-and-file machinists and militant local leaders or being captured as company unions.[14] As in Britain, the outcome of these dilemmas varied with organizational and ideological conditions. Conflicts in Bridgeport, Connecticut, clearly illustrate the dynamics of wartime factory politics, from radicalization to containment.

The Development of Radical Factory Politics in Bridgeport

Bridgeport saw only three work stoppages in 1914, and as late as March 1915, employers confidently predicted that, despite the efforts of outside agitators, "it is hardly likely that any serious trouble will occur."[15] But over the summer of 1915, fifty-five strikes swept the city. Machinists and ironworkers at Remington struck in mid-July to secure the eight-hour day, and IAM Lodge 30 gradually extended the dispute to Remington subcontractors. By July 22, Remington and its subcontractors (having been urged by Britain to grant demands and promised compensating price allowances) conceded the eight-hour day with ten hours' pay. This victory inspired new offensives against other Bridgeport firms, and on August 14 the Manufacturers' Association of Bridgeport recommended that all local firms adopt a fifty-hour weekly schedule. Thirty-one thousand Bridgeport employees, including thirty-seven hundred machinists, had won the eight-hour day by the end of August.[16]

The scale and success of this offensive was unprecedented, but the political character of industrial unrest in 1915 closely resembled the prewar norm. As before 1914, craftsmen from different departments and plants acted together solely in the interests of shorter hours and higher wages. Only in isolated cases did machinists put forward demands concerning workplace control (e.g., the abolition of piecework or shop committee recognition). This pattern reflects problems inherited from before the war. With machinists still poorly organized on the job, and ties between them and city union officials still insecure, general economic interests alone united craftsmen against Bridgeport employers. Machinists also lacked an independent base within the shops from which to pursue concerns other than those favored by established local and national union officials.

The same obstacles affected relations with less skilled workers. No organizational bridges between grades of workers laid the basis for either common action or alternatives to official craft union policies. Having won the eight-hour day for themselves, machinists took no part in a wave of strikes among less skilled workers in August. They offered no support to women as employers gradually retracted concessions on working hours for their female employees.[17] When specialists at Remington-UMC proposed to strike against the introduction of scientific management in 1916, the most highly skilled machinists made their indifference clear. "The tool and gauge makers who are getting 63 cents per hour are perfectly satisfied and a number of them remarked that in case of a strike they will stick to their jobs."[18] IAM leaders, for their part, were hardly disposed to lend less skilled workers a helping hand.

Neither rank-and-file organization nor local union officials, then, favored departures from economistic and sectional factory politics in the first two years of the war. Between 1916 and 1917, however, craftsmen gradually strengthened their position at work; and in May 1917, they voted in a new union leadership.

Machinists' efforts to organize on the job faced strong opposition from Bridgeport employers, who denounced shop committee recognition. The city's Manufacturers' Association declared publicly in 1915, "The members of this association will not be dictated to by any shop committee relating to the management or operation of their respective plants or the right to hire whom they see fit or to discharge for cause, and the members will continue . . . to run an absolutely open shop."[19] But with labor scarce and employers eager to avoid strikes, many smaller firms and some large ones grudgingly agreed to discuss grievances with shop representatives— grievances that included infringements on the eight-hour day, victimization of union activists, payment by results, and overtime.[20] Failure to meet shop delegates or consider demands sometimes resulted in strikes, called and managed by the committees.[21]

Contrary to conditions before the war or in Coventry in 1917, these committees were closely tied to Lodge 30 or to the newly formed District 55 (incorporating all local lodges) of the IAM. Local union officials were not, like their British counterparts, significantly constrained by national union or government policies in their conduct of trade policy. Lodge 30 urged "each shop [to] elect its own committee of three, and be ready for any advice from the business agent."[22] It was at union headquarters, in meetings led by lodge officials, that employees elected shop committees, discussed grievances, and formulated demands.[23] The union local delegated to shop committees responsibility for reporting on factory conditions and, given prior approval for a strike, calling members out if employers refused demands.[24] By mid-1917, district officials had developed an unprecedented capacity to coordinate rank-and-file action on a citywide basis.

Wartime organization among Bridgeport machinists also crossed skill and craft lines. Broadened solidarities expressed outside of and at odds with the Coventry ASE District Committee found a home within the IAM's local organization. Lodge 30 admitted to full membership many less skilled workers not eligible under the IAM constitution. Beginning in 1916, local leaders also made efforts to organize women and, with greater success, to establish lodges for Scandinavian machinists and Polish specialists.[25] Such experiments in solidary organization are visible in day-to-day procedures as well as formal policy. In many shop meetings convened to vote on demands or strikes, all attending participated, regardless of union affiliation, skill, or sex.[26] Similar procedures may have been adopted in the election of shop committees, giving them cross-sectional constituencies comparable to those of many Coventry stewards.[27] Lodge officials, representing the most powerful union in Bridgeport, also took the lead in arranging joint action among different crafts. Business Agent George Bowen, for example, secured the support of molders in several 1916 machinists' strikes; his successor, Sam Lavit, joined the local Metal Polishers' Union president in conducting a 1917 strike at Remington despite a settlement agreed to by national Metal Polishers' officials.[28]

By early 1917, then, many of the prewar obstacles to radical factory politics had been overcome. Machinists enjoyed greater security from employer reprisals. Cooperation with workers of other crafts and grades had become more firmly rooted in shop-floor and district institutions and practices, and shop committees, previously isolated, were more firmly integrated into citywide union organization.

Local IAM leadership, however, remained in moderate hands. From the war's outset until May 1917, "the Bowen clique" ruled Lodge 30.[29] Like many of his contemporaries in IAM office, George Bowen preferred his politics socialist and his trade unionism pure and simple. Militant in pursuit of shorter hours and higher wages, Bowen was reluctant to push control demands or support rank-and-file organizers within the factories. "He does not care what other conditions they have as long as they are working 48 hours with an hour for lunch."[30] When employees at the Bridgeport Projectile Company met to consider action against the firm's incentive pay scheme in April 1916, Bowen showed "very little interest in this movement for eliminating the piecework system."[31] In July, Remington-UMC workers proposed to strike in support of a victimized shop steward. The business agent thought otherwise. "Hearth's case has been dropped, and there is some hard feeling against Bowen, who neglected to call a special meeting in reference to this man's case. . . . Bowen said it was not the policy of the officials of this organization to call a special meeting for every man who gets discharged."[32] Nor had Bowen much concern for less skilled workers, dismissing auto repairman (who had applied for union membership) as "so cheap he does not like to have them in the organization."[33]

Against Bowen stood a group of industrial unionists (among them several former Wobblies) headed by Sam Lavit and actively involved in shop-floor organizing campaigns.[34] After a year of shouting matches and occasional fist fights between the two factions at chaotic union meetings, Lavit defeated Bowen for business agent of IAM District 55 in May 1917. The victory came in the midst of a new wave of resentment over Bowen's indifference toward two victimized activists at Remington-UMC, and fellow industrial unionists from Lavit's organizing committee won other local offices as well.[35] The election tentatively unified rank-and-file machinists under radical local leadership and appeared to be a mandate for the concerted pursuit of control demands.

The organizational changes consolidated by Lavit's election laid the groundwork for radical factory politics in Bridgeport. In August 1917, District 55 officials presented employers with an ambitious set of proposals worked out in shop and union meetings during the summer.[36] The union's key demand was for a classification of occupations into a relatively small number of job categories, each with a minimum wage rate. Toolmakers, diemakers, and gauge, jig, and fixture makers would receive no less than 60 cents per hour; machinists and toolsetters (machine setup men), 50 cents; automatic and hand-operated screw machine operators, 45 cents; specialists and machine operators, 43 cents; machinists' helpers, 38 cents; and apprentices, a scale of minimum rates increasing with each year of their terms. In addition machinists called for management recognition of shop committees to negotiate grievances. If plant conferences failed to reach an agreement, disputes would be referred to a committee of arbitration in which union officials could participate. It seems to have been assumed that shop committees would take part in administering the details of classification in each factory.[37]

These goals challenged prevailing management practices and advanced interests shared by a wide range of metalworkers. Classification certainly appealed to skilled workers because it guaranteed a standard minimum rate, curtailed "reclassification" to lower job titles, and prohibited the replacement of skilled men by dilutees at lower wages. But the principle of classification reflected neither sectional interests nor a nostalgic defense of craft standards. Protections sought by machinists were extended to less skilled machine operatives and helpers, and District 55 soon added to its platform the call for equal pay for women doing men's work—a demand that emerged from joint action by the IAM and the Metal Polishers against Remington's hiring of women at lower rates.[38] Machinists' efforts to win support from less skilled Bridgeport workers is suggested as well by their August request for a 10 percent wage hike for "all machinists and others employed in the machine industry."

The demand for classification also marked a progressive alternative to defending the craft status quo—but without abandoning the ethic of the trade. Bridgeport machinists clearly recognized that the traditional insistence on standard craft rates for skilled workers (ignoring those who failed to make the grade) was an unrealistic response to specialization and dilution. Conceding the division of labor and deskilling, they now aimed to replace *management* arrangements for organizing (or disorganizing) employees with an all-grades scheme of their own. In defending the machinists' program, moreover, Lavit attacked not specialization but specialization at the expense of workers. When an employer keeps a toolmaker on a single machine because it is profitable to do so, Lavit argued, that worker should still be paid the toolmaker's rate. Even if "he is not given the privilege of doing all of the work," such a worker should be rewarded according to his acquired skill, not his contribution to the firm's profits.[39] This argument adapts the craftsman's producer ethic to a radical critique of management control. By extending this principle down to specialists and machine operators, machinists proposed to prevent employers from diluting or subdividing tasks at the expense of workers as a whole.

The demand for shop committee recognition, similarly, both threatened management and appealed to a broad range of workers. Recognition would have consolidated union organization in Bridgeport at both the plant and city levels, thus violating cherished open-shop principles. Unionized machinists would not have been the only ones to gain from this concession. Regular grievance procedures supported by unions were attractive to many Bridgeport workers, long familiar with unaccountable and arbitrary supervision.

Labor militancy in Bridgeport had come a long way since 1915, when machinists had struggled for shorter hours and higher pay. The 1917 demands focused instead on workplace control, seeking to limit employers' discretion in classifying workers and to secure for representative shop committees a voice in factory management. Unlike the 1915 situation, this was the program of the entire machinists' organization, not of individual shop committees. The prewar isolation of control struggles had been overcome by a unification of shop and citywide bodies. Further, as local IAM organization in part transcended divisions of skill, so too did the demands advanced in late 1917, encompassing specialists, machine operators, helpers, and women. These strategies once again contrast with those of 1915, when machinists took no part in the activities of less skilled workers.

These initiatives did not, as in Coventry, pit rank-and-file machinists against their union local. Instead, the shift in factory politics between 1915 and 1917 depended on lodge officials' leadership. Bridgeport's radicalism did, however, involve a clear break with sectional trade union authority insofar as the local branch, contrary to national IAM policies and constitution, allowed less skilled workers and members of other crafts to participate in shop meetings and made semiskilled operatives the beneficiaries of union demands. The line of cleavage ran not between unofficial organization and national and district bodies, but between local organization (and its unauthorized policies) and Grand Lodge leadership. The contrast to Coventry reflects a difference in timing. Whereas in Britain the unofficial movement developed amid constraints on local leaders, by the time IAM and government restrictions took effect, Bridgeport radicals had already captured local control. Insurgence thus involved less friction between formal unions and rank-and-file organization and more between machinists and their local leaders on one side and national authority on the other.

A comparison of two 1917 strikes illustrates both the importance of local leadership and its relation to Grand Lodge authority. In March, Business Agent Bowen and IAM Executive Board member T. J. Savage threatened a strike against Remington when that company reinstated the ten-hour day and discharged several IAM activists. But Bowen called off the strike when IAM officials, government conciliators, and Remington representatives agreed to return to a basic eight-hour schedule and pay overtime rates, with Bowen defeating efforts by "certain so-called radicals" to mobilize a strike on the issue of discrimination.[40]

By July, Sam Lavit and his colleagues headed Bridgeport's union. When eight hundred metal polishers struck Remington over the hiring of women at lower wages, among other issues, some machinists came out in sympathy, and Lavit lent his union's support to local Metal Polishers' President Joseph Marchand. National union leaders and government mediators reached an agreement with Remington guaranteeing the piece rates of males along with a forty-eight-hour week and overtime pay. Lavit and Marchand, however, convinced strikers to hold out until the company promised equal pay to women for equal work and agreed to discuss grievances with a shop committee.[41] Under new leadership, Bridgeport metalworkers thus pressed new kinds of issues and departed from the sectional orientation clear before 1917. In doing so local unionists began moving away from their national leadership. The tension was heightened during 1918 as District 55 leaders and members defied the IAM's renunciation of strikes and the closed shop and, in pursuit of their goals, the AFL's no-strike pledge.[42]

The battle over classification and shop committee recognition pitted Bridgeport machinists against well-organized employers and, at times, government and IAM officials. Employers ignored the August demands except to seek criminal action against union leaders for conspiracy against the government. From September to February 1918, machinists pursued district demands through the threat of a general strike and by attempting to negotiate with (or downing tools at) individual firms. These efforts won only token concessions from a few manufacturers and, in February, a War Department promise to settle the dispute—a promise that remained empty for the next four months.[43]

At this point the dilemmas of radical factory politics in Bridgeport become clearer. The August program had emerged from a tenuous synthesis of craft power and industrial unionist goals. Innovations in local organization and progressive leadership had made that synthesis possible. But local officials' hold over rank-and-file machinists had limits, as did their ability to unite workers of varied skills behind an all-grades program of workers' control. Between February and June, craftsmen became increasingly frustrated by employer and government procrastination. The continued recruitment of women at lower wages, the differential between machinists' earnings and rates paid to their counterparts in shipbuilding, and the fact that skilled men were threatened with the draft if they left their employment all intensified the sectional grievances of craft workers.[44]

Under these conditions union officials were unable to prevent the most highly skilled workers from using their strategic power for exclusive ends. At the beginning of March, Remington toolmakers and machinists prepared for War Department consideration a set of demands that departed from the August program.

They retained their insistence on equal pay for women and, in somewhat veiled form, on shop committee recognition. But they requested minimum rates only for toolmakers, machinists, and machine shop specialists, dropping helpers and production workers from the classification scheme.[45] IAM members advanced this same, more sectional demand for minimum rates in strikes at Remington, Liberty Ordnance, and twenty-two subcontract shops from May 3 to May 11. The strikes took place over the objection of IAM and AFL officials and added a demand for the closed shop—a demand AFL leaders had agreed not to make during the war.[46] The strikes ended only after Major Rodgers of the War Department promised an award by June 1, retroactive to May 1, and pledged support for the principles of minimum rates and equal pay for women.

The War Department's decision, finally issued on June 8, was a qualified victory for District 55 members. The award laid down minimum rates for toolmakers, toolroom specialists, all-around machinists, and certain machine shop specialists. Machinists accepted the decision at a mass meeting June 14, although they protested the lower minimum rates assigned to some specialists and the apparent exclusion of others from the award. Many Bridgeport firms, however, refused to accept the War Department's ruling. Bridgeport machinists were outraged. On June 24, American and British Company employees came out. A mass meeting the same day voted for a general strike if manufacturers refused to comply with the award. Secretary of War Newton Baker then announced that matters would be taken up by the National War Labor Board; in the meantime "a strike if called will not be against the employers who are acting under instructions but against your government, such action directed against your government at a time of national emergency I cannot believe will be taken by any group of Americans."[47] This setting aside of the War Department's own settlement, together with the aspersions cast on the workers' patriotism, led to a reaffirmation of strike plans unless written assurances were forthcoming that a new award would be strictly enforced. Despite further pleas from NWLB officials, IAM President Johnston, and even Sam Lavit, seven thousand machinists at Remington, Liberty Ordnance, Bullard Machine Company, and the twenty-two subcontract shops struck June 26. A formal NWLB statement giv-

ing the requested promises persuaded strikers to resume work
June 28.[48]

The strikes between March and June indicate a partial retreat
from the all-grades program of 1917. Machinists' demands no
longer included production workers or helpers, but they did still
insist on the principle of classification and extended it to specialists
for whom the IAM generally had little concern. These strikes also
retained a commitment to equal pay for women. They also reflected a tremendous advance in local organization since 1915.
Classification had become the basis for a movement, which, by
June, mobilized seven thousand machinists at firms throughout
Bridgeport—and did so despite the fact that challenges to craft
standards varied enormously, from the factory conditions in Remington's tool rooms to the more bespoke methods of small subcontractors. When the NWLB began holding hearings early in July,
moreover, District 55 once again presented an all-grades program.
Local leaders asked the Board to grant classification and minimum
rates for "toolmakers, machinists, automatic and hand screw machines, toolsetters, specialists and operatives, and machinists'
helpers."[49]

The conflicting interests that had led to unsanctioned strikes
earlier in the year reappeared during hearings before the NWLB
in July. Employers, national union representatives, and local leaders found little common ground in debates over the proper goals
and organization of labor. Employers claimed that classification
would subject them to outside interference, disrupt war production, and undermine the time-proven method of rewarding individual merit. By assigning workers individualized rates along an
occupational scale, employers had channeled each employee's self-
interest into greater productivity for the enterprise—and the nation—as a whole. By providing a ladder for promotion and incentives to climb it, the tremendous task of recruiting and training
green hands was smoothly managed. Such a scheme, however,
could and should be laid down *only* by employers: they alone had
the experience and firsthand knowledge necessary to rate each
worker properly. Manufacturers wished to establish from the start
that classification was their business and wages the concern of the
NWLB. If justice could be done in wage matters, then why should
the Board meddle with management affairs, at great risk to effi-

ciency and, by implication, to national security? "We ask that the board leave that classification to us, provided we keep pace with the cost of living. (Mr. Walsh:) To you and your employees? (Mr. Merritt:) No, to the manufacturers and employers entirely. . . . What more have the workers the right to ask, under the circumstances, than that their wages have grown progressively with the cost of living?"[50]

IAM representatives countered that a principle of employment was at stake, not simply money. The right of machinists to safeguard their skill and the right of all metalworkers to protection from arbitrary reclassification justified restrictions on management's authority to classify and remunerate employees as they saw fit. "We are going to take it for granted, as already proved, that the cost of living does warrant a raise in wages. . . . As far as the other principles are concerned, they are, of course, different. . . . I contend that there should be established a minimum rate to apply to different classes of labor."[51]

The hearings also reveal more muted conflicts between national and local IAM officials. Fred Hewitt, representing the Executive Board, ultimately based labor's case on the increased cost of living and parity with the earnings of machinists elsewhere. This was a rationale compatible with employer arguments, and the concession smoothed the way for a massive investigation of local wages and prices with which manufacturers deluged the Board. Sam Lavit and J. J. Keppler (an IAM vice-president who worked closely with local leaders throughout the war), by contrast, maintained that "it is not so much the wage as it is classification."[52] When Lavit complained that in Bridgeport factories a man "breaks in a woman, and then he is politely removed, and the girl remains for 25 cents an hour," he emphasized, "I am speaking for the local situation, while my colleagues speak for the country."[53] By highlighting questions of wages and economic equity, however, national spokesmen defined the "problem" in such a way that local concerns would be ignored.

A second tension between local and national representatives concerned the proper beneficiaries of classification. The demands District 55 presented covered specialists, production workers, and helpers as well as machinists. Lavit insisted that specialists fell within the local machinists' jurisdiction. In rejecting employer arguments that the Board focus on wages alone, Keppler stated, "Until we hear from the other side, as to what they intend doing as to specialists, and classifying them, possibly we can not go further on the question of rates."[54] Yet Hewitt tended to speak on behalf of machinists and toolmakers alone, and he appeared uncomfortable with the involvement of specialists and operatives within District 55.[55] His attitude is clearer in a statement made at closed hearings before the War Department on May 23: "If you are going to load yourself up with specialists, men who do a certain part of a certain job, that is a different proposition. We haven't presented demands for a minimum rate covering from the highest skilled man down to a man who sweeps the floor."[56]

Ironically, it was the employers who urged that the NWLB award cover all workers—more than fifty thousand—in all fifty-three firms represented before the Board, from toolmakers, carpenters, and electricians to machine hands and floor sweepers. This charitable initiative was justified on the grounds that a sectional award would create unrest among those excluded. Perhaps as important, the inclusion of all crafts and grades helped define the Board's task as addressing the *economic* needs of *all* workers. Under this agenda, machinists' peculiar workplace concerns over dilution, piecework, and arbitrary authority were given short shrift. The NWLB, unable to agree on an award, referred the case to an umpire; meanwhile Bridgeport machinists staged a brief strike at Remington and Bullard to speed the decision. On August 28, the umpire issued an award denying classification in favor of a scale of wage increases pegged to an individual's existing pay rate. The higher one's earnings, the smaller the wage increase; those already making more than 78 cents an hour received no raise at all.[57]

Two days later seven thousand machinists—reiterating the demand for classification and minimum rates for all grades of metalworkers—struck in defiance of the Board.[58] The decision to strike was made in "open meetings where munitions workers, regardless of their affiliation with local 55, participated in the debate and voting."[59] Suggestions from IAM officials that members secure their back pay under the award in lieu of classification were "jeered"; threats that their charter would be withdrawn if a strike occurred were met with cries of "take it." "Local men have long counted on losing charter and have appealed to all Unions to join them in calling a convention to depose International officers if they outlaw a strike."[60]

The strike was a general one, including not only firms and subcontractors directly engaged in war work but also nonmunitions firms such as Locomobile and American Graphophone. Once again Bridgeport machinists demonstrated their ability to rally on a citywide basis for all-grades control demands. Some strikers, of course, were particularly outraged by the small wage increases awarded skilled men, especially given the high earnings of less qualified pieceworkers.[61] But under radical leadership sectional concerns were harnessed behind a progressive assault on management control. Widespread resentments over arbitrary and dictatorial management practices, government procrastination, and profiteering also helped cement an alliance behind progressive leaders. Indeed, a September 6, 1918, meeting of machinists requested President Woodrow Wilson "to take over all Munitions plants here." Unionists "will work for any wage for the government but not for private capital."[62]

Bridgeport's strike found sympathetic echoes elsewhere in the country. War Department agents in Hartford, Springfield, New York, and Philadelphia "report[ed] that production is slowing up perceptibly, and that the other scattering labor troubles at the munitions plants are all brought about by a determination of the organized workmen to back up the Bridgeport machinists and compel a classification of skilled workers." Some plans were allegedly made in these cities to strike September 11 if Bridgeport's demands were not met.[63] On September 11, however, IAM President Johnston issued an ultimatum that Bridgeport machinists had forty-eight hours to return to work and abide by the award; if they remained out, they would be expelled from the union. This action may have curbed sympathetic action in other munitions centers— unlike the British shop stewards' movement, there existed no national "unofficial" organization in the United States through which machinists might have organized a general strike in defiance of Grand Lodge authority. The ultimatum did not get the machinists back to work in Bridgeport, however. Instead, a September 11 mass meeting, after denouncing Johnston, voted to stay out until President Wilson responded to their appeal to take over Bridgeport's munitions plants.[64]

President Wilson's answer came on Friday, September 13. Machinists were reminded that classification could still be discussed under procedures laid down in the award. President Wilson then ordered strikers back to work. Any man still out after September 16 would lose his draft exemption and be blacklisted from all city munitions work for a year. Meeting September 16, the workers voted to comply, defending their strike and the principle of classification in a respectful but unrepentant reply to Wilson. At the same meeting machinists resolved "to form an 'American Labor Party,' for the express purpose of exercising their political rights, as an instrument of industrial emancipation, thus paving the way for an autonomous industrial republic (shop control) in the factories, mines, mills and other establishments wherein workers are employed."[65]

Containment

Bridgeport militancy was not turned back by presidential power alone. Government intervention to settle the 1918 disputes helped isolate radical leaders from rank-and-file machinists and limited the influence of craft interests on factory politics. At work, more systematic procedures for classifying, promoting, and disciplining employees undermined the solidarities among craftsmen and between grades that had developed during the war. Industrial relations reforms and features of the labor process combined to block the mobilization of control struggles in Bridgeport.

The NWLB sought a permanent solution for labor unrest by establishing a system of collective bargaining through shop committees (a common feature of NWLB and Shipbuilding Labor Adjustment Board awards)[66] and a local board of mediation. The plan required shop committee elections in every plant—elections not by members of particular unions or crafts but by all department employees. Chairmen from each department body, in turn, formed an Employees' General Committee. The NWLB's electoral procedures tended to dilute craft representation and union influence on shop committees because craft unionists were usually not strong enough to control departmentwide elections. In addition, management-initiated employee representation schemes won NWLB approval in at least five firms, while elsewhere NWLB committees replaced already-established union committees.[67] The NWLB committees set up to negotiate with employers were, in any case, powerless. Departmental and General Committees "shall not have Executive or veto powers, such as the right to decide who shall, or shall not, receive an increase in wage; how a certain operation shall, or shall not, be performed, etc."[69] Willard Aborn, NWLB administrator for Bridgeport, saw shop committees as vehicles for "inplant cooperation" rather than collective bargaining ("which included only the employees' side"). Employee representation would make it possible for manufacturers "to hear employee suggestions for improving operating methods, and to let the employees know something of the company's problems and to receive their assistance in solving them."[69]

The NWLB scheme operated against local union influence in another respect. Grievances not resolved by plant committees were forwarded to a Local Board of Mediation and Conciliation, with three labor and three employer representatives. Labor representatives were chosen in September 1918 at a citywide convention attended by delegates selected in earlier plant elections. That convention, dominated by the IAM, elected Sam Lavit, David Clydesdale (chairman of the strike committee in September), and Patrick Scollins (a UMC worker and former hatmaker in the ill-fated Danbury union).[70] Under the NWLB scheme, however, no union was formally involved in adjusting grievances, and government officials did their best to exclude union leaders from administering other aspects of the award. When the NWLB's Bridgeport administrator extended the period during which former employees could apply for retroactive pay, Lavit, Clydesdale, and Scollins requested a list of claimants so they could notify them of the extension. Willard Aborn cautioned NWLB officials against doing so, arguing that Lavit was merely trying to get credit for the extension. NWLB Secretary Jett Lauck agreed and telegrammed Lavit that claimants "will be notified directly by this office."[71]

The Local Board of Mediation guaranteed the impotence of individual shop committees. Employee representatives could, in principle, address issues of workplace control. Indeed, assurances that classification could be worked out through the collective bargaining scheme were important in getting machinists back to work on September 17. Because shop committees and employers were hardly likely to agree on classification, however, the issue would be referred to the Local Board, which, conveniently, had no permanent, voting chair. Employer and labor representatives, equally balanced, inevitably stalemated on any question of importance. A former mediator in the Ordnance Department who was involved in Bridgeport affairs found this failure to complete the Board "somewhat more than an accident."[72] In vain Lavit requested "such machinery that we can immediately press home [demands for classification and minimum rates] through each shop. . . . We submit that advancing demands through a balanced committee of six, with a powerless head, to the deadlocked War Labor Board will profit us nothing and merely waste our time."[73] After many fruitless conferences labor delegates to the Board finally resigned in March 1919 to protest its purely decorative role.[74]

The NWLB shop committee scheme undermined the organizational base for workers' control movements in Bridgeport. It did so, first, by breaking the links between shop committees and city-wide union leadership. George Hawley, general manager of Bridgeport's Manufacturers' Association, described the system as an "experiment in employee representation, through which collective bargaining has been combined with the open shop."[75] In effect the NWLB had reinstituted a modified form of prewar industrial relations, giving shop committees a somewhat more formal status but isolating them from union influences. Second, the NWLB's committees were elected by all workers, regardless of craft or union, and replaced union committees already in operation. Shop committees thus constituted diluted craft interests as well as union influence on the job.

This reorganization of workplace representation put radical local officials in a dilemma: although NWLB committees were nominally democratic and cross-sectional, they were ineffective for pursuing classification and other demands rooted in the craft tradition. Lavit and his colleagues could push these issues and strengthen the union's position in the factories only by demanding exclusive craft committees and abandoning the less skilled and the unorganized. In addition, a wedge had been driven between machinists on one side and specialists and production workers on the other by the NWLB's wage award, giving the greatest increases to those of lesser skill. Lavit was thus forced to request that "the workers who were not signatory to this case's complaint be not included in its administration, although asking that they share fully in its benefits. This ruling will produce a workers' committee of tried and true men and women who have been tested and found to be capable of truly representing the workers."[76] The request was denied.

By expanding the constituencies of nonunion shop committees, the government diluted the social base for control struggles and blocked the coordination of such protest by a radical union local. Under the new organizational conditions radicals could pursue control issues only on an exclusive basis; and as the strikes of 1919 would show, they could mount broadly based collective action only on economistic grounds. The NWLB's scheme and subsequent policies began the isolation of radical leaders that postwar unemployment and blacklisting would complete.

Some Bridgeport employers complained that the NWLB plan had been "really shoved down [their] throats," "in many instances against their will and better judgement."[77] In fact the Manufacturers' Association had considered and endorsed similar schemes for employee representation well before September 1918, partly to meet government collective bargaining requirements and partly in pursuit of "proper working relations between employer and employees, lower labor turnover, and increased efficiency and production."[78] When NWLB jurisdiction ceased and the Local Board of Mediation and Conciliation dissolved in March 1919, the Manufacturers' Association also had ready a new scheme for employee representation. This "Bridgeport Plan" was virtually identical to that of the NWLB, but it omitted a citywide mediation committee of the sort dominated, on labor's side, by Sam Lavit. Once again elections obscured occupational identities, grievance procedures shut out union influence, and employee committees lacked the authority to challenge management in any meaningful way. More than thirty-five local firms adopted the plan in April 1919, and although attrition was high, a year later twenty companies employing thirty thousand workers (about half the city's total) still maintained shop committees under the employers' plan. This record made Bridgeport "the industrial center in which the formation of Works Councils has progressed furthest"[79] in what was a national movement extending employee representation to about 500,000 workers in 1919 (a large majority of them in the metal trades) and to 1,400,000 by 1926.[80]

The NWLB and Bridgeport plans for employee representation dovetailed with workplace reforms intended to secure more harmonious relations between labor and management. During the war leading manufacturers showed increased concern to secure the willing cooperation of employees. With up to three thousand workers shifting jobs every week, thus bidding up wages and disrupting shop organization, employers hoped to lower the turnover rate.[81] Another aim was to secure labor peace and reduce the influence of "outside agitators." One strategy for meeting these goals involved welfare programs, which often made benefits contingent on loyalty to the firm and in some cases linked participation to schemes of employee representation.[82] More important, however, were efforts to rationalize wage grades and job ladders and to administer these systematically. Here, too, employers hoped to check turnover (in part by reducing foremen's discretion in hiring and firing); to meet the unprecedented need for recruiting, training, and upgrading inexperienced workers; and to soothe unrest over arbitrary changes and wage differentials.

Employment policies followed the principle of individualized reward for individual merit. Piecework satisfied this principle for less skilled employees engaged in repetitive machine tasks. On the more varied and demanding work machinists and toolmakers performed, it was rarely feasible to establish standardized piece rates or times. Instead, employers varied hourly wage rates according to the worker's skill, effort, and output. "A flexible hourly rate to meet each individual work is what takes the place of the incentive in the piece rate system."[83]

This approach could be chaotic for management and irritating to workers as wage rates proliferated and craftsmen of similar skills received different pay. Gradually, however, managers brought hourly wage incentives into a more systematic scheme of narrowly defined job categories and, within each category, pay grades. Individuals moved up the scale and from one classification to higher ones in accordance with their efficiency, skill, and discipline. This system retained the notion of offering different hourly rates as incentives but kept the "individuality" of wages within manageable limits laid down in a clear scale. At the same time, wage and job ladders provided an orderly mechanism for training and upgrading new workers on an unprecedented scale. At least two firms—Bullard, and Coulter and McKenzie—explicitly used job ladders as the basis for an internal labor market.[84]

Bridgeport employers also sought to ensure a more rule-bound and, if possible, tactful application of these employment policies. Job categories and pay scales would hardly systematize wages or encourage employee loyalty if foremen showed favoritism or whimsy in classifying and reclassifying workers. More clearly defining occupational classes and procedures for rating employees reduced the scope of foremen's discretion. In addition the Manufacturers' Association developed a variety of programs, manuals, and conferences to train foremen in managing workers.[85] Bridgeport firms also installed employment offices and specialized personnel to handle aspects of labor relations previously left to shop-floor supervisors, including hiring, promotion, and discharge.[86] These initiatives reflected a nationwide enthusiasm for personnel management during the war, inspired by tremendous increases in the size of work forces, a desire to hold on to employees at a time of labor shortage, and an effort to keep labor relations peaceful.[87] But in Bridgeport at least these developments survived the war and were even extended and elaborated in the early 1920s.[88]

These management practices seem to have inhibited movements for workers' control by dividing machinists, aggravating conflicts between skilled and less skilled workers, and defusing one widely shared source of hostility toward employers—arbitrary supervision. More specialized and narrowly defined job categories may have eroded the occupational identity of machinists in Bridgeport. Because job titles and conditions of pay and promotion varied from one firm to another, specific grievances and conflicts were confined to individual shops or departments and could no longer provide a common basis for struggles throughout the city. Within each plant competition for promotion further divided machinists, as local labor leaders warned: "So long as they can play the non-union man against the union by increasing the former's rate of pay, and not the latter, they feel they can prevent the workers from getting together and demanding any change with a chance of receiving it. This, and discrimination, blacklisting, and coercive slave driving methods, bonuses, pensions, and playing traitorous workers against their fellow men, rewarding such by promotion and other devious remuneration, are so well known and recognized by the true blue workman, that he is not deceived."[89] Finally, even the "true blue" craftsman could hardly look with favor on deskilling. Job ladders, by formalizing the promotion of less skilled workers at the expense of union apprenticeship and privilege, accentuated conflicts of interest between grades of labor.

The divide-and-conquer strategies attacked by Bridgeport IAM officials did not require "discrimination, blacklisting, and coercive slave driving methods." The best cure for outstanding troublemakers would always be to get rid of them. On a day-to-day basis, however, progressive managers endorsed the "square deal," with supervisors and workers alike adhering to known rules for hiring, job assignment, promotion, piece rates, and discharge. Such constitutional procedures helped defuse conflicts over unjust and inequitable management practices, coordinating the interests of employers and workers around the rule of law. Many members of the Bridgeport Manufacturers' Association recognized (at least in principle) the virtues of industrial government by law rather than by men; some made clear commitments to their employees to act accordingly.[90]

These changes in workshop authority had important consequences for factory politics. Of all grievances over workshop control, those focused on the unfair or abusive exercise of authority had the widest appeal. Machinists and production workers had rather different interests in questions of dilution and piecework, but both groups strongly resented foremen who bullied or played favorites. When machinists went on strike to protest the NWLB award in 1918, they justified their action to President Wilson on two grounds. First, they were entitled to a better standard of living. Second, they demanded classification "that will protect the worker from the arbitrary action of the employers with regard to the fixation of wage rates."[91] Replacing arbitrary action with constitutional procedures allowed employers to retain their own job ladders and pay scales while eliminating a major spur to *united* action over workshop control.

The emergence of employer classification schemes (particularly in their early and irregular forms) had spurred rather than impeded the solidary struggles of 1917–1918. Effective opposition to management control, however, presupposed joint organization bridging divisions among workers within and between the city's factories, and the NWLB's shop committee scheme broke that organization. As managers rationalized employment policies in the absence of effective counterorganization by workers, the conditions for mobilizing collective action on behalf of workers' control disappeared. The containment of radical factory politics thus involved a two-pronged offensive: by employers within the shops and by the NWLB outside them. This offensive's success—and the importance of its two components—is evident in the strike wave of 1919.

During the war Bridgeport's extraordinary economic boom relied on munitions production. The government began to cancel its military contracts after the armistice, and leading munitions firms and the subcontractors dependent on them laid off most of their workers or closed altogether. Increased demand for electrical goods, consumer products, and machine tools absorbed some of the slack, but during the winter of 1918–1919, unemployment increased, wage increases ceased, and inflation continued.[92] IAM Lodge 30's primary concern during this period was to lead workers in unemployment demonstrations and demands for relief rather than in strikes.[93]

On July 18, 1919, Lodge 30 members voted to present employers with demands for a forty-four-hour week, a 20 percent wage hike, and a minimum wage "for all machine shop workers."[94] The opening shot in the summer's battery of strikes was fired by unskilled workers, however, many of them foreign born.[95] On July 21, more than eight hundred record pressmen walked out at Columbia (formerly American) Graphophone, demanding a forty-four-hour week, wage hikes, nondiscrimination, and shop committee recognition. Most belonged to the Workers' International Industrial Union (WIIU), an offshoot of the IWW affiliated with the Socialist Labor Party. When toolmakers and machinists struck Bryant Electric Company the following day for the forty-four-hour week and a 25 percent wage increase, a large number of female employees came out with them—immigrant workers generally joining the WIIU, English-speakers coming to Lodge 30 for leadership. A similar split affected female employees who (together with machinists and toolmakers) walked out from Columbia Graphophone on July 24. Additional disputes (some involving less skilled workers alone, some craftsmen alone, and some both) affecting at least twenty-one other metal trades firms brought the total number of workers on strike between July 21 and mid-August to more than ten thousand, including fifteen hundred at Bryant and twenty-five hundred at Graphophone. Although Lodge 30 officials applied for national sanction on July 18, by the time a negative reply came back, thousands of strikers were already out and requesting local IAM sponsorship.[96]

These strikes demonstrated impressive unity among craftsmen and less skilled workers. Machinists, polishers and buffers, and molders came out together at several firms, and strike committees representing men and women of different trades and skills handled picketing and negotiations in some of the disputes. On July 29, officials of AFL unions (including federal unions organized for unskilled operatives) formed an executive committee, headed by Sam Lavit and State Federation of Labor Secretary Ira Ornburn, to coordinate strike policy throughout the city. As in 1915, however, demands for shorter hours and better pay unified the movement. Control issues around which solidary struggles had been based in 1918—classification, equal pay, shop committee recognition—once again appear only in isolated disputes, tacked on to an economistic program by individual strike committees. In only one strike did machinists and less skilled workers together raise the key demand of 1918, occupational classification. Even in matters of wages and hours, all-grades solidarities had an important limitation. Craft unionists cooperated with less skilled workers when the latter joined IAM Lodge 30 or AFL federal unions, as most natives did. But many production workers and laborers were foreigners and were affiliated with the WIIU. This overlapping division based on skill, ethnicity, and union politics was never bridged. AFL and IAM leaders refused to cooperate with the WIIU, and eventually their members returned to work at Graphophone under a settlement rejected by the WIIU (which had its strongest base, of about a thousand members, at that firm).

These strikes further demonstrate the significance of the NWLB's collective bargaining system. In a number of strikes IAM and AFL leaders sought to make good the losses inflicted the previous winter by demanding recognition for *union* shop committees. AFL Secretary Ornburn insisted, "We will not treat with the employers through the War Labor Board committees. The committees are in no small part elected by the manufacturers and in most cases there are non-union workers on them. . . . We will discuss questions and demands only through the shop committees of union employees."[97] Local officials appreciated that "employee representation" divorced from union organization amounted to company unionism.

Employers were equally clear on the issues at stake. Bryant's factory manager agreed to negotiate only with "properly constituted employees' committees, elected under rules laid down by the National War Labor Board. We will deal with no outside organization or influences."[98] Speaking for the Manufacturers' Association, George Hawley also endorsed NWLB committees—and only such committees—as "reasonable machinery for the adjustment of differences. . . . This association insists that these methods of adjustment be used rather than the arbitrary calling of strikes,"[99] and no metal trades firm agreed to recognize union shop committees. Employers had good reason to defend shop committees established under the NWLB and the Bridgeport Plan. Employee representatives at two firms persuaded workers not to strike, and shop committees established under (or approved by) the NWLB at Singer, UMC, Bridgeport Brass, and some others agreed to compromises on wages and hours without union involvement or strikes.[100]

Less decisive evidence suggests the success of new employment systems and welfare programs in containing militancy. Union officials were unable to get workers out on strike at three of the most progressive firms—Coulter and McKenzie, Crane, and Bullard. Bullard employees in particular had long been relatively immune to union agitation. The previous year employees had volunteered to work on Labor Day to get out war products, and when Lavit came to Bullard to call machinists out in September 1918, he was nearly thrown in a creek by a detachment of employees led by a flag-waving supervisor.[101]

By mid-August, many Bridgeport workers had won concessions on wages and hours. But Lodge 30 (and other AFL societies) had failed to substitute union shop committees for the Bridgeport Plan of employee representation. Combined with growing unemployment, this new structure of workshop organization enabled employers to effectively exclude unions from their plants. When local officials revived Bridgeport's Metal Trades Council in November, their support within the factory gates had returned to its sparse prewar levels. One organizer attributed this loss to management-sponsored employee representation: "The shop committees in the factories are suckers. . . . They are working, not for the laborer, but for the boss."[102]

Their grass-roots support ebbing, local radicals once more became vulnerable to union censure. At the beginning of August, the IAM Grand Lodge expelled Sam Lavit from the union, citing his leadership of unconstitutional strikes and his admission into the union of men and women unqualified for membership. Lavit's largest constituency—strikers at Bryant and Graphophone—promptly voted their confidence in him. When Lodge 30 members (by this time probably including larger numbers of less skilled Graphophone and Bryant strikers than machinists) followed suit, the Executive Board revoked Lodge 30's charter.[103]

Although Grand Lodge action could not deprive Lavit of his remaining support at Bryant and Graphophone, local government action could. On August 29, police prevented Lavit from addressing a group of Graphophone employees meeting to consider the company's final offer, escorting him instead to Bridgeport's mayor, who directed Lavit to leave town. WIIU leaders received the same advice several days later.[104] Lavit's experience mirrored that of other wartime radical leaders. In 1919 and 1920, national IAM officials expelled local officials who had been disrespectful of Executive Board authority and craft unionism in New York, Detroit, Philadelphia, Newark, and Chicago, as well as in Bridgeport,[105] and the Palmer raids and police roundups forced sympathizers underground.

Lodge 30 leaders sought a referendum vote in October to restore their charter. That effort failed. As many as eight hundred machinists from the lodge transferred to a new local set up by IAM officials;[106] others dropped union membership altogether. A much diminished Lodge 30 joined an outlaw Brooklyn IAM lodge in March 1920 to form the Amalgamated Metal Workers of America (AMWA), whose program articulated the ambitions of wartime movements for workers' control in unqualified form. Delegates to the first convention (held in Philadelphia in December 1920) endorsed "working class ownership of industries," "the amalgamation of all existing crafts and organizations in the industry," and "government of the workers, by the workers, and for the workers."[107] Organizers emphasized that although in the IAM "all the power lays [*sic*] in the hands of the Grand Lodge officials," in the AMWA "the workers through their shop stewards control at all times their affairs in their local conditions."[108]

Workers' control, local autonomy, and union democracy exercised through shop organization: these express the radical potential of craft traditions. Combined with industrial unionism, the platform represented a stark alternative to IAM policies, authority, and structure. Local militants could put forward the alternative only when they were "freed" from IAM authority and from the cautions required to retain support from metalworkers of varied skills and interests because, by mid-1920, the conditions that might have favored an alliance behind AMWA leaders had vanished. With manufacturing practices steadily diluting work, the craft constituency for workers' control narrowed. Management practices highlighted divisions of interest between workers of different skills and eroded occupational solidarity even among machinists. Company unionism and a renewed open-shop drive ensured that lingering conflicts over control would be isolated and free from union involvement. In short, issues of control could no longer bring workers together under radical leadership. From the start AMWA activists were forced to resort to the conventional organizing tactic of the industrial pariah: speeches *outside* the factory gates. Their support on the shop floor remained negligible.[109]

Chapter Eight

Patterns of Factory Politics in Comparative Perspective

Proposals for workers' control commanded wide support among engineers and machinists in 1917. That support developed during a transitional period, when craftsmen had not yet lost—and employers not yet won—control over factory production. Skilled men refused to sacrifice their traditional powers and standards for economic benefits. At times they combined with workers of varied trades and lesser skill in ambitious challenges to management rights. By the early 1920s, however, industrial conflict more closely approximated its contemporary form. Economic goals assumed priority; questions of workplace control were fought out, if at all, on a sectional and defensive basis.

This general trajectory did not assume identical forms in Britain and the United States. The distinctiveness of individual cases is useful in generating concrete explanations for the shifting fortunes of radical factory politics and the consolidation of more familiar agendas for industrial contention. Such historical explanations also lead to conclusions of broader applicability: they largely confirm Chapter One's analytical propositions concerning selective mobilization in craft protest.

Historical Conclusions

Wartime factory politics represented a clear alternative to the sectional and economistic priorities that have since come to dominate the British and American labor movements. Craft radicalism developed most fully during the war; however, it consummated longstanding trends. Skilled metalworkers had for some time expressed an intense concern with issues of workplace control; as war production speeded the demise of craft standards, this concern became more pressing. Insofar as radicalized craftsmen broadened their support through new types of organization, militancy moved beyond the defense of craft privilege to class-conscious assertions of workers' control. Shop steward and committee schemes that bridged divisions of trade and skill and freed the rank and file from national union constraints were pioneered before 1914; war conditions gave these institutions greater appeal and influence.

The specific structural foundations for radical factory politics differed in Coventry and Bridgeport. In prewar Coventry union and industrial relations constraints had confined conflicts over control to sectional goals and isolated disputes. These restrictions were overcome during the war. Within the shops unofficial organization developed independently of and at odds with craft union authority. In the city as a whole, the Coventry Engineering Joint Committee and (less effectively) the Coventry Workers' Committee challenged established district officials for leadership in local labor struggles. In different ways and degrees shop committees, the CEJC, and the CWC all repudiated divisions based on union affiliation, trade, and skill, bringing workers into common organizations and joint action. In Bridgeport, by contrast, machinists had before the war been cut off from union support and vulnerable to employer repression. Weak unions and open shops confined control struggles to individual shops and channeled joint action toward economic goals. By 1917, however, shop committees were far stronger and enjoyed much closer ties to union lodges. Policies and strategies could for the first time be coordinated on a citywide basis. IAM organization in Bridgeport, moreover, involved many semiskilled, immigrant, and female metalworkers in local membership, meetings, and demands—contrary to national rules and priorities.

These different patterns of local organization did share one key characteristic: both put local militants in a position to broaden their rank-and-file support and escape the constraints of sectional union authority. In Coventry radical leadership was exercised from the shop floor; in Bridgeport, from local union offices. The contrasting foundations for progressive factory politics may be attributed to the relative freedom of machinists and local IAM officials from national union or government restraints. When national restrictions tightened late in 1917, radicals had already gained local control. The division between official policies and unofficial movements, accordingly, did not develop along the same lines in Bridgeport as in Coventry. In both locations, however, the groundwork for radical factory politics had been completed by 1917. Independent, solidary organization made possible Coventry's shop stewards' strike in November 1917 and Bridgeport's August 1917 demands and September 1918 strike against the National War Labor Board decision.

The containment of radical factory politics involved reimposing union discipline over Coventry shop stewards and breaking union influence over Bridgeport shop committees. The effect was to again deprive radicals—on the shop floor in Coventry, in local union offices in Bridgeport—of their constituencies and influence over industrial action. In both cases the government played a major role in effecting these solutions.

The Shop Stewards' Agreement of 1917 incorporated shop stewards into formal union hierarchies and industrial relations procedures. This reform (made reluctantly by unions and employers under pressure from the Ministry of Munitions) consolidated craft union authority over workshop activism at the expense of progressive leaders in the CEJC and the CWC. The Agreement also undercut joint organization through works committees and the CEJC and sharply restricted the autonomy of reconstituted shop committees and stewards. In so doing, it at once subverted the organizational base for radical factory politics and ensured that control issues would be dealt with by union officials—ultimately national ones—and from a craft unionist perspective. A similar outcome was reached in Bridgeport by a different route. The shop committee plan established by the NWLB barred progressive union officials from having any role in organization and bargaining within the factory gates. The plan helped employers establish company unions under a scheme that denied influence or security to workers and systematically diluted the concerns and interests of skilled workers. Excluded from the shops, radicals were further isolated by IAM and AFL retribution against dissident leaders, locals, and metal trades councils.

The reform of workshop organization played a key role in these outcomes. The reconstruction and cooptation of Coventry's workshop organization by restrictive industrial relations rules and sectional unions undermined radical initiatives on the job. This finding agrees with those who see trade unions as checks on popular radicalism.[1] The experience of Bridgeport machinists, however, emphasizes the obvious caveat: independent shop-floor organization is not a sufficient condition for rank-and-file militancy. Here shop committees enjoyed unlimited independence from union authority but were more tightly controlled by employers. Strong unions and industrial relations laws may at times keep rebellious workers on a short leash; but these same conditions (as well as favorable economic circumstances) afforded rank-and-file organization some immunity from employers. Without that immunity shop committees could not become vehicles for solidary opposition to management control. This is clear not only from Bridgeport after the installation of the NWLB's employee representation scheme but also from the activities of nominally *union* shop stewards in Coventry during the 1920s.

Taking a broader view, the key to containment in Britain was the authority of sectional unions and the constraints of industrial relations rules and procedures. These kept the unofficial movement in check and allowed national union leaders to define the agenda for industrial conflict. In the United States, by contrast, the effects of the labor process—in eroding the social base for control struggles, dividing workers along occupational lines, and rewarding loyalty to the firm—were crucial.

The practical consequences for factory politics appear as early as 1918. Conflicts over control issues, when they occurred, were conducted along sectional and defensive lines. This pattern was especially characteristic of Britain, where the workshop apparatus for enforcing union rules and industrial relations agreements remained intact during the immediate postwar years. To the extent that labor struggles did unite workers of different crafts and skills, joint action focused on common economic interests rather than on demands for workplace control. This was most typical of the United States, where the relative weakness of craft traditions, the comparatively greater obstacles to solidarity at the plant level, and the frailty of organizational vehicles for concerted control struggles all favored an emphasis on the issues most widely shared and readily mobilized: wages and hours. These outcomes are clear from Coventry strikes in 1918, which aimed to protect exclusive craft privileges, and from those in Bridgeport in 1919, in which the common rallying cry concerned wage hikes and a shorter workweek.

The experiences of both Bridgeport and Coventry show how the impact of the labor process on factory politics is a contingent one. Theorists of the labor process commonly identify the divisive and hegemonic effects of particular management techniques, but the effects of production practices on industrial conflict will vary with the broader context of unionism and industrial relations. Under the favorable economic and organizational conditions of wartime Bridgeport, job classification and wage ladders, far from subduing workers, became the objects of militant and solidary struggles. The defeat of radical factory politics required, in effect, the reinstatement of prewar open shops and weak unions (under the formal guise of employee representation plans). Only after effective joint organization at work had been swept away did divisions and accommodation at the point of production prove decisive.

In Coventry, similarly, advanced dilution, widespread piecework, and the chargehand system limited the social base for control struggles, confined those struggles to individual shops, and accentuated conflicts of interest among engineering workers in matters of control. The consequences for factory politics are clear before 1914, when control struggles tended to be isolated; during World War I, when the CWC never secured the support enjoyed by Workers' Committees in Glasgow, Sheffield, or Manchester; and in the 1922 lockout, during which Coventry engineers proved reluctant to support craft standards. But here, too, the impact of the labor process was contingent on union and industrial relations conditions. Where craft unions were in a strong position, as in 1918, the defense of craft privileges could be mobilized on a citywide basis.

The containment of radical factory politics thus involved features of the labor process and of industrial relations in particular combinations. Production and management techniques in Bridgeport limited but did not eliminate disputes over control issues; when such disputes did occur, weak unions and open shops kept them quarantined. Manufacturing practices in Coventry were certainly advanced by British standards, and the labor process (as in Bridgeport) divided engineers and blocked solidary action on behalf of control demands. Even in the 1920s, however, Coventry firms employed skilled engineers in greater numbers than was typical in the United States, and conflicts over craft restrictions appear more frequently than in Bridgeport. In turn, employers' defense against such conflicts—union authority and industrial relations agreements—was characteristic of Britain rather than of the United States. Managers continued to recognize unions and adhere to industrial relations rules if it suited their needs, and when disputes occurred, they were kept within the boundaries of constitutional procedure and craft union policies.

Taken together, these conclusions point to contrasting strategies for containing radical factory politics during the transition from craft control to modern production.[2] The "British solution" relied on union authority and industrial rule of law to protect basic management rights and check rank-and-file militancy. The "American solution" attacked the problem more directly. Aggressive modernization of equipment and manufacturing techniques combined with open shops weakened the social base for control struggles, divided workers, and put production practices under the unilateral control of management. These different strategies had been clearly anticipated at the turn of the century: in Britain by the Terms of Agreement, in the United States by the open-shop drive and scientific management. After the war employers in effect returned to these same strategies, but with a difference. Factory politics during World War I had exposed the danger of workshop organization bypassing union and industrial relations restraints in Britain. The Shop Stewards' Agreement and the settlement of the 1922 lockout sought to close this loophole by formally incorporating shop-floor representation into union hierarchies and industrywide constitutional procedures. In the United States, wartime conflicts demonstrated that shop committees directed by "outside agitators" could challenge management authority even if employers avoided formal dealings with union officials. Company unionism represented a more conscientious effort to bring in-plant labor relations firmly under management control, insulated from union leadership.

The moves to incorporate shop stewards or install company unions after 1917 followed the same logic as had produced trade agreements and the open-shop drive.[3] British craft unions were too strong to ignore, and relatively traditional production techniques gave skilled engineers a secure foothold from which to thwart management. Under these conditions employers had little choice but to concede collective bargaining and, in exchange, require union leaders to respect management rights and discipline their members. The IAM, by contrast, was too weak either to force collective bargaining or to help employers control shop-floor unrest; advanced production techniques, in any case, limited craft militancy. Here management control could best be defended and craft protest defeated by keeping unions outside the factory gates.

Where conditions in either country departed from the norm, national identities did not prevent employers from adopting "foreign" strategies. Some American employers resorted to (and others advocated) "British solutions" to the labor problem when faced with effective labor organization. During the war, for example, shipbuilding firms endorsed formal union agreements and, with government help, encouraged centralized negotiations and tight union control over local shop committees and metal trades councils. Railroad managements adopted similar strategies to deal with their well-organized and rebellious repair shop craftsmen both before and after the war.[4] Where the labor process and union organization gave British employers the upper hand, they at least considered the attractions of open shops and in-house representation and welfare schemes—as in Coventry once victory in the 1922 lockout was assured. For the "average" British or American employer, however, the relative development of the labor process and trade unionism favored trade agreements and open shops, respectively, as the most effective strategies for controlling their shops and employees. Even where industrial conditions departed from national norms, historical traditions might prevail. Ever since 1898, the ASE and the Terms had been more or less taken for granted. The key problem for employers had long been how to buttress union authority and enforce industrial rules on rank-and-file engineers. The 1917 Shop Stewards' Agreement and 1922 Terms of Settlement were important steps in this direction. After 1901, the NMTA defined the problems of control in terms of keeping unions out of its factories and shifting its employees' loyalties from outside labor organizations to the firm.[5] Company unionism followed this agenda.

By the 1920s, these different solutions for common problems were firmly rooted in the manufacturing practices, trade union conditions, and industrial customs of each country. Employer strategies would be considerably modified (and in some cases abandoned) in later years, particularly with the revival of trade unions and the achievement of collective bargaining rights in the United States. But they proved effective in a critical transitional period during which skilled workers, though under siege, still retained their powers and traditions. It was in this crisis that broadly based movements for workers' control could flourish. Union authority and industrial relations rules in Britain, and the labor process and open shops in America, helped resolve the crisis in favor of sectional and economistic factory politics. The conditions favoring workers' control movements would not occur again.

Analytical Conclusions

The preceding conclusions outline two sets of conditions that undermined workers' control movements and ensured that sectional and economistic priorities would dominate industrial conflict in the metal trades. These two patterns combine particular features of the labor process, trade unionism, and industrial relations. To simplify, the contrast is between more or less traditional production organization, stronger or weaker unions, and industrial relations characterized by trade agreements or open shops. For most of the period examined here, British engineering combined the first sides of each dichotomy, American machine manufacturing the second. Although both configurations blocked movements for workers' control, the British one highlighted defensive and exclusive control struggles, the American one more economistic factory politics.

It is possible to analytically separate the influence of each factor on patterns of industrial conflict. Doing so serves two purposes. First, Chapter One advanced some propositions relating the labor process, unions, industrial relations, and workshop organization to selective mobilization in craft protest. These propositions outlined how each factor might be expected to favor some alliances on behalf of certain demands rather than other potential coalitions and goals. The accumulated evidence on factory politics in the British and American machine trades permits an assessment of these arguments. Second, presenting each factor in the guise of a sociological variable suggests applications to empirical settings different from those studied here.

The historical analysis of the labor process and factory politics confirms the dilemma outlined in Chapter One. Conflicts over control of shop practices, while challenging capital's right to manage, also tend to divide workers along trade and skill lines. Struggles for higher wages or shorter hours, by contrast, may bring different groups of workers together but do not usually threaten management. To unite workers in matters of control is a more challenging proposition. Normally, the labor process favors sectional struggles and exclusive goals if control issues are pursued, and it favors economistic goals when workers of varied skills and trades act together.

This is, of course, a static view. In historical perspective obstacles to radical factory politics assume different forms at different points in the development of the labor process. Where automatic machinery, the division of labor, and centralized management control are relatively limited, skilled workers enjoy considerable autonomy and power. The stronger the position of skilled workers, the firmer the social base for control struggles. More traditional production techniques, however, also preserve sharp cleavages between the status and interests of craftsmen and less skilled workers. Under these conditions craftsmen have both the incentive and the capacity to act alone in defense of their customary privileges. The mobilization of sectional control struggles is thus favored. By contrast, modern manufacturing practices blur distinctions between skilled workers and laborers. Semiskilled production operatives become the largest segment of the labor force, with craftsmen and laborers in smaller numbers and less sharply distinguished from the upper and lower ranks of machine tenders. These conditions lower workplace barriers to labor solidarity but also narrow the social base for control struggles. In this situation, which reflects a conflict pattern typical of mass production industries, economistic factory politics is favored.

In no period or case examined in this study had mass production fully arrived or craftsmen entirely lost their distinctive position and status at work. Between 1890 and 1922, British and American shops stood between the two ideal types of a traditional and a modern labor process—with manufacturing practices clearly headed in the latter direction. In comparative perspective, however, the contrasts made between the United States and Britain, Coventry and more traditional engineering centers, and American machine manufacturing and railroad repair shops all emphasize differences in the development of the labor process. Relative to British norms or American railroad shops, metalworking establishments in Coventry and the United States featured craftsmen in small numbers and a weak position. In each of these three comparisons, control struggles were less prominent where the labor process was more advanced.

The labor process appears to be most conducive to radical factory politics when craftsmen and craft traditions are still strong but face a relatively sudden and far-reaching challenge. Skilled workers are most likely to recognize the futility of customary, defensive strategies under these conditions. At the same time enduring commitments to craft standards and autonomy make skilled workers unwilling to abandon control interests for purely economic satisfactions. Demands for workers' control may mobilize support among craftsmen during these periods. Whether such possibilities are actually realized depends on many conditions other than the labor process. The argument that craftsmen are more likely to support radical programs where traditional work practices come under rapid and abrupt attack, though, is supported by the greater development of unofficial movements in Britain compared to the United States, and in Glasgow compared to Coventry.

It was argued that craft union officials may be expected to favor sectional action and conservative goals rather than broader solidarities and more ambitious demands for control. Such preferences reflect neither political biases nor complicity with capital. Rather, they are prudent estimates of what kinds of demands and strikes will bring the national organization the greatest benefits at the least risk and cost. IAM and ASE executives certainly conformed to this pattern, and they did so regardless of industrial relations agreements: IAM leaders were no more disposed to sanction sympathetic action or control struggles than were their British counterparts.

A comparative perspective emphasizes how union executives' ability to enforce their priorities on the rank and file vary. One source of variation is the business cycle: during economic booms, when labor is scarce and employers are eager to maintain production, workers will rely less on union benefits. They may thus pursue their own agenda with less fear of union sanctions. In both Britain and the United States, for example, wartime labor markets and business prosperity enabled engineers and machinists to strike frequently (and often successfully) in defiance of union orders and in pursuit of goals their officials explicitly renounced.

Labor unrest during World War I reveals another factor that reduces the weight of union policies. Employees have little reason to respect union authority when the government assumes responsibility for resolving disputes, quickly intervenes to avoid work stoppages, and restricts unions' rights to call strikes. In such cases, workers need not rely so heavily on their officials to negotiate with employers, they expect strikes will be short, and they know their union will not pay strike benefits in any case. In this situation, too, union constraints on rank-and-file action are lifted. State intervention clearly favored militancy among wartime engineers and machinists, with strikes typically lacking union support and at times involving demands and solidarities that repudiated the conservative policies and sectional authority of national union leaders. Paradoxically, the IAM's greater freedom from government restrictions during World War I may have curbed radical factory politics. The IAM, unlike the ASE, retained its powers and customary policies for most of the war, thus maintaining some legitimacy for and authority over its members. From the rank-and-file perspective, because the union was still useful, resorting to alternative organizations and leaders was not necessary.

National union policies have less influence on rank-and-file politics, finally, where members or locals have greater control over negotiations and decisions to strike. According to ASE and IAM constitutions and customs, engineers and machinists enjoyed similar controls over local trade policy. In practice, however, local autonomy is also bound up with industrial relations practices. Formal or informal rights to prepare demands and conduct negotiations have little value if employers ignore demands and refuse to bargain. By this standard machinists exercised less local autonomy before 1914 than they did during the war and at all times less than did engineers. These contrasts in local autonomy are consistent with differences in factory politics. In the United States, prewar radicals were free to put forward demands at odds with IAM policies. But rank-and-file action on those demands in defiance of their unions became widespread only during World War I, and even then unofficial action never achieved the scope of Britain's Shop Stewards' Movement.

Industrial relations have been conceptualized as a further influence on selective mobilization. Employers typically are more reluctant to accept restrictions on production techniques and management authority than they are to negotiate wage increases, and this preference often channels conflict toward economistic issues. Workers know that demands for wage increases are more likely to win concessions, workers are better able to judge what an employer can pay and when the best time is to make the demand, and they can expect that a strike on economic issues will be less protracted and uncertain than one challenging management prerogatives. Comparing the machine trades in the two countries, American firms were clearly more vehement and successful in fighting encroachments on managerial rights than were British employers. In the engineering industry, moreover, formal trade agreements reinforced craft policies by recognizing unions, enhancing the role of union leaders in disputes procedures, and accepting at least some union concerns over workshop practices as legitimate topics for negotiation. Open shops and union busting, by contrast, prevailed in the United States. Contrasting patterns of factory politics found for much of the period 1890–1922 are consistent with these differences: engineers were more actively involved in defending craft restrictions, machinists in pursuing economic concessions.

The same conditions that weaken the influence of union policies on factory politics will also ease the constraints of industrial relations. Broadly based movements for workers' control in the United States developed most fully during World War I, when an advantageous labor market and government intervention temporarily muted employers' open shop practices. In Britain, similarly, wartime economic boom, state policies, and shop-floor leaders' increased role in managing labor unrest all gave workers some independence from industrial relations rules and their accompanying inhibitions. The British experience also suggests how trade agreements may themselves contribute to local autonomy and thus lower obstacles to radical factory politics. Engineers resented concessions made by union executives in the national agreement of 1898, including the curbs on their freedom of action. They responded by organizing more effectively at the local level to bypass new restrictions. A marked increase in unconstitutional strikes and unofficial bargaining followed—at least during business booms when engineers could afford to defy their unions. The engineering trade agreement did more than strengthen local autonomy. By bringing union officials into disrepute, it also expanded the appeal of alternative leaders. Advocates of industrial unionism and syndicalism became especially prominent in rank-and-file insurgence between 1910 and 1914. Radical leaders had less influence among machinists before World War I, partly because the IAM was not discredited by contractual obligations to defend management rights and limit strikes.

Finally, it has been argued that rank-and-file organization within the factories can offset the divisive impact of the labor process, the sectional influence of craft unions, and the restrictive effects of industrial relations. Workshop organization may play this role when it combines employees of different unions and skills on the job and gives them an independent base for protest. Industrial conflict in the British and American cases confirms these propositions. Engineers developed far more effective shop steward organization than did machinists, especially after 1900. During the war, when the suspension of normal trade union functions favored cooperation on the job without regard for craft distinctions, shop-floor organization formed the basis for radical insurgence.

The relative weakness of workplace unionism in America, by contrast, kept industrial conflict more closely circumscribed by AFL policies. The exceptions confirm the rule. Before World War I joint action for control demands (in some cases under radical leadership) was most prominent in the railroad repair shops, where system federations gave craftsmen, specialists, and clerks a common, independent organizational base. Elsewhere war conditions greatly strengthened the position of shop committees and local unionists. These activists initiated solidary strikes (in defiance of government agencies as well as national union leaders) in support of ambitious proposals for workshop control. The importance of rank-and-file organization for mobilizing radical factory politics is clear, finally, from the reversal of wartime trends. Once the power of shop committees was broken at the end of the war (with government awards often replacing such bodies with employer-dominated employee representation plans), radical initiatives collapsed. By different means Britain's Shop Stewards' Movement met a similar fate. Where union controls and industrial relations checks on workplace organization were reimposed in 1918, engineering protest once again turned to conservative goals and sectional action.

This analysis of selective mobilization in factory politics has been focused narrowly in two respects: it concentrates on industrial life, and it attends to a transitional period between craft production and modern manufacture. In both respects the conclusions have implications for a broader understanding of working-class radicalism. First, a consideration of selective mobilization can help clarify the roles of community and state institutions in the development of working-class politics. Second, the study of transitional periods in economic development raises questions about traditional Marxist views of revolutionary class formation.

Recent work on labor's community life and local political activity shows how associations outside the workplace (e.g., bars, neighborhood organizations, and political clubs) enhance workers' ability to mobilize collective action. Some findings of this study concur: citywide metal trades councils, union lodges, and Amalgamation and Workers' Committees often supported rank-and-file strikes when government and national union policies discouraged protest. It has been emphasized, however, that such organizations did not merely augment workers' *capacity* for action. The analysis highlighted instead how different kinds of capacities favored mobilization in support of different interests and goals. By organizing new alliances and offering local activists some independence from official union policies, citywide associations helped channel protest toward new goals.

Studies of the contributions of community institutions to working-class politics more broadly may be reinterpreted in similar ways. The general model Ronald Aminzade adopts in his study of mid-nineteenth-century Toulouse, for example, roots workers' grievances in changing relations of production. The larger political expression of those grievances, however, is shaped outside the shops by the development of local political and cultural institutions linking workers to members of other shops, trades, and classes.[6] In most of Aminzade's historical analysis, such institutions—cafés, dance halls, political clubs—are seen as an expression of new (socialist) ideas and broadened solidarities; these institutions, in turn, enhance workers' capacity to act on behalf of their interests and goals.[7] Approaching these dynamics from the perspective of selective mobilization suggests a different interpretation. Rather than reflecting new solidarities and ideas, more inclusive institutions, which developed for pragmatic political or recreational purposes, may themselves have helped dissolve occupational identities and highlighted interests and goals of wider appeal to workers.[8]

John Foster's conclusions regarding class consciousness in early-nineteenth-century Oldham may be interpreted in the same way. He argues that labor's connections to local political institutions gave radicals leadership among Oldham employees; the economics of the cotton industry, in turn, helped this vanguard lead workers from a sectional to a class consciousness. By altering the emphasis, one can read Foster's narrative as a chronicle of selective mobilization. Efforts to pursue illegal collective bargaining and to capture local political positions created alliances among Oldham workers of different shops and skills. Although defensive in origin, these alliances created a more favorable terrain for the mobilization of class (as against sectional) interests and programs.[9]

The kind of solidarity Oldham workers achieved is exceptional. Ira Katznelson's analysis of working-class ideology in the United States suggests similar processes leading in the opposite direction. With the country's early franchise, decentralized government, and locally based mass parties, workers entered the political arena as members of neighborhoods and ethnic groups rather than as members of an economic class. American workers consequently developed a split personality. At work they defined themselves in terms of class, but their political consciousness was based on ethnic and residential categories.[10] The argument may be pushed further: institutionalizing alliances based on sectional identities discouraged the mobilization of class interests and goals in the political arena.

Treating citywide labor organization in Bridgeport and Coventry as a channel for industrial protest is clearly consistent with studies of broader working-class politics. More important, the analysis of selective mobilization—applied here more to workplaces than to experiences outside the factory gates—may help explain the role of community associations in shaping labor's alliances and goals.

Although this study of factory politics concentrates on craft workers and their responses to industrial change, it also raises larger issues in the development of working-class radicalism. According to the traditional Marxist view, revolutionary class formation is favored (though not assured) by three tendencies, each embedded in the dynamics of capitalism: divisions within the working class diminish (proletarianization); the gap between labor and capital widens, eroding solidarities across class lines (polarization); and labor increasingly faces alienation at work and a decline (relative or absolute) in living standards. Such circumstances make working-class unity and class conflict likely. Whether class conflict assumes a revolutionary form depends, in effect, on the lessons workers learn in the course of their struggles.

All three factors favoring class formation are bound up with the labor process. Deskilling is largely responsible for producing a more homogeneous working class. Polarization involves the decline of small masters and subcontractors and the growing gulf between those who conceive and those who execute. Alienation (in at least one sense) is associated with mass production techniques, impoverishment with the expropriation of surplus value.

In the British and American metal trades these dynamics appear to be less straightforward. As Marx well knew, even an ethnically homogeneous working class was divided into two factions: skilled men on their way down the industrial hierarchy and less skilled men and women on their way into industry from traditional occupations or on their way up within industry, from laborers to machine tenders.[11] In such circumstances the prospects for working-class unity and radicalism appear uncertain. Engineers and machinists were well to the left in their respective labor movements. Their alliances with less privileged workers in the industry, however, developed only under specific and rather fleeting historical conditions; and those coalitions proved difficult to sustain even in the best of circumstances.

A second problem (and one often cited) with Marx's view of class formation is that, although modern production techniques are hardly conducive to "worker satisfaction," the standard of living for most workers has risen (absolutely). Indeed, alienated labor has made available growing economic benefits to compensate workers for their dull and repetitive jobs. Less skilled workers have generally accepted this trade-off. Their pursuit of economic concessions has at various times involved considerable militancy. But especially where wage struggles have been institutionalized through unions and collective bargaining, they have posed no real challenge to capitalist control.

The same holds true for skilled workers in contemporary times. This could not always be taken for granted, however. In the transitional period from craft control to modern production, when the power of craftsmen was still high and their traditions remained strong, they often refused to sacrifice their standards and control for better pay. Under attack, craftsmen could and frequently did simply cling to their accustomed status and reject any alliances with the workplace rabble. But skilled workers' traditions of shop-floor autonomy and their noninstrumental ethic also made them sympathetic to more progressive and aggressive attacks on the rights of capital at work. Under favorable conditions radicalized craftsmen proved willing to abandon their exclusive ways and ally with less skilled labor in pursuit of workers' control.

One kind of revolutionary action, then, may be associated less with a homogeneous proletariat than with alliances between radicalized craftsmen and militant semiskilled workers. Such alliances might have turned the labor movement in new directions, behind more ambitious goals. To *sustain* rank-and-file movements for workers' control, of course, would have demanded more than the innovative organization within the factories discussed here. It also would have required a political party to coordinate local struggles, develop common policies, and reinforce solidarity among groups with varied occupational interests and identities.[12]

Ultimately, these two strands of working-class protest—the radicalism of besieged craftsmen and the militancy of less skilled employees—failed to coalesce. Tentative alliances formed in the era of World War I were broken. Mass production and a semiskilled work force subsequently developed in industrial sectors and under organizational conditions isolated from craft traditions and radicalism; elsewhere, the foundations of craft radicalism gradually disappeared. With the transitional crisis resolved on the basis of management prerogative and sectional, economistic factory politics, the conditions that favored alliances supporting workers' control were safely consigned to the past.

Notes

Chapter 1

1. The classic formulation is Selig Perlman, *A Theory of the Labor Movement* (New York: Augustus M. Kelley, 1949). See also Clark Kerr et al., *Industrialism and Industrial Man* (Cambridge, Mass.: Harvard University Press, 1960); and Peter Stearns, *Lives of Labor: Work in a Maturing Industrial Society* (New York: Holmes and Meier, 1975).

2. For present purposes the "labor process" refers to the social and technical organization of production and how this organization influences workers' relations to their work, workmates, and management. Especially relevant are the skill levels "required" by production techniques, how workers are assigned to specific tasks or machines, how they are supervised, and how they are paid.

3. Prominent examples include Bernard Moss, *The Origins of the French Labor Movement: The Socialism of the Skilled Workers, 1830–1914* (Berkeley and Los Angeles: University of California Press, 1976); William H. Sewell, Jr., *Work and Revolution in France: The Language of Labor from the Old Regime to 1848* (Cambridge: Cambridge University Press, 1980); Ronald Aminzade, *Class, Politics, and Early Industrial Capitalism: A Study of Mid-Nineteenth-Century Toulouse, France* (Albany: State University of New York Press, 1981); Barrington Moore, Jr., *Injustice: The Social Bases of Obedience and Revolt* (White Plains, N.Y.: M. E. Sharpe, 1978), esp. pp. 287–289, 319–320; Victoria Bonnell, *Roots of Rebellion: Workers' Politics and Organizations in St. Petersburg and Moscow, 1900–1914* (Berkeley and Los Angeles: University of California Press, 1983); Steve Smith, "Craft Consciousness, Class Consciousness: Petrograd, 1917," *History Workshop* 11 (Spring 1981): 33–56; John

Laslett, *Labor and the Left: A Study of Socialist and Radical Influences in the American Labor Movement, 1881–1924* (New York: Basic Books, 1970); Bryan Palmer, *A Culture in Conflict: Skilled Workers and Industrial Capitalism in Hamilton, Ontario, 1860–1914* (Montreal: Queen's University Press, 1979); and Craig Heron, "Labourism and the Canadian Working Class," *Labour/Le Travail* 13 (Spring 1984): 45–75.

4. In addition to the works cited in note 3, above, see Michael P. Hanagan, *The Logic of Solidarity: Artisan and Industrial Workers in Three French Towns, 1871–1914* (Urbana: University of Illinois Press, 1980); James Hinton, *The First Shop Stewards' Movement* (London: George Allen and Unwin, 1973); David Montgomery, *Workers' Control in America: Studies in the History of Work, Technology, and Labor Struggles* (Cambridge: Cambridge University Press, 1979); Wayne Roberts, "Toronto Metal Workers and the Second Industrial Revolution," *Labour/Le Travail* 6 (Autumn 1980): 49–72. Some comparative conclusions are found in E. J. Hobsbawm, *Labouring Men: Studies in the History of Labour* (London: Weidenfeld and Nicolson, 1964), pp. 359–360; David Brody, "Radical Labor History and Rank and File Militancy," *Labor History* 16, no. 1 (1975): 117–120; Michael Hanagan and Charles Stephenson, "The Skilled Worker and Working-Class Protest," *Social Science History* 4, no. 1 (1980): 5–13; Carmen Sirianni, "Workers' Control in the Era of World War I," *Theory and Society* 9, no. 1 (1980): 29–88; and James Cronin, "Labor Insurgency and Class Formation: Comparative Perspectives on the Crisis of 1917–1920 in Europe," *Social Science History* 4, no. 1 (1980): 125–152.

5. "Craftsmen who made machinery" include those who cut pieces of metal to the dimensions of configurations required to assemble complete machines. Traditionally, fitting the pieces together was also a skilled task for which machinists and engineers were responsible.

6. A preoccupation with jurisdictional turf was especially common in British engineering, where numerous unions competed in the same occupations. See Alan Aldridge, *Power, Authority and Restrictive Practices* (Oxford: Basil Blackwell, 1976), pp. 39–40. In the United States the International Association of Machinists often quarreled with other craft societies over what jobs (e.g., the repair of printing presses) constituted "machinists'" work. But for all practical purposes there were no competing unions for machinists. The problem in the United States, in other words, was one of demarcation rather than jurisdiction.

7. Some of the practical incentives for economistic union policies are discussed by Michael Mann, *Consciousness and Action among the Western Working Class* (London: Macmillan, 1973), p. 21. Specific considerations tending in the same direction are noted in Chapter Three.

8. Similar conclusions are reached by Stearns, *Lives of Labor*, pp. 323–325; Richard Hyman, "Trade Unions, Control and Resistance," *The Politics of Work and Occupations*, ed. Geoff Esland and Graeme Salaman (Toronto: University of Toronto Press, 1980), p. 310; and James Cronin, "Strikes 1870–1914," in *A History of British Industrial Relations, 1875–1914*, ed. Chris Wrigley (Brighton, Sussex: Harvester Press, 1982), p. 80.

9. This argument is developed and applied in Chapter Five. H. A. Turner (*Trade Union Growth Structure and Policy: A Comparative Study of the Cotton Unions* [London: George Allen and Unwin, 1962], p. 317) makes a similar point in explaining the relative absence of unofficial movements in the cotton industry.

10. This approach to the role of ideology in industrial conflict is suggested by Liston Pope, *Millhands and Preachers: A Study of Gastonia* (New Haven, Conn.: Yale University Press, 1942), ch. 11–14; Alvin Gouldner, *Wildcat Strike* (Yellow Springs, Ohio: Antioch Press, 1954), pp. 34–37; John Foster, *Class Struggle and the Industrial Revolution: Early Industrial Capitalism in Three English Towns* (London: Weidenfeld and Nicolson, 1974), pp. 123–124; and Huw Beynon, *Working for Ford* (East Ardsley, Wakefield: EP Publishing, 1975), p. 175 and ch. 9, passim.

11. A similar argument concerning the wide support enjoyed by demands for checks on management authority is made by Richard Price, *Masters, Unions and Men: Work Control in Building and the Rise of Labour, 1830–1914* (Cambridge: Cambridge University Press, 1980), pp. 8–11.

12. For the United States, see Sumner H. Slichter et al., *The Impact of Collective Bargaining on Management* (Washington, D.C.: Brookings Institution, 1960); I. W. Kuhn, "Business Unionism in a Laboristic Society," in *The Business of America*, ed. I. Berg, pp. 284–309 (New York: Harcourt, Brace and World, 1968); Richard Herding, *Job Control and Union Structure: A Study of Plant-Level Industrial Conflict in the United States with a Comparative Perspective on West Germany* (Rotterdam: Rotterdam University Press, 1972); and Richard B. Freeman and James L. Medoff, *What Do Unions Do?* (New York: Basic Books, 1984). For Britain, see Hugh Armstrong Clegg, *The System of Industrial Relations in Great Britain*, 3rd ed. (Oxford: Basil Blackwell, 1976); and John Elliott, *Conflict or Cooperation? The Growth of Industrial Democracy* (London: Kogan Page, 1984). See also the comparative conclusions in Mann, *Consciousness and Action*; Anthony Giddens, *The Class Structure of Advanced Societies* (New York: Harper and Row, 1973); and Hugh Armstrong Clegg, *Trade Unionism Under Collective Bargaining: A Theory Based on Comparisons of Six Countries* (Oxford: Basil Blackwell, 1976).

13. Carter L. Goodrich, *The Frontier of Control: A Study of British Workshop Politics* (New York: Harcourt, Brace and Howe, 1920), ch. 19.

14. These rules are much less likely to assume a written contractual form in Britain than in the United States.

15. The components of management's attacks and the grievances they generated are discussed in detail in Chapter Two.

16. Chapter Three considers these competing possibilities at greater length.

17. This is the question traditionally asked by students of social movements: under what conditions do dissatisfied individuals act together to remedy their grievances? In most of this book, collective action of some kind can be taken for granted. Analytical attention shifts instead to explaining which collectivities were involved and which dissatisfactions and goals were expressed or supported.

18. This reduction in craftsmen's privileges and the lowering of barriers between employees of different skills was anticipated by classical Marxism.

19. Cf. the analysis of "proletarianization" and its possible consequences for worker solidarity in Charles F. Sabel, *Work and Politics: The Division of Labor in Industry* (Cambridge: Cambridge University Press, 1982), e.g., pp. 18–19, 92, 176–178.

20. Metal trades union leaders confirm this interpretation in words as well as deeds, as Chapter Three notes. See also E. T. Hiller, *The Strike: A Study in Collective Action* (Chicago: University of Chicago Press, 1928), pp. 213–214; Stearns, *Lives of Labor,* pp. 323–325; and Claus Offe and Helmut Wiesenthal, "Two Logics of Collective Action: Theoretical Notes on Social Class and Organizational Form," in *Political Power and Social Theory: A Research Annual,* vol. 1 (Greenwich, Conn.: JAI Press, 1980), p. 83.

21. For the period covered here, see, for example, George Milton Janes, *The Control of Strikes in American Trade Unions* (Baltimore: Johns Hopkins University Press, 1916).

22. Gouldner, in *Wildcat Strike,* applies these general principles in his interpretation of the issues fought out in the "General Gypsum Company" dispute.

23. The role of the state in shaping industrial conflict has received considerable attention in recent years, particularly through discussions of corporatism. The most historically sophisticated treatment is Charles S. Maier, *Recasting Bourgeois Europe: Stabilization in France, Germany, and Italy in the Decade After World War I* (Princeton, N.J.: Princeton University Press, 1975), esp. pp. 582–585. See also Leo Panitch, "The Development of Corporatism in Liberal Democracies," *Comparative Po-*

litical Studies 10, no. 1 (1977): 61–90; Suzanne D. Berger, ed., *Organizing Interests in Western Europe: Pluralism, Corporatism, and the Transformation of Politics* (Cambridge: Cambridge University Press, 1981); John H. Goldthorpe, ed., *Order and Conflict in Contemporary Capitalism: Studies in the Political Economy of Western European Nations* (Oxford: Clarendon Press, 1984); and, from different angles, Giddens, *Class Structure of Advanced Societies*, pp. 290–292; and Jürgen Habermas, *Legitimation Crisis* (Boston: Beacon Press, 1973), pp. 45–55, 68–75.

24. See, for example, Katherine Stone, "The Origins of Job Structures in the Steel Industry," in *Labor Market Segmentation,* ed. Richard Edwards, Michael Reich, and David Gordon, pp. 27–84 (Lexington, Mass.: D. C. Heath, 1975); Richard Edwards, *Contested Terrain: The Transformation of the Workplace in the Twentieth Century* (New York: Basic Books, 1979); David Gordon, Richard Edwards, and Michael Reich, *Segmented Work, Divided Workers: The Transformation of Labor in America* (Cambridge: Cambridge University Press, 1982); and David Gartman, *Auto Slavery: The Labor Process in the American Automobile Industry, 1897–1950* (New Brunswick, N.J.: Rutgers University Press, 1986), ch. 11.

25. Michael Burawoy, *The Politics of Production: Factory Regimes Under Capitalism and Socialism* (London: Verso, 1985). See also Michael Burawoy, *Manufacturing Consent: Changes in the Labor Process Under Monopoly Capitalism* (Chicago: University of Chicago Press, 1979); and Stone, "Origins of Job Structures," p. 76.

26. Aminzade, *Class, Politics, and Early Industrial Capitalism*, especially Preface and ch. 1–4.

27. Theoretical statements of the resource mobilization perspective are generally much less subtle than Aminzade's historical study in the connections they make among interests, goals, and collective action. See, for example, Anthony Oberschall, *Social Conflict and Social Movements* (Englewood Cliffs, N.J.: Prentice-Hall, 1973); Michael Schwartz, *Radical Protest and Social Structure: The Southern Farmers' Alliance and Cotton Tenancy, 1880–1890* (New York: Academic Press, 1976); John D. McCarthy and Mayer N. Zald, "Resource Mobilization and Social Movement: A Partial Theory," *American Journal of Sociology* 82, no. 6 (1977): 1212–1239; Charles Tilly, *From Mobilization to Revolution* (New York: Random House, 1978); Mayer N. Zald and John D. McCarthy, eds., *The Dynamics of Social Movements: Resource Mobilization, Social Control, and Tactics* (Cambridge, Mass.: Winthrop Publishers, 1979); and Mayer N. Zald, "Issues in the Theory of Social Movements," in *Current Perspectives in Social Theory: A Research Annual*, ed. Scott G. McNall and Gary N. Howe, pp. 61–72 (Greenwich, Conn.: JAI Press, 1980).

28. See note 3 above.

29. In principle, aggregate strike data compiled by government agencies could be used for a statistical analysis of factory politics. There is some value in attempting to do so, as David Montgomery has shown in his study of control strikes (*Workers' Control in America*, ch. 4). Unfortunately, strike data have serious shortcomings. Smaller disputes, which are the most likely to involve unofficial action and conflicts over shop management, usually are not recorded. And in comparing government reports with more detailed accounts of the same incidents in newspapers or union minutes, discrepancies are often found. Whether because government investigators recorded only the "leading" cause of the dispute or because their information was faulty, demands may in fact have been put forward that do not appear in official accounts. Less commonly, smaller numbers of workers belonging to other trades or skill levels may have come out in sympathy with (for example) striking machinists; yet this fact is not mentioned in official sources. For these reasons the analysis of strikes in this study is confined as far as possible to incidents for which more detailed information is available. Collecting such information requires patient searching through recalcitrant sources; the sample will thus be small. On the interpretive value of strikes, see, e.g., W. Lloyd Warner and J. O. Low, *The Social System of the Modern Factory. The Strike: A Social Analysis* (New Haven, Conn.: Yale University Press, 1947), p. 1; Richard Hyman, *Strikes* (Glasgow: Fontana/Collins, 1977); and Joseph White, *The Limits of Trade Union Militancy: The Lancashire Textile Workers, 1910–1914* (Westport, Conn.: Greenwood Press, 1978), pp. 10–11. On strike statistics, see Hyman, *Strikes*, pp. 17–19; and Clegg, *The System of Industrial Relations*, pp. 311–314.

Chapter 2

1. For surveys of craft control in Britain, see, e.g., Raphael Samuel, "The Workshop of the World: Steam Power and Hand Technology in Mid-Victorian Britain," *History Workshop* 3 (Spring 1977): 6–72; and Craig Littler, "Deskilling and Changing Structures of Control," in *The Degradation of Work? Skill, Deskilling, and the Labour Process*, ed. Stephen Wood, pp. 122–145 (London: Hutchinson, 1982). For the United States, see Benson Soffer, "A Theory of Trade Union Development: The Role of the 'Autonomous' Workman," *Labor History* 1, no. 2 (1960): 141–163; and Montgomery, *Workers' Control in America*, ch. 1.

2. Thomas Wright, *Some Habits and Customs of the Working Classes* (New York: Augustus Kelly, 1967 [1867]), pp. 84, 100–105; *Machinists' Monthly Journal* (hereafter *MMJ*), January 1890, p. 2; Monte Calvert, *The*

Mechanical Engineer in America, 1830–1910: Professional Cultures in Conflict (Baltimore: Johns Hopkins University Press, 1967), p. 8.

3. Samuel, "The Workshop of the World," p. 40; Charles More, "Skill and the Survival of Apprenticeship," in Wood, *The Degradation of Work*, pp. 116–118; Fred J. Miller, "The Machinist," *Scribner's Magazine* 14 (September 1893): 318–319.

4. The *American Machinist* survey is summarized in Calvert, *The Mechanical Engineer*, p. 72. See also More, "Skill and the Survival of Apprenticeship."

5. This was often the case even in the absence of formal subcontracting systems. See David F. Schloss, *Methods of Industrial Remuneration*, 3rd ed. (London: Williams and Norgate, 1898); Montgomery, *Workers' Control in America*, p. 11; John H. Ashworth, *The Helper and American Trade Unions* (Baltimore: Johns Hopkins University Press, 1915).

6. W. Burns, "New Shop Methods from the Machinist's Point of View," *Engineering Magazine* 31 (April 1906): 93.

7. Samuel, "The Workshop of the World," pp. 40–41; Dan Clawson, *Bureaucracy and the Labor Process: The Transformation of U.S. Industry, 1860–1920* (New York: Monthly Review Press, 1980), pp. 142–143; Egbert P. Watson, "The Changes in One Lifetime in the Machine Shop," *Engineering Magazine* 30 (March 1906): 890.

8. Watson, "Changes in One Lifetime," p. 890.

9. R. O. Clarke, "The Dispute in the British Engineering Industry, 1897–98: An Evaluation," *Economica*, new series, 24 (May 1957): 131; B. C. M. Weekes, "The Amalgamated Society of Engineers, 1880–1914. A Study of Trade Union Government, Politics, and Industrial Policy," Ph.D. thesis, University of Warwick, 1970, pp. 82–89; Jonathan Hart Zeitlin, "Rationalization and Resistance: Skilled Workers and the Transformation of the Division of Labor in the British Engineering Industry, 1830–1930," B.A. thesis, Harvard University, 1977, p. 68; Mark Perlman, *The Machinists: A New Study in American Trade Unionism* (Cambridge, Mass.: Harvard University Press, 1961), pp. 247–250; Bruno Ramirez, *When Workers Fight: The Politics of Industrial Relations in the Progressive Era, 1898–1916* (Westport, Conn.: Greenwood Press, 1978), p. 91.

10. *The Engineer*, December 25, 1885, p. 449; Alfred Williams, *Life in a Railway Factory* (Newton Abbot, Devon: David and Charles Reprints, 1969 [1915]), p. 78; *American Machinist*, May 21, 1891, p. 8; Miller, "The Machinist," p. 322; John Craig, "The Premium System and Its Relation to Discipline in the Factory," *The Open Shop* 4 (March 1905): 137.

11. Engineering Employers' Federation (Broadway House, Tothill St., London SW1), General Letter No. 22, January 8, 1898; Arthur Bar-

ker, *The Management of Small Engineering Workshops* (Manchester: Technical Publishing, 1903), p. 166; Eric Wigham, *The Power to Manage: A History of the Engineering Employers' Federation* (London: Macmillan, 1973), pp. 17–18; W. D. Forbes, "Foremen vs. New Appliances," *Machinery* 5 (January 1899): 143; Report by F. S. North on Superintendents' and Foremen's Clubs, Proceedings of the 7th Annual Convention of the National Metal Trades Association, in *The Open Shop* 4 (1905): 222–224.

12. Employers' abdication of control appears most clearly in the subcontract (or piecemaster) system. See Alan Fox, "Industrial Relations in Nineteenth-Century Birmingham," *Oxford Economic Papers*, new series, 7, no. 1 (1955): 57–62; G. C. Allen, *The Industrial Development of Birmingham and the Black Country, 1860–1927* (London: Frank Cass, 1966), pp. 159–162; Littler, "Deskilling and Changing Structures of Control", Henry Roland, "Six Examples of Successful Shop Management," *Engineering Magazine* 12 (1896–1897): 400–406, 994–1000; John Buttrick, "The Inside Contract System," *Journal of Economic History* 12, no. 3 (1952): 205–221; Alfred Chandler, *The Visible Hand: The Managerial Revolution in American Business* (Cambridge, Mass.: Harvard University Press, 1977), pp. 271–275; Clawson, *Bureaucracy and the Labor Process*, pp. 72–80, 101–108, 110–123.

13. *Amalgamated Engineers' Monthly Journal* (hereafter *AEMJ*), July 1901, p. 3; "Economical Workshop Production," *Mechanical World*, October 29, 1909, pp. 206–207, and February 18, 1910, pp. 74–75; A. L. Levine, "Industrial Change and Its Effects upon Labour, 1900–1914," Ph.D. thesis, University of London, 1954, p. 413; Burns, "New Shop Methods," pp. 93–94; "The Present State of the Art of Industrial Management," American Society of Mechanical Engineers, *Transactions* 34 (1912): 1139; Fred Rogers et al., "Developments in Machine Shop Practice During the Last Decade," American Society of Mechanical Engineers, *Transactions* 34 (1912): 852; L. P. Alford, "Ten Years' Progress in Management," *Mechanical Engineering* 44 (November 1922): 701; Stephen Meyer III, *The Five Dollar Day: Labor Management and Social Control in the Ford Motor Company, 1908–1921* (Albany: State University of New York Press, 1981), pp. 22, 58.

14. Charles Booth, *Life and Labour of the People in London* (New York: AMS Press, 1970 [1902–1904]), second series: Industry, vol. 1, p. 295; Morris Yates, *Wages and Labour Conditions in British Engineering* (London: Macdonald and Evans, 1937), pp. 17–19; James Jefferys, *The Story of the Engineers, 1800–1945* (London: Lawrence and Wishart, 1945), p. 122; *MMJ*, May 1913, p. 475; Victor S. Clark, *History of Manufactures in the United States* (New York: Peter Smith, 1949), vol. 2, p.

144; Harless Wagoner, *The U.S. Machine Tool Industry from 1900 to 1950* (Cambridge, Mass.: MIT Press, 1968), p. 20. At Armstrong Whitworth in 1906, "hundreds" of milling machine specialists earned 25–28s a week, and management claimed little need for time-served turners, at 36–38s a week, on these machines (Keith Burgess, *The Challenge of Labour: Shaping British Society, 1850–1930* [London: Croom Helm, 1980], p. 115). Smith Premier Typewriter in 1909 placed women on drilling machines at $4–10 a week, as against the $14–18 previously earned by men (*MMJ*, September 1909, p. 845).

15. *Engineering Magazine* 16 (1899): 826; *AEMJ*, February 1909, p. 5; Yates, *Wages and Labour Conditions*, pp. 20–23; Jefferys, *The Story of the Engineers*, p. 123; Henry Roland, "The Revolution in Machine Shop Practice," *Engineering Magazine* 18 (1899): 180–188; Clark, *History of Manufactures*, vol. 1, p. 420; Meyer, *The Five Dollar Day*, p. 51.

16. *Engineering Magazine* 20 (1900): 106; Tariff Commission, *Report of the Tariff Commission*, vol. 4: *The Engineering Industries* (London: P. S. King and Son, 1909), paragraph 449; "Economical Workshop Production," *Mechanical World*, October 29, 1909, p. 207; Jefferys, *The Story of the Engineers*, pp. 125–126; E. H. Phelps Brown, *The Growth of British Industrial Relations: A Study from the Standpoint of 1906–14* (New York: St. Martin's Press, 1959), pp. 91–98; U.S. Congress, Senate Committee on Education and Labor, *Report of the Committee of the Senate upon the Relations Between Capital and Labor* (Washington, D.C.: Government Printing Office, 1885), vol. 1, p. 755; Roland, "The Revolution in Machine Shop Practice," pp. 42–48; Burns, "New Shop Methods," pp. 93–95; "Developments in Machine Shop Practice," pp. 850–858; Sterling H. Bunnell, "Jigs and Fixtures as Substitutes for Skill," *Iron Age* 93 (March 5, 1914): 610–611.

17. Joyce Shaw Peterson, "Auto Workers and Their Work, 1900–1933," *Labor History* 22, no. 2 (1981): 220.

18. Meyer, *The Five Dollar Day*, pp. 46, 51.

19. Yates, *Wages and Labour Conditions*, p. 32.

20. Ibid.

21. Meyer, *The Five Dollar Day*, pp. 46, 51.

22. Calculated from figures in Montgomery, *Workers' Control in America*, p. 118.

23. Unskilled workers constituted 20 percent of the engineering work force in Britain in 1914, 13 percent in 1928 (Yates, *Wages and Labour Conditions*, p. 32). Meyer (*The Five Dollar Day*, pp. 46, 50–51) found Ford employees to include 34 percent laborers in 1910, 21 percent in 1913, and 14.6 percent "unskilled workers" in 1917.

24. The decline of apprenticeship programs occurred more slowly in

Britain, but by 1925 only 32 percent of those under twenty-one were working under such programs—and far less than this in engineering and automobile production. Jefferys, *The Story of the Engineers*, p. 205; More, "Skill and the Survival of Apprenticeship"; U.S. Industrial Commission, *Report* (Washington, D.C.: Government Printing Office, 1901–1902), vol. 7, pp. 18, 266, 620–621, vol. 8, p. 489; Daniel Nelson, *Managers and Workers: Origins of the New Factory System in the United States, 1880–1920* (Madison: University of Wisconsin Press, 1975), pp. 96–97; Wagoner, *The U.S. Machine Tool Industry,* pp. 346–347.

25. U.S. Industrial Commission, *Report*, vol. 19, pp. 812–813; *The Open Shop* 5 (January 1906); *MMJ*, March 1908, pp. 257, 261, July 1909, p. 627; National Metal Trades Association, *Synopsis of Proceedings of the Fourteenth Annual Convention*, April 11, 1912, pp. 94–95; Wagoner, *The U.S. Machine Tool Industry,* pp. 88–92. See also the debate in *American Machinist*, July–December 1916, on "Where are the Good Mechanics?" In Britain these tendencies appear later, especially after the war. See, e.g., Great Britain Board of Trade, *Report of the Departmental Committee Appointed by the Board of Trade to Consider the Position of the Engineering Trades After the War* (London: HMSO, 1918), pp. 15–16.

26. Clegg, *The System of Industrial Relations*, p. 170; Jefferys, *The Story of the Engineers*, p. 129; Great Britain, Committee on Industry and Trade, *Survey of Industrial Relations* (London: HMSO, 1926), p. 105; Great Britain, Ministry of Munitions, *History of the Ministry of Munitions* (London: HMSO, 1922), vol. 5, pt. 1, p. 6.

27. *MMJ*, October 1909, p. 928; Arthur Shadwell, *Industrial Efficiency: A Comparative Study of Industrial Life in England, Germany and America* (New York: Longmans, Green, 1906), p. 141.

28. Alford, "Ten Years' Progress in Management," p. 701.

29. A lucid introduction to the varieties and complexities of incentive pay is G. D. H. Cole, *The Payment of Wages* (London: Labour Research Department, 1918).

30. *The Engineer,* April 4, 1902, p. 328; Jefferys, *The Story of the Engineers*, pp. 63, 129; Littler, "Deskilling and Changing Structures of Control"; Craig, "The Premium System," p. 139; William H. Buckler, "The Minimum Wage in the Machinists' Union," in *Studies in American Trade Unionism*, ed. Jacob Hollander and George Barnett (New York: Henry Holt, 1907), pp. 139–140; *The Open Shop* 7 (1908): 103–104; Clawson, *Bureaucracy and the Labor Process*, p. 169.

31. Great Britain, Royal Commission on Labour, *Minutes of Evidence* (London: HMSO, 1893), vol. 3, paragraphs 25,296; 25,515; 25,662; 25,772–775; J. Slater Lewis, "Works Management for the Maximum of Production," *Engineering Magazine* 18 (1899): 202; "Economical Work-

shop Production," *Mechanical World*, October 29, 1909, p. 206, September 9, 1910, p. 122; U.S. Industrial Commission, *Final Report*, vol. 19, pp. 735–736; U.S. Bureau of Labor, 11th Special Report, *Regulation and Restriction of Output* (Washington, D.C.: Government Printing Office, 1904), pp. 114, 118; *The Open Shop* 8 (1908): 99.

32. Coventry District Committee, Amalgamated Society of Engineers, Minutes (hereafter CDC Minutes), September 17, 1907; "Economical Workshop Production," *Mechanical World*, October 29, 1909, p. 206, February 18, 1910, p. 74; M. W. Bourdon, "Production Methods in the British Automobile Plants," *Automotive Industries*, June 24, 1920, p. 1462; *American Machinist*, September 7, 1916, p. 435; L. P. Alford, "Introduction of Shop Management in Typewriter Plants," *American Machinist*, October 5, 1916, pp. 537–540; Montgomery, *Workers' Control in America*, p. 119.

33. Williams, *Life in a Railway Factory*, pp. 304–305; Jefferys, *The Story of the Engineers*, pp. 132, 135; U.S. Congress, House Committee on Labor, *Hearings Before a Special Committee of the House of Representatives to Investigate the Taylor and Other Systems of Shop Management* (Washington, D.C.: Government Printing Office, 1912), vol. 1, p. 458; Records of the Manufacturers' Research Association, Report of the Time Study Code Committee (undated, c. 1928), Harvard Business School, Baker Library, MSS 883.

34. Quoted in Jefferys, *The Story of the Engineers*, p. 132.

35. Meyer, *The Five Dollar Day*, p. 56.

36. "Economical Workshop Production," *Mechanical World*, September 9, 1910, p. 122; J. T. Towlson, "A British View of Shop Efficiency," *American Machinist*, August 24, 1911, p. 362; Robert Stelling, "The Foreman in Relation to Workshop Organization," *Engineering and Industrial Management*, September 4, 1919, p. 294; Littler, "Deskilling and Changing Structures of Control"; W. R. Garside and H. F. Gospel, "Employers and Managers: Their Organizational Structure and Industrial Strategies," in *A History of British Industrial Relations, 1875–1914*, ed. Chris Wrigley (Brighton, Sussex: Harvester Press, 1982), pp. 102–103; *The Open Shop* 5 (1906): 219; *American Machinist*, March 16, 1911, p. 503, June 8, 1911, p. 1069; G. G. Weaver, "The Foreman—Past and Future," *American Machinist*, October 26, 1922, p. 652; Nelson, *Managers and Workers*, p. 57.

37. Treatments of scientific management, serving varied polemical purposes, include Milton Nadworny, *Scientific Management and the Unions, 1900–1932* (Cambridge: Harvard University Press, 1955); Reinhard Bendix, *Work and Authority in Industry: Ideologies of Management in the Course of Industrialization* (Berkeley and Los Angeles: University

of California Press, 1974); Harry Braverman, *Labor and Monopoly Capital: The Degradation of Work in the Twentieth Century* (New York: Monthly Review Press, 1974); Bryan Palmer, "Class, Conception, and Conflict: The Thrust for Efficiency, Managerial Views of Labor, and the Working Class Rebellion, 1903–1922," *Review of Radical Political Economy* 7, no. 2 (1975): 31–49; Craig Littler, "Understanding Taylorism," *British Journal of Sociology* 25, no. 2 (1978): 185–202; Montgomery, *Workers' Control in America*, ch. 2; Clawson, *Bureaucracy and the Labor Process;* Daniel Nelson, *Frederick Taylor and the Rise of Scientific Management* (Madison: University of Wisconsin Press, 1980); and Tony Elger and Bill Schwarz, "Monopoly Capitalism and the Impact of Taylorism: Notes on Lenin, Gramsci, Braverman, and Sohn-Rethel," in *Capital and Labour: Studies in the Capitalist Labour Process*, ed. Theo Nichols, pp. 358–369 (London: Athlone Press, 1980).

38. *Handling Men* (Chicago: A. W. Shaw, 1917), p. 23; Braverman, *Labor and Monopoly Capital*, p. 85.

39. U.S. Bureau of Labor, *Regulation and Restriction of Output*, p. 128; U.S. Congress, *Hearings Before a Special Committee*, vol. 1, p. 83; Littler, "Understanding Taylorism," pp. 188–189; Montgomery, *Workers' Control in America*, p. 114.

40. Joseph A. Litterer, "Systematic Management: Design for Organizational Recoupling in American Manufacturing Firms," *Business History Review* 37, no. 4 (1963): 369–391; Nelson, *Managers and Workers*, pp. 55–57, 75–76.

41. On scientific management and incentive pay, see P. J. Darlington, "Methods of Remunerating Labor," *Engineering Magazine* 17 (June 1899): 444–454 and 17 (September 1899): 925–936; U.S. Bureau of Labor, *Regulation and Restriction of Output*, pp. 114, 118; U.S. Congress, *Hearings Before a Special Committee*, vol. 1, p. 55; *MMJ*, June 1912, p. 541; Alford, "Introduction of Shop Management"; Montgomery, *Workers' Control in America*, p. 114; and Clawson, *Bureaucracy and the Labor Process*, pp. 235–239.

42. This point is developed most clearly by Littler, "Understanding Taylorism," pp. 189–195. See also Clawson, *Bureaucracy and the Labor Process*, p. 31 and ch. 6, passim.

43. W. F. Watson, *Machines and Men: An Autobiography of an Itinerant Mechanic* (London: George Allen and Unwin, 1935), pp. 186–195; Wagoner, *The U.S. Machine Tool Industry*, pp. 21, 83; Meyer, *The Five Dollar Day*, pp. 54–55, 58.

44. Rogers et al., "Developments in Machine Shop Practice," p. 852; Dexter Kimball, "Basic Principles of Industrial Organization," NMTA, *Proceedings of the Annual Convention*, 1914, p. 162; Alford, "Introduc-

tion of Shop Management," pp. 537–540; Littler, "Understanding Taylorism," pp. 189–193; Clawson, *Bureaucracy and the Labor Process*, pp. 217–223; Meyer, *The Five Dollar Day*, pp. 54–56.

45. For discussions of British scientific management in the fifteen years before the war, see *Engineering*, March 1, 1912, p. 290; the series of articles on scientific management in the Workers' Union *Record*, February–July 1914; James F. Whiteford, "Development of Management in the United Kingdom," *Mechanical Engineering*, November 1922, pp. 703–704; Watson, *Machines and Men*, pp. 60, 89–98; Jefferys, *The Story of the Engineers*, pp. 124–125, 132; L. Urwick and E. F. L. Brech, *The Making of Scientific Management*, vol. 2: *Management in British Industry* (London: Management Publications Trust, 1949); Asa Briggs, "Social Background," in *The System of Industrial Relations in Great Britain: Its History, Law, and Institutions*, ed. Allan Flanders and H. A. Clegg (Oxford: Basil Blackwell, 1954), pp. 35–36; Phelps Brown, *The Growth of British Industrial Relations*, pp. xv–xvi; Littler, "Deskilling and Changing Structures of Control"; Garside and Gospel, "Employers and Managers," pp. 102–103.

46. Theoretical statements of how product markets shape the labor process include *Cambridge Journal of Economics* 3, no. 3 (1979), special issue, "The Labour Process, Market Structure, and Marxist Theory"; and Michael Piore and Charles Sabel, *The Second Industrial Divide: Possibilities for Prosperity* (New York: Basic Books, 1984).

47. *Engineering Magazine* 16 (1899): 826; Jefferys, *The Story of the Engineers*, p. 120; S. B. Saul, "The Motor Industry in Britain to 1914," *Business History* 5, no. 1 (1962): 38, and "The Engineering Industry," in *The Development of British Industry and Foreign Competition, 1875–1914*, ed. Derek H. Aldcroft (London: George Allen and Unwin, 1968), pp. 190, 215; Allen, *The Industrial Development of Birmingham*, pp. 292–297, 302–303; F. W. Carr, "Engineering Workers and the Rise of Labour in Coventry, 1914–1939," Ph.D. thesis, University of Warwick, 1978, pp. 5–7; Roland, "The Revolution in Machine Shop Practice," pp. 42–48, 369–370; Clark, *History of Manufactures*, vol. 3, pp. 154–156; Fred H. Colvin, *60 Years with Men and Machines: An Autobiography* (New York: McGraw-Hill, 1947), pp. 84–87; L. T. C. Rolt, *A Short History of Machine Tools* (Cambridge, Mass.: MIT Press, 1965), p. 215; Wagoner, *The U.S. Machine Tool Industry*, p. 21.

48. H. F. L. Orcutt, "Machine Shop Management in Europe and America," *Engineering Magazine* 16 (1899): 551.

49. Ibid., pp. 551–554; Tariff Commission, *Report of the Tariff Commission*, paragraphs 1041–1042; Great Britain, Board of Trade, *Report of the Departmental Committee*, p. 12; Calvert, *The Mechanical Engineer*,

pp. 5–6; Wagoner, *The U.S. Machine Tool Industry*, pp. 19, 272–273. Although similar trends existed in Britain, they clearly came later and moved more slowly. The issue is discussed in Tariff Commission, *Report of the Tariff Commission*; Saul, "The Engineering Industry," pp. 186–187, and "The Machine Tool Industry in Britain to 1914," *Business History* 10, no. 1 (1968): 26, 36–40; and Roderick Floud, *The Machine Tool Industry, 1850–1914* (Cambridge: Cambridge University Press, 1976), pp. 11–17.

50. The influence of labor supply on technical innovation is analyzed in detail by H. J. Habakkuk, *American and British Technology in the Nineteenth Century: The Search for Labor Saving Inventions* (Cambridge: Cambridge University Press, 1967). See also Orcutt, "Machine Shop Management," *Engineering Magazine* 16 (1899): 703–707, and 17 (1899): 386–389.

51. Hobsbawm, *Labouring Men*, pp. 348–358; Hinton, *The First Shop Stewards' Movement*, pp. 58–59; Jonathan Zeitlin, "Craft Control and the Division of Labour: Engineers and Compositors in Britain, 1890–1930," *Cambridge Journal of Economics* 3, no. 3 (1979): 267; Tariff Commission, *Report of the Tariff Commission*, p. 845.

52. *Engineering Magazine* 16 (1899): 826; "Economical Workshop Production," *Mechanical World*, February 18, 1910, p. 74; Jefferys, *The Story of the Engineers*, pp. 122–123, 202–203; Allen, *The Industrial Development of Birmingham*, pp. 315–316; Floud, *The Machine Tool Industry*, pp. 23–26; Bunnell, "Jigs and Fixtures," pp. 610–611; Clark, *History of Manufactures*, vol. 2, pp. 22, 96; vol. 3, p. 155; Rolt, *A Short History of Machine Tools*, pp. 200–201; Wagoner, *The U.S. Machine Tool Industry*, pp. 17–18.

53. Jefferys, *The Story of the Engineers*, pp. 124–125.

54. More ("Skill and the Survival of Apprenticeship," p. 112) estimates that nearly 50 percent of skilled engineering workers were unionized as early as 1861. By 1911, some 29.2 percent of *all* metal and engineering workers, skilled and less skilled alike, were unionized, and most union members were skilled workers (George Sayers Bain and Robert Price, *Profiles of Union Growth: A Comparative Statistical Portrait of Eight Countries* [Oxford: Basil Blackwell, 1980], p. 50). The figure for machinists is offered by Montgomery, *Workers' Control in America*, p. 63.

55. Phelps Brown, *The Growth of British Industrial Relations*, p. 24; Andrew Dawson, "The Paradox of Dynamic Technological Change and the Labor Aristocracy in the United States, 1880–1914," *Labor History* 20, no. 3 (1979): 331.

56. Tariff Commission, *Report of the Tariff Commission*, paragraphs 568, 580, 618, 630, 664, 715.

57. John Upp, "The Woman Worker," American Society of Mechanical Engineers, *Transactions* 39 (December 1917): 1134. See also National

Industrial Conference Board, *Wartime Employment of Women in the Metal Trades* (Boston: NICB, 1918), pp. 48–50.

58. Quoted by P. W. Kingsford, *Engineers Inventors and Workers* (London: Edward Arnold, 1964), p. 138. For similar views and other examples, see Habakkuk, *American and British Technology,* p. 153; and U.S. Industrial Commission, *Report,* vol. 8, p. 40.

59. This is a point Clawson (*Bureaucracy and the Labor Process,* pp. 122–123) makes with respect to subcontractors, but it is more broadly applicable.

60. *The Engineer,* April 4, 1902, p. 328; "Economical Workshop Production," *Mechanical World,* September 9, 1910, p. 122; Cole, *The Payment of Wages,* p. 73; Forbes, "Foremen vs. New Appliances," p. 143; *The Open Shop* 5 (1906): 219; U.S. Senate, Commission on Industrial Relations, *Final Report and Testimony* (Washington, D.C.: Government Printing Office, 1916), vol. 1, p. 838; Montgomery, *Workers' Control in America,* p. 42.

61. Engineering Employers' Federation, General letters, no. 22 (January 8, 1898) and no. 25 (February 7, 1898), offices of the EEF, London.

62. Synopsis of Proceedings of the 7th Annual Convention of the NMTA, March 23–24, 1905, in *The Open Shop* 4 (1905): 222.

63. *The Engineer,* November 5, 1897, p. 455; *AEMJ,* January 1898, pp. 54–55, March 1907, p. 12, April 1907, p. 14; *MMJ,* July 1904, p. 637; *The Open Shop* 4 (1905): 223–224.

64. Judith A. Merkle, *Management and Ideology: The Legacy of the International Scientific Management Movement* (Berkeley and Los Angeles: University of California Press, 1980), p. 75.

65. Meyer Bloomfield, "The Aim and Work of Employment Managers' Associations," *Annals of the American Academy of Political and Social Science* 65 (May 1916): 83. Similar arguments were advanced in Britain by the Welfare Workers' Institute (forerunner of the Institute of Personnel Management). M. M. Niven, *Personnel Management, 1913–1963: The Growth of Personnel Management and the Development of the Institute* (London: Institute of Personnel Management, 1967), pp. 44, 48.

66. Bloomfield, "The Aim and Work," p. 76.

67. Calvert, *The Mechanical Engineer in America,* pp. 65, 281.

68. Merkle, *Management and Ideology,* pp. 71–75, 86–92. See also David Noble, *America by Design: Science, Technology, and the Rise of Corporate Capitalism* (New York: Knopf, 1977).

69. James Arthur, "American and British Workmen and Machinery," *American Machinist,* November 24, 1892, p. 4; *The Engineer,* September 24, 1897, p. 303, January 21, 1898, p. 66; Orcutt, "Machine Shop Management," *Engineering Magazine* 16 (1899): 552–553, 703–707, and 17

(1899): 386–389; Alfred Mosley, "British Views of American Workshops," *Cassier's Magazine* 23, no. 3 (1903): 477–478; Shadwell, *Industrial Efficiency*, pp. 141–143; National Metal Trades Association, *Synopsis of Proceedings*, 1911, p. 200; Joseph Wickham Roe, *English and American Tool Builders* (New Haven, Conn.: Yale University Press, 1916), pp. 105–106; Urwick and Brech, *The Making of Scientific Management;* Saul, "The Engineering Industry," pp. 231, 235.

70. A. L. Levine, *Industrial Retardation in Britain, 1880–1914* (London: Weidenfeld and Nicolson, 1967), p. 16.

71. "Men and Output," *The Times Engineering Supplement*, September 29, 1916, p. 146.

72. Saul, "The Motor Industry," pp. 43–44. See also Colvin, *60 Years*, pp. 130–131.

73. S. B. Saul, "The Market and the Development of the Mechanical Engineering Industries in Britain, 1860–1914," *Economic History Review*, second series, 20, no. 1 (1967): 116–117, 124; Habakkuk, *American and British Technology*, p. 218.

74. Orcutt, "Machine Shop Management," *Engineering Magazine* 16 (1899): 551–554; Great Britain, Board of Trade, *Report of the Departmental Committee*, p. 7; Habakkuk, *American and British Technology*, p. 219.

75. Habakkuk, *American and British Technology;* Samuel, "The Workshop of the World," pp. 47–48.

76. Orcutt, "Machine Shop Management," *Engineering Magazine* 17 (1899): 268; "American and British Workmen," p. 243; Levine, *Industrial Retardation*, pp. 79–94; Habakkuk, *American and British Technology*, p. 143.

77. Great Britain, Board of Trade, *Report of the Departmental Committee*, p. 11; Saul, "The Engineering Industry," p. 231.

78. Habakkuk, *American and British Technology*, pp. 105–106, 218.

79. Saul, "The Market and the Development," p. 124.

80. These statistics are calculated from Great Britain, Business Statistics Office, *Historical Record of the Census of Production, 1907–1970* (London: Government Statistical Service, n.d.), Tables 1 and 6; Great Britain, Census of Production, 1907, *Parliamentary Papers*, Cmd. 6320, 1912–1913, cix, p. 204; U.S. Department of Commerce, Bureau of the Census, *Thirteenth Census of the United States*, vol. 8, Manufactures, 1909 (Washington, D.C.: Government Printing Office, 1913), Table 19.

81. Jefferys, *The Story of the Engineers*, p. 198. Gross output of textile machinery was 13 million pounds, of railway locomotives (including repair) 12.4 million. The next largest category was steam engines (excluding locomotive and agricultural) at 6.9 million, followed by cycles and motor cars (including parts) at 5.6 million, and motor vehicles and parts at 5.2 million. Saul, "The Market and the Development," p. 113.

82. Tariff Commission, *Report of the Tariff Commission*, Tables 41 and 49.

83. Barbara Drake, *Women in the Engineering Trades* (London: Labour Research Department, 1918), pp. 8–9; Hinton, *The First Shop Stewards' Movement*, p. 218; Keith Burgess, *The Origins of British Industrial Relations: The Nineteenth Century Experience* (London: Croom Helm, 1975), p. 50; Andrew L. Friedman, *Industry and Labour: Class Struggle at Work and Monopoly Capitalism* (London: Macmillan, 1977), p. 192; Carr, "Engineering Workers and the Rise of Labour," pp. 10, 107; Keith McClelland and Alastair Reid, "Wood, Iron and Steel: Technology, Labour and Trade Union Organisation in the Shipbuilding Industry, 1890–1914," in *Divisions of Labour: Skilled Workers and Technological Change in Nineteenth Century England*, ed. Royden Harrison and Jonathan Zeitlin, pp. 151–184 (Urbana: University of Illinois Press, 1985).

84. *American Machinist*, November 2, 1922, p. 704; Colvin, *60 Years*, p. 95.

85. E.g., in 1901, Bridgeport machinists demanded one worker to a machine, even though they realized that manufacturers could go out "and hire any ordinary man with common sense to come in the shop and after a week's tutoring that man can run half a dozen automatic machines as well as a machinist can. . . . At the present time in any of the factories in Connecticut men will be found running from two to as high as ten and twelve machines" (*Bridgeport Herald*, April 14, 1901). Having a worker run half a dozen automatic machines was not beyond the technical competence of many British manufacturers. The difference is rather between a weak union demanding an end to established practices and a strong one defending the status quo against managerial encroachments.

86. On specialists, see Levine, *Industrial Retardation*, pp. 46–49. In 1914, females accounted for 15.7 percent of electrical engineering employees and 14.3 percent of small arms manufacturing employees in Britain. In the United States women (not including girls under the age of sixteen) constituted 19.9 and 19.7 percent, respectively, in these branches. Great Britain, Ministry of Munitions, *History of the Ministry*, vol. 4, pt. 4, p. 139; National Industrial Conference Board, Research Report No. 8, *Wartime Employment of Women in the Metal Trades* (Boston: NICB, 1918), p. 2. On the persistence of apprenticeship in Britain, see More, "Skill and the Survival of Apprenticeship," pp. 112–118. The underdevelopment of British tool room practice is reviewed by *The Foreman*, September 1921, p. 16.

87. Hinton, *The First Shop Stewards' Movement*, pp. 61–62; Roger Penn, *Skilled Workers in the Class Structure* (Cambridge: Cambridge University Press, 1985).

88. Tariff Commission, *Report of the Tariff Commission*, paragraphs

1017, 1026; CDC Minutes, July 21, 1909; Cole, *The Payment of Wages*, p. 92; Watson, *Machines and Men*, p. 92.

89. *AEMJ*, January 1902, p. 10; National Metal Trades Association, *Synopsis of Proceedings*, April 12–13, 1911, p. 200; P. J. O'Neill, "British and American Industrial Methods Compared and Contrasted," *Machine Tool Review*, June–July 1917, pp. 25–26; Great Britain, Board of Trade, *Report of the Departmental Committee*, p. 11; Saul, "The Engineering Industry," p. 231.

90. The term "noninstrumental aspects of the craft tradition" is from Hinton (*The First Shop Stewards' Movement*), who clearly emphasizes the importance of craft traditions in the development of British factory politics.

91. U.S. Congress, Senate Committee on Education and Labor, *Report of the Committee*, vol. 1, p. 743.

92. Watson, "Changes in One Lifetime," p. 890.

93. U.S. Congress, Senate Committee on Education and Labor, *Report of the Committee*, vol. 1, p. 755.

94. Commission on Industrial Relations, *Final Report and Testimony* (Washington, D.C.: Government Printing Office, 1916), vol. 3, p. 2840.

95. *AEMJ*, February 1909, p. 5.

96. Ibid., March 1897, pp. 19–20.

97. *MMJ*, March 1914, p. 274.

98. Great Britain, Royal Commission on Labour, *Minutes of Evidence*, vol. 3, paragraph 22,658; CDC Minutes, October 8, 1907, March 9, 1908, July 8, 1909, August 25, 1909; Williams, *Life in a Railway Factory*, pp. 6, 37, 184; Goodrich, *The Frontier of Control*, p. 163; *MMJ*, March 1896, pp. 70–71, July 1907, p. 667; U.S. Bureau of Labor, *Regulation and Restriction of Output*, p. 142; Colvin, *60 Years*, p. 275.

99. *MMJ*, April 1914, p. 367.

100. CDC Minutes, January 20, June 10, 1909, and passim; Jefferys, *The Story of the Engineers*, pp. 154–155; Wigham, *The Power to Manage*, p. 74; *MMJ*, February 1900, pp. 104–105; U.S. Bureau of Labor, *Regulation and Restriction of Output*, p. 141.

101. U.S. Congress, House Committee on Labor, *Hearings Before a Special Committee*, vol. 1, p. 279. See also Great Britain, Royal Commission on Labour, *Minutes of Evidence*, vol. 3, paragraph 22,658; Trades Union Congress, *The Premium Bonus System: Report of an Inquiry* (London: TUC, 1910); and *MMJ*, January 1893, p. 356.

102. *AEMJ*, September 1921, pp. 59–60; Urwick and Brech, *The Making of Scientific Management*, p. 106; *MMJ*, January 1893, p. 357, March 1902, p. 186.

103. Goodrich, *The Frontier of Control*, p. 172; *AEMJ*, September

1921, pp. 59–60; Jefferys, *The Story of the Engineers*, p. 100; Wigham, *The Power to Manage*, p. 73; *Bridgeport Herald*, April 10, 1898; *MMJ*, June 1911, p. 557; Colvin, *60 Years*, p. 275.

104. *MMJ*, May 1897, p. 139. See also *MMJ*, October 1907, p. 967, September 1908, p. 789, June 1911, p. 557; U.S. Congress, House Committee on Labor, *Hearings Before a Special Committee*, vol. 2, pp. 924, 929, 1005, 1032, vol. 3, pp. 1660, 1760–1761, 1812. For Britain, see Great Britain, Royal Commission on Labour, *Minutes of Evidence*, vol. 3, paragraph 22,658; CDC Minutes, July 8, 1909; *AEMJ*, September 1921, p. 60.

105. Commission on Industrial Relations, *Final Report and Testimony*, vol. 1, p. 874. See also U.S. Bureau of Labor, *Regulation and Restriction of Output*, p. 141; CDC Minutes, March 9, 1908, July 26, August 25, 1909; W. F. Watson, *The Worker and Wage Incentives* (London: Hogarth Press, 1934), pp. 23–24; Urwick and Brech, *The Making of Scientific Management*, p. 106; Wigham, *The Power to Manage*, p. 73.

106. *The Engineer*, December 25, 1885, p. 499.

107. U.S. Congress, House Committee on Labor, *Hearings Before a Special Committee*, vol. 1, pp. 22–23.

108. J. D. Lawrence, "Prussianism in the Workshop," *Amalgamated Engineers' Monthly Journal*, September 1919, p. 53.

109. Commission on Industrial Relations, *Final Report and Testimony*, vol. 1, p. 903.

110. *Bridgeport Herald*, May 12, 1901.

111. For example, CDC Minutes, September 17, 1913 (at Rover), November 18, 1913 (at Daimler), February 4, 1914 (at Swift Motor Company), and May 9, 1914 (at the Coventry Ordnance Works).

112. Fred J. Miller, "Scientific Management: Its Installation and Operation," *Efficiency Society Journal* 5 (March 1916): 121–125. Such views were particularly popular during the war and the early 1920s.

113. *MMJ*, September 1893, p. 346. ASE officials and members sometimes made similar arguments. See, e.g., CDC Minutes, October 6, 1910, and May 21, 1914; *AEMJ*, September 1919, p. 53.

114. Frank Hudson, "The Machinist's Side of Taylorism," *American Machinist*, April 27, 1911, p. 773; U.S. Congress, House Committee on Labor, *Hearings Before a Special Committee*, passim; Commission on Industrial Relations, *Final Report and Testimony*, vol. 1, pp. 132–141, 838, 903, 945; U.S. Congress, House Committee on Labor, *Hearings on a Bill to Regulate the Method of Directing Work of Government Employees* (Washington, D.C.: Government Printing Office, 1916); Montgomery, *Workers' Control in America*, pp. 114–123; Clawson, *Bureaucracy and the Labor Process*, pp. 235–239.

115. U.S. Congress, House Committee on Labor, *Hearings Before a Special Committee*, vol. 1, p. 20.

116. *MMJ*, November 1911, p. 1108.

117. Montgomery, *Workers' Control in America*, p. 117. Although less afflicted with scientific management, British engineers voiced many of the same criticisms. See, e.g., *AEMJ*, January 1903, p. 3; Towlson, "A British View of Shop Efficiency," p. 362; Cole, *The Payment of Wages*, p. 73; Watson, *Machines and Men*, p. 188; Littler, "Deskilling and Changing Structures of Control"; and Garside and Gospel, "Employers and Managers," pp. 102–103.

118. *MMJ*, March 1890, p. 30.

119. U.S. Congress, House Committee on Labor, *Hearings Before a Special Committee*, vol. 3, p. 1870.

120. *MMJ*, July 1918, p. 640.

121. For example, Hiram Maxim, "The Effects of Trade Unionism upon Skilled Mechanics," *Engineering Magazine* 14 (November 1897): 193; "English and American Methods in the Engineering and Iron Trades," *Engineer*, January 21, 1898, p. 66; George Barnes [General Secretary of the ASE], letter to the *Engineer*, May 19, 1899, p. 489; "American and British Workmen," *Engineering* 76 (1903): 205–207, 242–244.

122. U.S. Congress, House Committee on Labor, *Hearings Before a Special Committee*, vol. 3, p. 1668, vol. 1, p. 691.

123. Ibid., vol. 1, p. 1812.

124. "The Present State of the Art of Industrial Relations," American Society of Mechanical Engineers, *Transactions* 34 (1912): 1160.

125. U.S. Congress, House Committee on Labor, *Hearings Before a Special Committee*, vol. 2, p. 1008; Commission on Industrial Relations, *Final Report and Testimony*, vol. 1, p. 900.

126. Ibid., vol. 1, p. 527.

127. The relative importance of class identities among English and American workers is analyzed by Ira Katznelson, "Working-Class Formation and the State: Nineteenth-Century England in American Perspective," in *Bringing the State Back In*, ed. Peter B. Evans, Dietrich Rueschemeyer, and Theda Skocpol, pp. 257–284 (New York: Cambridge University Press, 1985).

Chapter 3

1. F. W. Hirst, "The Policy of the Engineers," *Economic Journal* 8 (March 1898): 126; Jefferys, *The Story of the Engineers*, p. 137; Weekes, "The Amalgamated Society of Engineers," pp. 87–88; Burgess, *The Origins of British Industrial Relations*, pp. 35–41; *MMJ*, May 1897, p. 140,

April 1899, p. 182, June 1899, pp. 403–404; Perlman, *The Machinists*, p. 303.

2. *MMJ*, January 1891, p. 107; Perlman, *The Machinists*, p. 9.

3. Jefferys, *The Story of the Engineers*, pp. 140–142; E. H. Hunt, *British Labour History, 1815–1914* (Atlantic Highlands, N.J.: Humanities Press, 1981), p. 284; Perlman, *The Machinists*, p. 11.

4. *AEMJ*, January 1899, p. 43; George Nicol Barnes, "Uses and Abuses of Organisation Among Employers and Employees: The Old Trade Unionism vs. Wisely Organised Labour," *Engineering Magazine* 20 (January 1900): 563; *MMJ*, July 1899, p. 481; Janes, *The Control of Strikes*, pp. 71–73.

5. The clearest formulation of these points is Gouldner, *Wildcat Strike*, pp. 34–37. See also Warner and Low, *The Social System of the Modern Factory*, p. 131; Mann, *Consciousness and Action*, p. 32; and Offe and Wiesenthal, "Two Logics of Collective Action," p. 83.

6. *MMJ*, June 1897, pp. 214–216. See also Perlman, *The Machinists*, p. 12; U.S. Industrial Commission, *Report*, vol. 19, pp. 968–969.

7. *MMJ*, May 1897, p. 140, June 1899, pp. 390, 403–405; James O'Connell, "Piece-Work Not Necessary for Best Results in the Machine Shop," *Engineering Magazine* 19 (June 1900): 373; Perlman, *The Machinists*, p. 25.

8. Amalgamated Society of Engineers, *Notes on the Engineering Trade Lock-Out of 1897–8* (London: Charles Mitchell, n.d.), Appendix, pp. 13–14; Weekes, "The Amalgamated Society of Engineers," p. 82; Stearns, *Lives of Labor*, p. 323.

9. Phelps Brown, *The Growth of British Industrial Relations*, pp. 124–125; Hinton, *The First Shop Stewards' Movement*, p. 79; Burgess, *The Origins of British Industrial Relations*, pp. 35–41; Clegg, *The System of Industrial Relations*, pp. 155–157; *MMJ*, March 1893, p. 108; U.S. Bureau of Labor, 11th Special Report, *Regulation and Restriction of Output*, pp. 103–104; Perlman, *The Machinists*, pp. 151–153.

10. *AEMJ*, July 1897, p. 59; Amalgamated Society of Engineers, *Jubilee Souvenir* (London: Co-operative Printing Society, 1901), p. 102; Burgess, *The Origins of British Industrial Relations*, pp. 37–39, 53, 60; Clegg, *The System of Industrial Relations*, p. 38; Hunt, *British Labour History*, p. 284. In the United States, too, many accounts of strikes in the *MMJ* show that initial negotiations were handled by a deputation or a shop committee. See, e.g., *MMJ*, April 1899, p. 210, August 1899, p. 502, March 1900, p. 165, and February 1901, p. 102. See also U.S. Industrial Commission, *Report*, vol. 17, p. 230; and U.S. Bureau of Labor, 11th Special Report, *Regulation and Restriction of Output*, p. 105

11. Jefferys, *The Story of the Engineers*, p. 69; Richard Croucher,

"The Amalgamated Society of Engineers and Local Autonomy, 1898–1914," M.A. thesis, University of Warwick, 1971, p. 3; *MMJ*, January 1892, p. 375, November 1894, p. 432, February 1896, p. 26, February 1897, p. 19, June 1899, p. 404; H. M. Norris, "Actual Experience with the Premium Plan," *Engineering Magazine* 18 (January 1900): 575; U.S. Bureau of Labor, 11th Special Report, *Regulation and Restriction of Output*, p. 105.

12. Burgess, *The Origins of British Industrial Relations*, p. 41; Zeitlin, "Rationalization and Resistance," p. 68; *MMJ*, January 1893, p. 355, July 1893, p. 236, October 1897, p. 504, May 1898, p. 316; Perlman, *The Machinists*, p. 249.

13. CDC Minutes, April 26, 1899; Jefferys, *The Story of the Engineers*, pp. 103–104, 142–143; Weekes, "The Amalgamated Society of Engineers," pp. 82, 87–88.

14. Wage rates were attached to machines in Coventry, where the union was in a weaker position and employers had made more headway in rationalizing production (CDC Minutes, July 2, 1901). See also Amalgamated Society of Engineers, *Notes on the Engineering Trade Lockout*, Appendix, pp. 13–14; Clarke, "The Dispute in the British Engineering Industry," p. 131.

15. CDC Minutes, 1902 District Rules; Watson, *Machines and Men*, pp. 13, 17–20.

16. Hinton, *The First Shop Stewards' Movement*, p. 61; H. A. Clegg, Alan Fox, and A. F. Thompson, *A History of British Trade Unions Since 1889*, vol. 1: 1889–1910 (London: Oxford University Press, 1964), p. 141.

17. Jefferys, *The Story of the Engineers*, p. 139; CDC Minutes, May 6, 1901, quoting 1897 agreement with Webster and Bennet, September 3, 1900, October 3, 1901; Clegg, Fox, and Thompson, *A History of British Trade Unions*, p. 141.

18. E.g., in Coventry, CDC Minutes, April 21 and 26, May 2, 1899. See also Shadwell, *Industrial Efficiency*, pp. 21–22.

19. Amalgamated Society of Engineers, *Jubilee Souvenir*, p. 102; Weekes, "The Amalgamated Society of Engineers," pp. 9–11; Croucher, "The Amalgamated Society of Engineers," p. 4; Burgess, *The Origins of British Industrial Relations*, p. 60.

20. *AEMJ*, April 1899, p. 60; Croucher, "The Amalgamated Society of Engineers," pp. 3–4; Burgess, *The Origins of British Industrial Relations*, pp. 53, 56.

21. Burgess, *The Origins of British Industrial Relations*, p. 47. See also Hirst, "The Policy of the Engineers," p. 126; Jefferys, *The Story of the Engineers*, p. 137; Croucher, "The Amalgamated Society of Engineers," p. 3; Hinton, *The First Shop Stewards' Movement*, p. 79; Burgess, *The Origins of British Industrial Relations*, pp. 35–41.

22. Burgess, *The Origins of British Industrial Relations*, pp. 41–56.

23. Jefferys, *The Story of the Engineers*, pp. 91, 108–109, 140–141; Burgess, *The Origins of British Industrial Relations*, pp. 38–41.

24. General information on the lockout and settlement is available in *AEMJ, Engineering*, and *The Engineer;* Ernest Aves, "Labor Notes: The Dispute in the Engineering Trade, &c.," *Economic Journal* 7 (December 1897): 625–630; and "The Dispute in the Engineering Trades," *Economic Journal* 8 (March 1898): 115–124; Amalgamated Society of Engineers, *Notes on the Engineering Trade Lock-Out;* Jefferys, *The Story of the Engineers*, pp. 143–149; Clarke, "The Dispute in the British Engineering Industry"; Clegg, Fox, and Thompson, *A History of British Trade Unions*, pp. 161–167.

25. Arthur Shadwell, *The Engineering Industry and the Crisis of 1922: A Chapter in Industrial History* (London: John Murray, 1922), pp. 21–22.

26. Nigel Todd, "Trade Unions and the Engineering Industry Dispute at Barrow-in-Furness, 1897–1898," *International Review of Social History* 20, no. 1 (1975): 35–41.

27. This was the opening statement of the Terms of Settlement, under the heading "General Principle Agreed To of Freedom to Employers in the Management of Their Works."

28. *Engineering*, September 24, 1897, p. 386.

29. Ibid., October 21, 1898, p. 527.

30. *MMJ*, June 1897, p. 218; Buckler, "The Minimum Wage in the Machinists' Union," p. 117; Ashworth, *The Helper and American Trade Unions*, pp. 32–33; Perlman, *The Machinists*, p. 303; Montgomery, *Workers' Control in America*, p. 15.

31. *MMJ*, November 1894, p. 432, June 1899, p. 404; Norris, "Actual Experience with the Premium Plan," pp. 575–576; U.S. Industrial Commission, *Report*, vol. 8, pp. 119, 130; Colvin, *60 Years*, p. 275.

32. Perlman, *The Machinists*, pp. 247–259. The IAM won few such contracts outside of its strongholds—railroad repair shops, breweries, hand tool manufacture, small shops, and a few well-organized cities (especially Chicago and San Francisco).

33. Montgomery, *Workers' Control in America*, pp. 15–17; see also *MMJ*, February 1891, p. 19.

34. Perlman, *The Machinists*, pp. 229–235. Although the definition of machinists' work was not at issue, conflicts with the International Machinists' Union in the mid to late 1890s and with the American branches of the ASE in the late 1890s and early 1900s indicate the same sectional orientation on the IAM's part.

35. *MMJ*, January 1892, p. 375. See also February 1896, p. 26, February 1897, p. 19.

36. Perlman, *The Machinists*, pp. 151–159. From June 1899 to June 1901, 200 local lodges reported settling 759 grievances, securing apprenticeship agreements with 409 firms, and gaining the closed shop in 163 firms, among other achievements. *MMJ*, July 1901, p. 464.

37. *MMJ* reports of disputes typically refer to an initial deputation to management. See also *MMJ*, April 1899, p. 210, March 1900, p. 165; U.S. Industrial Commission, *Report*, vol. 8, p. 127; P. J. Conlon, "Past, Present and Future of Our Association," *MMJ*, February 1909, p. 164. In response to a questionnaire prepared for the U.S. Industrial Commission, IAM officials noted that, although their experience with written agreements was good, "as much may be accomplished by a sensible shop committee." IAM Miscellaneous Pamphlet #5, Department of Labor Library.

38. E.g., *MMJ*, April 1898, pp. 194–195, July 1898, p. 390, August 1899, p. 502.

39. See the work histories of machinists testifying before the U.S. Congress, House Committee on Labor, *Hearings Before a Special Committee*, and the discussion of "boomers" (migratory machinists) by Clinton S. Golden, "The Militants of the Metal Trades—The Machinists," in *The Amalgamated Illustrated Almanac—1924* (New York: Amalgamated Clothing Workers of America, Education Department, 1924), p. 143.

40. On sympathy strikes and craft control, see Montgomery, *Workers' Control in America*, pp. 18–26.

41. Ibid., pp. 23–24.

42. Perlman, *The Machinists*, p. 12.

43. Ibid., pp. 151–152. See also Janes, *The Control of Strikes*, p. 111.

44. *MMJ*, July 1901, p. 464.

45. Ibid., March 1893, p. 108.

46. Basic secondary sources on the strike and its settlement are Ernest L. Bogart, "The Machinists' Strike, 1900," *Yale Review* 9 (November 1900): 302–313; Perlman, *The Machinists*, pp. 25–27; Montgomery, *Workers' Control in America*, pp. 49–52.

47. U.S. Industrial Commission, *Report*, vol. 8, pp. 501–502; Clarence E. Bonnett, *Employers' Associations in the United States: A Study of Typical Associations* (New York: Macmillan, 1922), pp. 103–104; Montgomery, *Workers' Control in America*, p. 50.

48. *MMJ*, May 1900, p. 254.

49. U.S. Industrial Commission, *Report*, vol. 8, pp. 502–503.

50. *MMJ*, June 1899, pp. 348–349.

51. See, e.g., the statement by Duncan Douglas Wilson, IAM vice-president, to the U.S. Industrial Commission, *Report*, vol. 8, p. 490.

52. Ibid.

53. *MMJ*, April 1900, p. 210; U.S. Industrial Commission, *Report*, vol. 8, p. 490.

54. *MMJ*, July 1902, p. 424.

55. See especially Bogart, "The Machinists' Strike," p. 305, n. 5; Montgomery, *Workers' Control in America*, p. 51. Stuart Reid referred to the Chicago demands for seniority and shop committees as "minor points" (*MMJ*, April 1900, p. 210).

56. The Murray Hill Agreement.

57. The NMTA made this charge in 1901 (U.S. Industrial Commission, *Report*, vol. 17, pp. 358–359). That the charge had some truth is suggested in testimony by Vice-President Wilson. Presented with a copy of the Murray Hill Agreement published by the NMTA and asked if it was the correct version, he replied, "I see one or two little points here that it was agreed would not be made public . . . just merely in connection with shop management." U.S. Industrial Commission, *Report*, vol. 8, p. 491.

58. Ibid., vol. 8, pp. xxx, 7.

59. *MMJ*, June 1900, p. 349.

60. U.S. Industrial Commission, *Report*, vol. 8, p. 10.

61. Ibid., p. xxx.

62. Ibid., pp. viii, 10–11, 19, 30, 513–514.

63. *MMJ*, May 1900, p. 255.

64. U.S. Industrial Commission, *Report*, vol. 8, pp. cxxv, 510.

65. Although the Murray Hill Agreement followed the precedent set by the National Founders' Association and the National Stove Founders' Association (ibid., p. cxxxviii), the NMTA's decision to reach a similar agreement with the IAM followed, by a week, the reading of a paper, "A History of the English Engineering Strike," at its annual convention. Clarence E. Bonnett, *History of Employers' Associations in the United States* (New York: Vintage Press, 1956), p. 449.

66. Montgomery, *Workers' Control in America*, p. 54.

67. Resolution passed at the 3rd annual NMTA convention, April 9–10, Detroit. Quoted in *Iron Age*, April 18, 1901, p. 24. The NMTA also sent a letter to its members, *before* the breakdown in negotiations between the NMTA and the IAM, stating that "it was the opinion of your Administrative Council that no further concessions should be granted to the members of the Machinists' Union" (*Iron Age*, May 16, 1901, p. 49).

68. The background and course of the strike are reviewed in *Iron Age*, May 23–June 27, 1901; *MMJ*, May–September 1901; U.S. Industrial Commission, *Report*, vol. 17, pp. 357–359; Perlman, *The Machinists*, p. 27; and Montgomery, *Workers' Control in America*, pp. 54–57.

69. Statement by the NMTA, quoted in U.S. Industrial Commission,

Report, vol. 17, p. 359. See also *MMJ*, February 1901, p. 102; *Engineering Magazine* 21 (1901): 590; and *Iron Age*, April 18, 1901, p. 23.

70. Statement by Charles Piez, president of the Link Belt Company, Commission on Industrial Relations, *Final Report and Testimony*, vol. 4, p. 3177. See also U.S. Industrial Commission, *Report*, vol. 8, pp. 513–514.

71. Perlman, *The Machinists*, p. 206.

72. *Iron Age*, June 6, 1901, p. 23.

73. *MMJ*, June 1902, pp. 329–330.

74. Montgomery, *Workers' Control in America*, p. 56.

75. Jefferys, *The Story of the Engineers*, pp. 98, 107, 137, 141–142; Perlman, *The Machinists*, pp. 5–7, 12–13, 16–21; Laslett, *Labor and the Left*, pp. 147–153 and ch. 5, passim.

76. Montgomery, *Workers' Control in America*, pp. 54–56, 62–63.

77. Ibid., p. 63; More, "Skill and the Survival of Apprenticeship," p. 112; Bain and Price, *Profiles of Union Growth*, p. 50.

78. A similar pattern is found in other industries. See Bonnett, *Employers' Associations in the United States*, pp. 22–25.

79. Montgomery, *Workers' Control in America*, pp. 49, 56–58.

80. Burgess, *The Origins of British Industrial Relations*, pp. 3–4.

81. Tariff Commission, *Report of the Tariff Commission*, paragraph 422.

82. Samuel L. Haber, "A History of the International Association of Machinists," B.A. thesis, University of Wisconsin, 1924, p. 192. See also Montgomery, *Workers' Control in America*, p. 48. Ronald Dore (*British Factory–Japanese Factory: The Origins of National Diversity in Industrial Relations* [Berkeley and Los Angeles: University of California Press, 1973], ch. 14–15) emphasizes the importance for industrial relations of the relative development of production techniques and craft unionism in his comparison of Britain and Japan. Michael Burawoy ("The Anthropology of Industrial Work," *Annual Review of Anthropology* 8 [1979]: 257–259) elaborates the point in more general terms.

83. Levine, *Industrial Retardation*, pp. 65–78, 145–147.

84. Montgomery, *Workers' Control in America*, pp. 59–60. Particularly during the 1890s, there were many cases in Britain of troops protecting blacklegs and dispersing strikers. Richard Price ("The Labour Process and Labour History," *Social History* 8 [1983]: 70–72) notes that in individual decisions justices often dealt more harshly with picketing than statutory law would indicate. In the 1890s and after, however, these measures applied almost exclusively to less skilled workers. See also E. H. Phelps Brown, *The Origins of Trade Union Power* (Oxford: Clarendon Press, 1983), pp. 203–207; and Howard F. Gospel and Craig R.

Littler, eds., *Managerial Strategies and Industrial Relations: An Historical and Comparative Study* (London: Heinemann, 1983).

Chapter 4

1. Jefferys, *The Story of the Engineers*, pp. 163–164. The question of amalgamation is debated on a regular basis in *AEMJ*. The demand that the ASE Executive Council ballot its members on the subject of amalgamation and convene a meeting of trade union representatives (one-third chosen by the Executive Council, two-thirds by members) to formulate a plan of amalgamation was put forth by the London District Committee and endorsed by the Coventry District Committee among others. CDC Minutes, November 6, 1913. See also CDC Minutes, July 26, 1909.

2. This is the title of W. F. Watson's 1913 pamphlet, issued by the Metal, Engineering and Shipbuilding Amalgamation Committee.

3. Bob Holton, *British Syndicalism 1900–1914: Myths and Realities* (London: Pluto Press, 1976), p. 153.

4. In Coventry, for example, the ASE and the Steam Engine Makers' Executives sought to secure for themselves veto power over Coventry Engineering Joint Committee decisions affecting their own union members. CDC Minutes, March 5, July 24, 1912.

5. Holton, *British Syndicalism*, pp. 66–68, 140–141, 152–153.

6. Meyer Bloomfield, *Management and Men: A Record of New Steps in Industrial Relations* (New York: Century, 1919), pp. 365–367; Watson, *Machines and Men*, pp. 120–122; Jefferys, *The Story of the Engineers*, p. 159; Clegg, Fox, and Thompson, *A History of British Trade Unions*, pp. 431–432.

7. CDC Minutes, April 9, 1906; Jefferys, *The Story of the Engineers*, pp. 156–157.

8. CDC Minutes, August 25, November 19, 1909, October 23, 24, December 4, 17, 1913; Cole, *The Payment of Wages*, pp. 90–95; Watson, *Machines and Men*, pp. 92–93; Wigham, *The Power to Manage*, p. 75.

9. CDC Minutes, July 21, 1909.

10. Watson, *Machines and Men*, pp. 97–98; Wigham, *The Power to Manage*, p. 74.

11. CDC Minutes, February 21, December 14, 1913; *AEMJ*, June 1914, pp. 35–36; Hinton, *The First Shop Stewards' Movement*, pp. 311–312; Burgess, *The Origins of British Industrial Relations*, pp. 70–71.

12. U.S. Bureau of Labor, 11th Special Report, *Regulation and Restriction of Output*, p. 799; Wigham, *The Power to Manage*, p. 68.

13. *AEMJ*, June 1908, pp. 12, 15; Jefferys, *The Story of the Engineers*, p. 159; Wigham, *The Power to Manage*, pp. 63–64.

14. U.S. Bureau of Labor, 11th Special Report, *Regulation and Restriction of Output*, p. 791; Jefferys, *The Story of the Engineers*, p. 151.

15. *AEMJ*, May 1913, Abstract Report of Provisional Executive Council Proceedings; CDC Minutes, February 26, November 6, December 14, 1913; Croucher, "The Amalgamated Society of Engineers," pp. 85–89.

16. *AEMJ*, January 1899, p. 43; CDC Minutes, July 21, 1909, April 16, December 4, 1913, May 6, 1914.

17. Jefferys, *The Story of the Engineers*, pp. 153–154; Croucher, "The Amalgamated Society of Engineers," pp. 65–66; Wigham, *The Power to Manage*, p. 81. Comparable developments appear in the Lancashire textile industry. See White, *The Limits of Trade Union Militancy*, e.g., pp. 85–87, 176.

18. *Engineering*, April 17, 1908, p. 524; *AEMJ*, May 1908, p. 8; Burgess, *The Origins of British Industrial Relations*, pp. 70–71.

19. Weekes, "The Amalgamated Society of Engineers," pp. 310–311; Wigham, *The Power to Manage*, pp. 63–64, 68–71.

20. *AEMJ*, June 1914, pp. 35–36. See also *AEMJ*, June 1908, pp. 12–15; CDC Minutes, April 11, 21, 1911, February 21, April 16, November 5, 6, 17, 1913; Croucher, "The Amalgamated Society of Engineers," pp. 85–89.

21. The arguments that follow draw on Hinton, *The First Shop Stewards' Movement*. They differ by emphasizing more strongly the mediating role played by solidary organization in channeling shop-floor discontent into more radical factory politics.

22. Weekes, "The Amalgamated Society of Engineers," pp. 315–316.

23. *AEMJ*, May 1908, p. 8.

24. Wigham, *The Power to Manage*, pp. 83–84.

25. The term is from Holton, *British Syndicalism*.

26. Hinton, *The First Shop Stewards' Movement*, pp. 79, 311–312; Holton, *British Syndicalism*, pp. 67, 153–154; Hunt, *British Labour History*, p. 327.

27. This statement reflects a systematic review of monthly reports by Organizing District Delegates in the *AEMJ*. See also Wigham, *The Power to Manage*, p. 83.

28. By 1914, for example, Manchester engineers were electing their own rate fixers to conduct negotiations. *AEMJ*, February 1914, p. 35.

29. Goodrich, *The Frontier of Control*, pp. 27–34; Branko Pribicevic, *The Shop Stewards' Movement and Workers' Control, 1910–1922* (Oxford: Basil Blackwell, 1959), pp. 70–72; Holton, *British Syndicalism*, pp.

30–33; Van Gore, "Rank-and-File Dissent," in Wrigley, *A History of British Industrial Relations*, pp. 67–69.

30. Watson, *Men and Machines*, p. 32; Pribicevic, *The Shop Stewards' Movement*, pp. 26, 65–69; Holton, *British Syndicalism*, pp. 153–154.

31. Jefferys, *The Story of the Engineers*, pp. 156–157; Richard Hyman, *The Workers' Union* (Oxford: Clarendon Press, 1971), p. 72.

32. *AEMJ*, May 1911, p. 31.

33. CDC Minutes, March 31, 1914; Great Britain, Ministry of Labour, *Report of an Inquiry as to Works Committees* (reprinted by the Industrial Relations Division, United States Shipping Board Emergency Fleet Corporation, 1919), pp. 67–68; G. D. H. Cole, *Workshop Organization* (Oxford: Clarendon Press, 1923), p. 18.

34. Cole, *Workshop Organization*, p. 18.

35. J. R. Richmond, *Some Aspects of Labour and Its Claims in the Engineering Industry* (Glasgow: n.p., 1916), p. 6; James Hinton, "The Rise of a Mass Labour Movement," in Wrigley, *A History of British Industrial Relations*, p. 25.

36. *AEMJ*, May 1911, p. 31; CDC Minutes, March 31, 1914; Turner, *Trade Union Growth Structure and Policy*, p. 317; Holton, *British Syndicalism*, pp. 140–153.

37. CDC Minutes, shop steward lists, 1907–1908, passim; Carr, "Engineering Workers and the Rise of Labour," p. 28.

38. On the protracted COW strike, see CDC Minutes, February 20, 23, March 9, 27, April 26, May 4, September 17, 24, October 1, 8, 1907. For Daimler, see CDC Minutes, March 9, 20, 1908.

39. Hyman, *The Workers' Union*, pp. 71–72.

40. Arthur Gleason, "The Shop Stewards and Their Significance," *The Survey*, January 4, 1919, pp. 417, 421; Great Britain Ministry of Munitions, *History of the Ministry*, vol. 6, pt. 2, p. 33.

41. *AEMJ*, September 1914, p. 3.

42. E.g., Phelps Brown, *The Growth of British Industrial Relations*, pp. 332–333; Clegg, Fox, and Thompson, *A History of British Trade Unions*, pp. 328, 362.

43. *MMJ*, July 1903, pp. 537, 591, November 1911, pp. 1134–1135, June 1912, pp. 535–536, May 1913, p. 475; Ashworth, *The Helper and American Trade Unions*, pp. 83, 92, 100–102, 108–109; Perlman, *The Machinists*, p. 34.

44. *MMJ*, June 1904, pp. 489–490, November 1905, p. 1024; American Federation of Labor, Metal Trades Department, *Proceedings of Annual Conventions*, passim.

45. Metal trades councils and their relations with the AFL Metal Trades Department and individual unions are discussed in Ramirez,

When Workers Fight, pp. 105–116. See also American Federation of Labor, Metal Trades Department, *Proceedings of the Third Annual Convention* (1911), pp. 30–31. On system federations, see Perlman, *The Machinists*, pp. 40–42; Montgomery, *Workers' Control in America*, pp. 81–82, 107, 124.

46. *MMJ*, February 1903, p. 87, September 1908, p. 815, January, 1911, p. 15; Perlman, *The Machinists*, p. 256.

47. U.S. Bureau of Labor, 11th Special Report, *Regulation and Restriction of Output*, p. 113; *MMJ*, August 1903, p. 718, February 1904, p. 136, January 1905, p. 60, March 1909, p. 230, June 1909, p. 533, April 1913, p. 375.

48. *MMJ*, August 1903, pp. 717–718, September 1905, p. 840, September 1910, p. 836; U.S. Bureau of Labor, 11th Special Report, *Regulation and Restriction of Output*, pp. 103–105, 108–109; U.S. Congress, House Committee on Labor, *Hearings Before a Special Committee*, vol. 2, p. 1010.

49. *MMJ*, March 1900, p. 165, August 1903, p. 718, January 1911, p. 15, October 1912, p. 895; U.S. Bureau of Labor, 11th Special Report, *Regulation and Restriction of Output*, pp. 103–105, 108–109, 113, 138–139.

50. *MMJ*, May 1907, p. 476, May 1913, p. 483; U.S. Congress, House Committee on Labor, *Hearings Before a Special Committee*, vol. 2, pp. 1004, 1032, 1251.

51. Montgomery, *Workers' Control in America*, p. 107.

52. U.S. Bureau of Labor, 11th Special Report, *Regulation and Restriction of Output*, p. 118; *MMJ*, May 1908, pp. 425–427, May 1910, p. 445, July 1910, pp. 645–646, October 1912, p. 920; Montgomery, *Workers' Control in America*, pp. 124–125.

53. Bonnett, *Employers' Associations in the United States*, pp. 109–117.

54. *MMJ*, June 1903, p. 479, September 1904, p. 788, January 1906, p. 71, October 1909, p. 928; Montgomery, *Workers' Control in America*, p. 65.

55. *Bridgeport Herald*, May 10, 1903. Similar tactics were used in 1907 (*Bridgeport Herald*, April 14, 21, June 2, 1907) and during the strike wave of 1915.

56. Bonnett, *Employers' Associations in the United States*, pp. 102–103.

57. *MMJ*, September 1910, p. 836.

58. American Federation of Labor, Metal Trades Department, *Proceedings of the Third Annual Convention* (1911), pp. 2–3, 13; Ramirez, *When Workers Fight*, pp. 118, 120–121.

59. *MMJ*, May 1905, p. 430, December 1905, p. 1125, January 1906, pp. 51, 54, 55–56. March 1906, p. 249; *Bridgeport Post*, July 16, 17, 20, 1907.

60. *MMJ*, January 1906, p. 46, November 1909, pp. 1044–1079; Perlman, *The Machinists*, p. 36.

61. American Federation of Labor, Metal Trades Department, *Proceedings of the Annual Conventions* (1909–1914); Ramirez, *When Workers Fight*, pp. 105–116.

62. Laslett, *Labor and the Left*, pp. 157–158, 161–162.

63. *MMJ*, March 1912, p. 239.

64. U.S. Congress, House Committee on Labor, *Hearings Before a Special Committee*, vol. 2, pp. 1007–1008.

65. Ibid., p. 527. See also Montgomery, *Workers' Control in America*, pp. 68–69.

66. Over 1910–1912 alone, machinists initiated disputes over scientific management at the Starrett Tool Company, American Locomotive, Watertown Arsenal, Illinois Central Railroad, John Deere Plow Company, Norfolk and Charlestown Navy Yards, and the Newport News Shipbuilding Company. U.S. Congress, House Committee on Labor, *Hearings Before a Special Committee*, vol. 1, p. 535, vol. 2, p. 917; *MMJ*, February 1912, p. 141; *AEMJ*, October 1912, p. 33; Montgomery, *Workers' Control in America*, pp. 115–116. On political action, see Perlman, *The Machinists*, p. 43.

67. Montgomery, *Workers' Control in America*, pp. 69, 123.

68. Laslett, *Labor and the Left*, p. 180; Montgomery, *Workers' Control in America*, pp. 79–80.

69. Montgomery, *Workers' Control in America*, p. 116.

70. *MMJ*, January 1893, p. 357, December 1893, p. 494, July 1901, p. 465, November 1904, p. 998, September 1908, p. 789; Maxim, "The Effects of Trade Unionism," p. 193; U.S. Bureau of Labor, 11th Special Report, *Regulation and Restriction of Output*, p. 115; U.S. Congress, House Committee on Labor, *Hearings Before a Special Committee*, vol. 2, pp. 924, 929, vol. 3, pp. 1660, 1684–1685, 1760–1761, 1812.

71. Commission on Industrial Relations, *Final Report and Testimony*, vol. 1, pp. 135–136, 141.

72. For this reason, specialists were reluctant to join the IAM, with its constitutional ban on piecework. *MMJ*, November 1910, p. 1050.

73. *AEMJ*, May 1902, p. 22.

74. Manufacturers' Association of the City of Bridgeport, Bulletin (Bridgeport Public Library, Accession 1977.25, Box 1), June 14, 1907, July 19, 1912.

75. *Bridgeport Herald*, April 24, 1898; "A.W. Reports," typescript of

reports from a labor spy, planted in the Bridgeport IAM, to the Manufacturers' Association of Bridgeport (Bridgeport Public Library), September 27, 1916.

76. Amalgamated Society of Engineers, American and Canadian Council, *Monthly Report*, August 1910. See also *MMJ*, July 1911, p. 683, September 1911, p. 878, July 1913, p. 680; *AEMJ*, October 1912, p. 33.

77. American Federation of Labor, Metal Trades Department, *Proceedings of the Third Annual Convention* (1911), pp. 2–3; Albert Berres, "Metal Trades Department," *American Federationist* 23 (1916): 949; Ramirez, *When Workers Fight*, pp. 116–120.

78. American Federation of Labor, Metal Trades Department, *Proceedings of the Annual Conventions* (1909–1914).

79. Ramirez, *When Workers Fight*, pp. 117–121.

80. Janes, *The Control of Strikes*, p. 111.

81. Laslett, *Labor and the Left*, p. 158.

82. *MMJ*, May 1907, p. 476, July 1913, p. 680; *Bridgeport Post*, July 16, 17, 20, 1907; Montgomery, *Workers' Control in America*, p. 94.

83. *MMJ*, December 1905, p. 1125, January 1906, p. 46; Laslett, *Labor and the Left*, p. 159. See also Montgomery, *Workers' Control in America*, pp. 72, 93.

84. Information on strikes is drawn from Connecticut Bureau of Labor Statistics *Annual Reports*, local newspapers, and in one case from the *MMJ*, July 1913, p. 680.

85. Peterson, "Auto Workers and Their Work," pp. 232–234.

86. E.g., Edwards, *Contested Terrain;* Stone, "The Origins of Job Structures"; Clawson, *Bureaucracy and the Labor Process;* Meyer, *The Five Dollar Day*, esp. ch. 5.

87. This view is advanced most unequivocally by Jeremy Brecher, "*Who* Advocates Spontaneity?" *Radical America* 7, no. 6 (1979): 91–112; Stanley Aronowitz, *False Promises: The Shaping of American Working Class Consciousness* (New York: McGraw-Hill, 1973), ch. 4; and, with greater subtlety, James Hinton, *Unions and Strikes* (London: Sheed and Ward, 1968), and Hyman, "Trade Unions, Control and Resistance," esp. pp. 324–325.

88. *American Machinist*, November 2, 1922, p. 704; Colvin, *60 Years*, p. 95.

89. The IAM sought arbitration procedures in all its contracts. It is clear from the *MMJ*, which reports on agreements reached, that the union had far more success in securing such contracts in railroad shops than elsewhere. See also Perlman, *The Machinists*, p. 29; and Montgomery, *Workers' Control in America*, p. 63.

90. *MMJ*, August 1908, pp. 425–427, October 1912, p. 920, October

1914, p. 978; Perlman, *The Machinists*, pp. 30, 40–41, 43; Montgomery, *Workers' Control in America*, pp. 81–82, 107–108, 124.

91. Drake, *Women in the Engineering Trades*, pp. 8–9; Hinton, *The First Shop Stewards' Movement*, p. 218; Burgess, *The Origins of British Industrial Relations*, p. 50, Friedman, *Industry and Labour*, p. 192, Carr, "Engineering Workers and the Rise of Labour," pp. 10, 107.

92. C. Ford, "The Political Behavior of the Working-Class in Coventry 1870–1900," M.A. thesis, Department of Social History, University of Warwick, 1973, pp. 39–40; Carr, "Engineering Workers and the Rise of Labour," pp. 40, 48, 233–234.

93. CDC Minutes, July 12, 26, 1907, and lists of shop stewards, passim; Carr, "Engineering Workers and the Rise of Labour," p. 28.

94. CDC Minutes, October 10, 1911. See also July 18, August 30, November 15, 1911, September 15, 1914.

95. Ibid., March 7, 1902, and passim. On District Committee censure of errant members, see, e.g., September 3, 1900, April 9, 1906, May 9, 1912.

96. Strike information is drawn from the CDC Minutes and local newspapers. See also Carr, "Engineering Workers and the Rise of Labour," p. 231.

Chapter 5

1. John Prest, *The Industrial Revolution in Coventry* (London: Oxford University Press, 1960), p. x; Saul, "The Motor Industry," p. 30; Ford, "The Political Behavior," p. 1; Friedman, *Industry and Labour*, p. 191; Carr, "Engineering Workers and the Rise of Labour," p. 8.

2. Coventry and District Engineering Employers' Association [Coventry EEA], Application for Admission to Membership of the Engineering Employers' Federation. In "Historical Documents" box of the Coventry EEA.

3. Great Britain, Ministry of Munitions, *History of the Ministry*, vol. 2, pt. 2, p. 101.

4. "The Works of the Daimler Co., Ltd.," *Automobile Engineer* 11 (August 1921): 285; "The Works of Messrs. Alfred Herbert, Limited, Coventry," *Engineering* 90 (July 22, 1910): 113; "Famous British Works: Messrs. Alfred Herbert, Ltd., Coventry," *Engineering Production* 3 (August 18, 1921): 148; Great Britain, Ministry of Munitions, *History of the Ministry*, vol. 5, pt. 5, p. 50; Annual Reports of the Registrar-General, 1916 [Cd 8206], p. 14 and 1920 [Cmd 608], p. 19.

5. Great Britain, Ministry of Munitions, *History of the Ministry*, vol. 5, pt. 5, pp. 52–53; Great Britain, Commission of Enquiry into Industrial

Unrest, *Report of the Commissioners for the West Midlands Area* (London: HMSO, 1917); George Hodginson, *Sent to Coventry* (N.p.: Robert Maxwell, 1970), p. 41.

6. Hinton, *The First Shop Stewards' Movement*, p. 217, n. 3; Carr, "Engineering Workers and the Rise of Labour," pp. 32–33, 75–76, 246.

7. For general views see Drake, *Women in the Engineering Trades;* G. D. H. Cole, *Trade Unionism and Munitions* (Oxford: Clarendon Press, 1923); Jefferys, *The Story of the Engineers*, pp. 125–126, 135, 174–175; Hinton, *The First Shop Stewards' Movement,* pp. 62–67.

8. Great Britain, Ministry of Munitions, *History of the Ministry,* vol. 6, pt. 3, pp. 22–32, Tables 6, 8, 9, 24.

9. Ibid., p. 65, Table 19. Machine tool and ordnance manufacture involved heavier and less repetitive work than did ammunition production, and the large-scale employment of women in these sectors broke more sharply with prewar practices.

10. CDC Minutes, March 2, 16, 23, April 6, 1915; "Works and Workers," *Times Engineering Supplement*, February 22, 1918, p. 46; Great Britain, Ministry of Munitions, *History of the Ministry,* vol. 5, pt. 1, pp. 121, 127, 165–166; Cole, *Workshop Organization,* pp. 63–65; Cole, *Trade Unionism and Munitions*, pp. 166–167.

11. CDC Minutes, March 2, June 15, 26, October 20, November 2, 24, 1915, March 14, 21, 1916; Great Britain, Ministry of Munitions, *History of the Ministry,* vol. 2, pt. 3, p. 68.

12. On the "skilled timeworkers' grievance," see Great Britain, Ministry of the Munitions, *History of the Ministry,* vol. 5, pt. 1, pp. 167–168; Cole, *Workshop Organization,* pp. 60–62.

13. *AEMJ*, January–April 1915; Great Britain, Ministry of Munitions, *History of the Ministry,* vol. 1, pt. 4, pp. 6–16; Cole, *Trade Unionism and Munitions*, pp. 53–77.

14. J. T. Murphy, *The Workers' Committee: An Outline of Its Principles and Structure* (London: Pluto Press, 1972 [1917]), p. 13; CDC Minutes, February 1, 1916.

15. Great Britain, Ministry of Munitions, *History of the Ministry,* vol. 5, pt. 1, pp. 128, 138–139, 150–152.

16. Cole, *Workshop Organization,* pp. 48–49; Cole, *Trade Unionism and Munitions,* pp. 106–114; James Hinton, "The Clyde Workers' Committee and the Dilution Struggle," in *Essays in Labour History 1896–1923*, ed. Asa Briggs and John Saville (London: Macmillan, 1971), pp. 174–175.

17. Great Britain, Ministry of Munitions, *History of the Ministry,* vol. 4, pt. 2, pp. 2–3; Cole, *Trade Unionism and Munitions*, pp. 104–105, 157–162.

18. Gleason, "The Shop Stewards," p. 419; Great Britain, Ministry of Munitions, *History of the Ministry*, vol. 6, pt. 1, p. 92.

19. Cole, *Trade Unionism and Munitions*, pp. 130–133; Hinton, *The First Shop Stewards' Movement*, pp. 38–39.

20. Cole, *Trade Unionism and Munitions*, pp. 115–116; Samuel J. Hurwitz, *State Intervention in Great Britain: A Study of Economic Control and Social Response, 1914–1919* (New York: Columbia University Press, 1949), pp. 98–102; Hinton, *The First Shop Stewards' Movement*, pp. 35–36.

21. For conflicts between skilled and less skilled engineering workers over government policies, see the Workers' Union *Record*, September 1916, January and November 1917; Great Britain, Ministry of Munitions, *History of the Ministry*, vol. 6, pt. 1, pp. 44, 97–98.

22. Great Britain, Ministry of Munitions, *History of the Ministry*, vol. 4, pt. 2, pp. 26–32, vol. 5, pt. 3, p. 143.

23. CDC Minutes, August 31, September 7, October 12, November 24, 1915, January 11, March 21, June 27, 1916.

24. S. G. Hobson, "War Conditions and the New Shop Stewards," *New Age*, September 19, 1918, p. 332; Great Britain, Ministry of Munitions, *History of the Ministry*, vol. 4, pt. 2, p. 30; Cole, *Trade Unionism and Munitions*, p. 116; Jefferys, *The Story of the Engineers*, p. 135.

25. *Coventry Herald and Free Press*, November 17–18, 1916; CDC Minutes, November 18, 1916.

26. Great Britain, Ministry of Munitions, *History of the Ministry*, vol. 6, pt. 1, pp. 92–93. See also the series of reports by the Commission of Enquiry into Industrial Unrest. For some general assessments of the role of communitywide grievances in mobilizing broadly based workers' struggles during the war, see Moore, *Injustice*, p. 289; and Cronin, "Labor Insurgency and Class Formation," p. 145.

27. *Iron Age*, July 22, 1915, p. 201, February 3, 1916, pp. 296–298, January 3, 1918, pp. 28, 126; Zenas Potter, "War-Boom Towns I: Bridgeport," *The Survey*, December 4, 1915, p. 238; *Bridgeport Post*, January 4, 1916, March 26, 1922; *New York Times*, January 16, 1916, sec. 4; George C. Waldo, *History of Bridgeport and Vicinity* (New York: S. J. Clarke, 1917), pp. 171, 179; Elsie Nicholas Danenberg, *The Story of Bridgeport* (Bridgeport: The Bridgeport Centennial, 1936), p. 112; Cecelia F. Bucki, "Dilution and Craft Traditions: Bridgeport, Connecticut, Munitions Workers, 1915–1919," *Social Science History* 4, no. 1 (1980): 107.

28. Amy Hewes, "Bridgeport on the Rebound," *The Survey*, October 14, 1916, p. 50; Waldo, *History of Bridgeport*, p. 153; *Iron Age*, July 18, 1918, p. 147.

29. *New York Times*, January 16, 1916, sec. 4; Amy Hewes, *Women as*

Munitions Makers: A Study of Conditions in Bridgeport, Connecticut (New York: Russell Sage Foundation, 1917), pp. 80, 88; *Bridgeport Herald*, December 26, 1915, March 26, 1916; Danenberg, *The Story of Bridgeport*, p. 112.

30. *MMJ*, August 1915, p. 748; Manufacturers' Association of the City of Bridgeport, Minutes of Executive Board and Committee Meetings (Bridgeport Public Library, Accession 1981.06), November 4, 1915. My estimate of peak IAM strength is based on the facts that in March 1916 there were two thousand members ("A.W. Reports," March 22, 1916), and in April 1916 alone sixteen hundred more were initiated (*MMJ*, June 1916, p. 553).

31. Manufacturers' Association of Bridgeport, Minutes, November 4, 1915; Hewes, *Women as Munitions Makers*, p. 18. On "boomers," see Golden, "The Militants of the Metal Trades," p. 143.

32. "A.W. Reports," March 22, 1916.

33. *Iron Age*, July 18, 1918, pp. 146–147, October 24, 1918, p. 1018.

34. Calculated from data presented by Remington Arms-UMC at Hearings before the National War Labor Board, July 17, 1918. National Archives, Record Group 2 (hereafter N.A., RG2), Box 3, Docket No. 132: IAM District #55 vs. Bridgeport, Connecticut, employers.

35. *Iron Trade Review*, "Teaching Efficiency," July 20, 1916, p. 136; *Automotive Industries*, "Training 150 Operators Per Week," August 15, 1918, p. 277.

36. Testimony of Mr. Freeland, NWLB Hearings, July 18, 1918, N.A., RG2, Box 3, Docket No. 132.

37. See the information provided by the Manufacturers' Association of Bridgeport to the NWLB, N.A., RG2, Box 21, Docket No. 132; testimony by Mr. Sutton and Mr. Edge, National War Labor Board, Hearings, July 17, 1918, N.A., RG2, Box 3; and by Mr. Freeland, July 18, 1918.

38. *Bridgeport Herald*, September 8, 1918; *Bridgeport Post*, September 14, 1918.

39. Bucki, "Dilution and Craft Traditions," p. 118.

40. Alexander Bing, *War-Time Strikes and Their Adjustment* (New York: E. P. Dutton, 1921), pp. 171–172, 238.

41. *MMJ*, February 1918, p. 162; American Federation of Labor, Metal Trades Department, *Proceedings of the Ninth Annual Convention* (1917), pp. 13, 30, and *Proceedings of the Tenth Annual Convention* (1918), p. 8.

42. National Industrial Conference Board, *Wartime Employment of Women*, p. 44; Bing, *War-Time Strikes*, p. 66. The records of the National War Labor Policies Board (National Archives, Record Group 1) detail a number of government proposals and employers' opposition to them, including conflicts over a planned Metal Trades Adjustment Board with

authority over wages, hours, labor conditions, and worker classification in munitions production.

43. Minutes of the War Labor Policies Board (N.A., RG1), Boxes 1–2, May 29, June 7, 21, 1918; "The Substitution of Women for Men," undated paper, no author given, Records of the WLPB (N.A., RG1), Box 17; September 24, 1918, memo from Mr. Clayton (director of the Training and Dilution Service) to William Chenery, Chenery correspondence, Records of the WLPB (N.A., RG1), Box 9.

44. American Federation of Labor, Metal Trades Department, *Proceedings of the Ninth Annual Convention* (1917), pp. 47–48.

45. *MMJ*, May 1918, p. 468.

46. Hewes, *Women as Munitions Makers*, p. 7.

47. U.S. War Department, *A Report of the Activities of the War Department in the Field of Industrial Relations During the War* (Washington, D.C.: Government Printing Office, 1919), pp. 26–32, 54–55; Bing, *War-Time Strikes*, pp. 66–67, 117–121; Robert D. Cuff, "The Politics of Labor Administration During World War I," *Labor History* 21, no. 4 (1980): 546–569.

48. *MMJ*, May 1918, p. 469; U.S. War Department, *A Report of the Activities*, p. 31; Bing, *War-Time Strikes*, pp. 155–156.

49. Minutes of the Local Board of Mediation and Conciliation, November 4, 8, 1918 (Records of the National War Labor Board, N.A., RG2, Box 21, Docket No. 132).

50. See, e.g., Meyer, *The Five Dollar Day*, pp. 174–175, 185.

51. Bing, *War-Time Strikes*, pp. 233–235.

52. Ibid., pp. 66, 69–70, 171, 309–311; Selig Perlman and Philip Taft, *History of Labor in the United States, 1896–1932* (New York: Macmillan, 1935), pp. 408–409.

53. American Federation of Labor, Metal Trades Department, *Proceedings of the Tenth Annual Convention* (1918), pp. 10–12; U.S. War Department, *A Report of the Activities*, p. 31.

54. *Bridgeport Herald*, September 8, 1918; *Labor Leader* (weekly paper of Bridgeport IAM Lodge 30), January 31, 1918.

55. *MMJ*, July 1918, p. 640.

56. *Bridgeport Herald*, August 8, 15, 22, 1915, June 30, 1918; Bucki, "Dilution and Craft Traditions," p. 116.

Chapter 6

1. Surveys of the Shop Stewards' Movement include Cole, *Workshop Organization*; Pribicevic, *The Shop Stewards' Movement*; and especially Hinton, *The First Shop Stewards' Movement*.

2. Great Britain, Ministry of Labour, Industrial Report No. 2: *Works*

Committees (London: HMSO, 1918), pp. 10–12, 37–38; Cole, *Workshop Organization*, p. 47.

3. Great Britain, Ministry of Munitions, *History of the Ministry*, vol. 6, pt. 1, pp. 116–117; Hinton, *The First Shop Stewards' Movement*, p. 15.

4. Great Britain, Ministry of Munitions, *History of the Ministry*, vol. 1, pt. 2, pp. 98–99, vol. 6, pt. 1, pp. 92–93.

5. Ibid., vol. 6, pt. 1, pp. 114–115, vol. 6, pt. 2, pp. 29–30; Cole, *Workshop Organization*, pp. 82–83; Pribicevic, *The Shop Stewards' Movement*, pp. 93–98, 101–102; Hinton, *The First Shop Stewards' Movement*, pp. 201–204.

6. Great Britain, Ministry of Labour, Industrial Report No. 2: *Works Committees*, p. 40; Cole, *The Payment of Wages*, p. 96; Great Britain, Ministry of Munitions, *History of the Ministry*, vol. 4, pt. 1, p. 31; Cole, *Workshop Organization*, p. 47.

7. Great Britain, Ministry of Labour, Industrial Report No. 2: *Works Committees*, pp. 10, 17–18; Gleason, "The Shop Stewards," p. 418; Cole, *Trade Unionism and Munitions*, p. 206; Hyman, *The Workers' Union*, p. 117.

8. Great Britain, Ministry of Munitions, *History of the Ministry*, vol. 6, pt. 1, pp. 93–94, vol. 6, pt. 2, pp. 29–30; Cole, *Workshop Organization*, pp. 35–36, 54–55; Pribicevic, *The Shop Stewards' Movement*, p. 86; James Hinton, "Introduction," in Murphy, *The Workers' Committee*, pp. 6–7.

9. S. G. Hobson, "The Industrial Unit and the New Shop Steward," *The New Age*, September 26, 1918, p. 347; Cole, *Workshop Organization*, pp. 76–77, 85–94; Pribicevic, *The Shop Stewards' Movement*, pp. 85–93.

10. Murphy, *The Workers' Committee*, p. 18.

11. Hinton, *The First Shop Stewards' Movement*, pp. 65–69 and passim.

12. CDC Minutes, March 2, 16, 23, April 6, 1915. See also notes on the October 4, 1915, conference between the Coventry Engineering Employers' Federation and engineering unions, "Historical Documents, Including Local Conferences" box, Offices of the Coventry and District Engineering Employers' Association.

13. CDC Minutes, November 2, 1915. Original emphasis.

14. On the two-machine system, see ibid., March 2, 16, June 26, 1915; on women, ibid., June 15, October 20, 1915, March 14, 21, 1916.

15. Ibid., March 7, April 12, 1916.

16. Ibid., December 18, 1917, February 5, 1918.

17. Ibid., March 7, 1916.

18. Ibid., October 23, 1916. See also ibid., July 27, 1915; Great Britain, Ministry of Munitions, *History of the Ministry*, vol. 6, pt. 1, p. 93, pt. 2, pp. 32–33.

19. CDC Minutes, August 13, 1915. The same year stewards also led strikes at COW and Daimler (ibid., February 9, August 13, 1915). Such action became more frequent from the beginning of 1917.

20. Ibid., April 7, 1917; Great Britain, Commission of Enquiry into Industrial Unrest, *Report of the Commissioners*, pp. 9–10; Great Britain, Ministry of Labour, Industrial Report No. 2: *Works Committees*, pp. 15–16 (it is clear from information given that the Works Committee described here is at Daimler); Hodginson, *Sent to Coventry*, p. 37; Friedman, *Industry and Labour*, p. 194; Carr, "Engineering Workers and the Rise of Labour," p. 80.

21. CDC Minutes, April 12, 1916.

22. Ibid., January 10, February 6, 20, March 6, 17, April 3, October 16, 1917.

23. On the CWC, see Carr, "Engineering Workers and the Rise of Labour," pp. 79–84.

24. Great Britain, Ministry of Munitions, *History of the Ministry*, vol. 6, pt. 1, p. 114, n. 1.

25. Carr, "Engineering Workers and the Rise of Labour," p. 85.

26. *Midland Daily Telegraph*, May 21, 1917; Hinton, *The First Shop Stewards' Movement*, p. 216; Carr, "Engineering Workers and the Rise of Labour," pp. 80–81.

27. CDC Minutes, April 7, 1917.

28. Quoted by Carr, "Engineering Workers and the Rise of Labour," pp. 80–81. See also CDC Minutes, April 7, 1917.

29. Letter dated April 14, 1917. EEF Correspondence, Offices of the Engineering Employers' Federation.

30. CDC Minutes, April 10, 11, 1917.

31. Great Britain, Ministry of Munitions, *History of the Ministry*, vol. 6, pt. 2, pp. 32–33.

32. April 17, 1917, letter from the Secretary of the EEF to the Coventry EEA, EEF Correspondence.

33. The Hotchkiss Works Committee constitution is reproduced in Great Britain, Ministry of Labour, *Report of an Inquiry*, pp. 80–81.

34. Carr, "Engineering Workers and the Rise of Labour," p. 81.

35. Great Britain, Ministry of Munitions, *History of the Ministry*, vol. 6, pt. 1, pp. 52–63.

36. CDC Minutes, May 14, 1917.

37. Ibid., April 29, 1917.

38. Ibid., May 6, 1917.

39. Ibid.; Carr, "Engineering Workers and the Rise of Labour," pp. 82–83.

40. CDC Minutes, May 14, 1917; Great Britain, Ministry of Munitions, *History of the Ministry*, vol. 6, pt. 1, pp. 113–114; Hinton, *The First Shop Stewards' Movement*, p. 217; Carr, "Engineering Workers and the Rise of Labour," pp. 82–83.

41. Great Britain, Ministry of Munitions, *History of the Ministry*, vol. 6, pt. 1, p. 63.

42. CDC Minutes, October 16, 1917; Carr, "Engineering Workers and the Rise of Labour," p. 89.

43. Carr, "Engineering Workers and the Rise of Labour," pp. 86–90.

44. CEJC Shop Rules and Instructions for Stewards. Reprinted in Great Britain, Ministry of Labour, *Report of an Inquiry*, pp. 124–125; Hinton, *The First Shop Stewards' Movement*, pp. 221–222; Carr, "Engineering Workers and the Rise of Labour," p. 85.

45. Hinton, *The First Shop Stewards' Movement*, p. 223.

46. CDC Minutes, September 22, November 6, 13, 1917.

47. Ibid., October 16, 1917.

48. Ibid., November 6, 1917; Circular Letter No. 38, November 21, 1917, from C. Martin (EEA Secretary) to controlled establishments in Coventry, "Historical Documents, Including Local Conferences" box, Coventry EEA.

49. CDC Minutes, November 6, 1917.

50. *Coventry Herald and Free Press*, November 23–24, 1917; Great Britain, Ministry of Munitions, *History of the Ministry*, vol. 6, pt. 2, p. 26; Hodginson, *Sent to Coventry*, p. 48; Hinton, *The First Shop Stewards' Movement*, p. 223.

51. CDC Minutes, November 20, 22, 1917; *Birmingham Gazette*, November 30, 1917.

52. CDC Minutes, November 25, 1917; *Birmingham Post*, November 28, 1917; *Birmingham Gazette*, November 29, 1917; Great Britain, Ministry of Munitions, *History of the Ministry*, vol. 6, pt. 2, pp. 30–31; Hinton, *The First Shop Stewards' Movement*, pp. 223–224; Carr, "Engineering Workers and the Rise of Labour," p. 95. For a view that celebrates the strike as a left-wing triumph, see Ken Biggs, "Coventry and the Shop Stewards' Movement, 1917," *Marxism Today* 13, no. 1 (1969): 14–23.

53. *Midland Daily Telegraph*, December 8, 1917.

54. Notes on December 4 and 5, 1917, conferences, Coventry EEA, "Historical Documents, Including Local Conferences" box.

55. CDC Minutes, November 28, 29, 1917.

56. Ibid., December 3, 1917; *Birmingham Mail*, December 3, 1917.

57. Great Britain, Ministry of Munitions, *History of the Ministry,* vol. 6, pt. 2, p. 33.

58. *Birmingham Mail,* December 3, 1917.

59. Great Britain, Ministry of Munitions, *History of the Ministry,* vol. 6, pt. 2, p. 32. See also Hinton, *The First Shop Stewards' Movement,* pp. 213–215, 233–234.

60. Memorandum of Conference Between the Engineering Employers' Federation and Thirteen Trade Unions, Regulations Regarding the Appointment and Functions of Shop Stewards, reprinted in Great Britain, Ministry of Labour, *Report of an Inquiry.* See also Great Britain, Ministry of Munitions, *History of the Ministry,* vol. 6, pt. 2, p. 31; Cole, *Workshop Organization,* pp. 76–79; Hinton, *The First Shop Stewards' Movement,* p. 225; Carr, "Engineering Workers and the Rise of Labour," pp. 94–95.

61. Hodginson, *Sent to Coventry,* p. 46.

62. Cole, *Trade Unionism and Munitions,* p. 153.

63. Great Britain, Ministry of Munitions, *History of the Ministry,* vol. 6, pt. 2, p. 31; Cole, *Workshop Organization,* pp. 76–77.

64. Carr, "Engineering Workers and the Rise of Labour," pp. 94–95.

65. January 23, 1918, letter from Secretary Martin to members of the Coventry EEA, "Historical Documents, Including Local Conferences" box; Hinton, *The First Shop Stewards' Movement,* p. 226.

66. Carr, "Engineering Workers and the Rise of Labour," p. 96.

67. Workers' Union *Record,* February 1918, p. 2.

68. CDC Minutes, January 2, 6, 1918.

69. Great Britain, Ministry of Munitions, *History of the Ministry,* vol. 6, pt. 2, p. 46.

70. CDC Minutes, June 18, 1918.

71. Ibid., April 23, 1918; Carr, "Engineering Workers and the Rise of Labour," p. 98.

72. CDC Minutes, January 2, 1918.

73. Carr, "Engineering Workers and the Rise of Labour," pp. 96–97.

74. *Midland Daily Telegraph,* July 20, 1918; *Birmingham Gazette,* July 20, 1918; *Birmingham Daily Mail,* July 22, 1918; Great Britain, Ministry of Munitions, Justice McCardie's Committee of Inquiry, *Interim Report on Labour Embargoes* (London: HMSO, 1918); Great Britain, Ministry of Munitions, *History of the Ministry,* vol. 6, pt. 2, p. 65.

75. Hinton, *The First Shop Stewards' Movement,* p. 231.

76. Great Britain, Ministry of Munitions, *History of the Ministry,* vol. 6, pt. 2, p. 66; Ministry of Munitions poster displayed in Coventry, Birmingham, and Manchester, reprinted in *Birmingham Post,* July 22, 1918.

77. Hinton, *The First Shop Stewards' Movement*, p. 231.

78. *Midland Daily Telegraph*, July 23, 1918; CDC Minutes, July 26, 1918.

79. CDC Minutes, July 23, 1918; Hinton, *The First Shop Stewards' Movement*, p. 231.

80. *Birmingham Daily Mail*, July 24, 1918; *Midland Daily Telegraph*, July 29, 1918; Great Britain, Ministry of Munitions, *History of the Ministry*, vol. 6, pt. 2, pp. 67–69.

81. Carr, "Engineering Workers and the Rise of Labour," pp. 98, 174–182.

82. CDC Minutes, November 30, 1920.

83. Shadwell, *The Engineering Industry*, p. 43; Labour Research Department, *Labour and Capital in the Engineering Trades* (London: Labour Publishing Co., 1922); Cole, *Workshop Organization*, p. 125.

84. Cole, *Workshop Organization*, p. 128; Pribicevic, *The Shop Stewards' Movement*, pp. 37–38, 102–108; Hinton, *The First Shop Stewards' Movement*, p. 308.

85. Hinton, *The First Shop Stewards' Movement*, pp. 218–221; Carr, "Engineering Workers and the Rise of Labour," p. 107.

86. Carr, "Engineering Workers and the Rise of Labour," e.g., pp. 237, 452, 499–501.

87. Hinton, *The First Shop Stewards' Movement*, p. 218.

88. Prest, *The Industrial Revolution*, p. x; Ford, "The Political Behavior," pp. 1, 4; Friedman, *Industry and Labour*, p. 192.

89. The political implications of Coventry's weak craft traditions are noted for the war period by Hinton, *The First Shop Stewards' Movement*, pp. 218–221.

90. Examples of these agreements include those with Webster and Bennet in 1897 (noted in CDC Minutes, May 6, 1901) and with another company in 1901 (CDC Minutes, October 3, 1901).

91. Ibid., December 17, 1913, March 25, 1919, January 18, 25, 1927; Coventry EEA, Executive Committee Minutes, January 10, 1921.

92. Carr, "Engineering Workers and the Rise of Labour," p. 249.

93. Coventry employers credited incentive pay with the city's relative freedom from labor unrest in the 1920s. When the EEF threatened a national lockout over an unofficial strike in London, the Coventry EEA Executive Committee complained that in "districts such as Lancashire and Northern Industrial Areas, where payment by results had not been developed, the Engineering workpeople were generally *very dissatisfied* . . . whilst the Employers and workmen in Coventry were working in harmony together" (Minutes, March 22, 1926; original emphasis).

94. Carr, "Engineering Workers and the Rise of Labour," p. 231.

95. At one time or another the CDC Minutes note chargehand arrangements at Webster and Bennet, Herberts, and Selson Engineering (machine tool firms); Coventry Chain Company; Coventry Ordnance Works; Calcott Cycle and Triumph Motor Cycle; and the motor car plants of Daimler, Rover, Swift, Hillman, Riley, Maudslay, and Standard. These account for most of the city's leading firms. For historical background on this system, see Allen, *The Industrial Development of Birmingham;* and Carr, "Engineering Workers and the Rise of Labour," pp. 4–5. See also Littler, "Deskilling and Changing Structures of Control."

96. CDC Minutes, October 9, 1901. See also March 18, 1903.

97. Ibid., May 3, 1927.

98. Ibid., February 17, March 10, 1914. See also August 27, 1919.

99. Ibid., February 7, 1927.

100. This split is discussed in general terms by Carr, "Engineering Workers and the Rise of Labour."

101. On the 1922 lockout and its background, see *AEMJ*, 1920–1922, passim; Great Britain, Parliament, *Report by a Court of Inquiry Concerning the Engineering Trades Dispute, 1922* (London: HMSO, 1922 [Cmd. 1653]); Labour Research Department, *Labour and Capital;* Shadwell, *The Engineering Industry;* Jefferys, *The Story of the Engineers*, pp. 217–227; and Wigham, *The Power to Manage*, pp. 117–124.

102. Memorandum of conference between the Engineering and National Employers' Federation and the AEU, November 17–18, 1921. Reprinted in Great Britain, Parliament, *Report by a Court of Inquiry,* p. 3.

103. Poster in "Historical Documents, Including Local Conferences" box, Coventry EEA. Original emphasis. See also Great Britain, Parliament, *Report by a Court of Inquiry,* p. 17. The EEF did threaten to open the workshops to individual employees, but the agreement that blacklegs were to be asked to sign included the same procedures for appeal and union conferences as the eventual national settlement. See letters of April 25 and 27 from James Brown (EEF secretary) to the AEU and Negotiating Committee of the other unions, EEF Correspondence, Offices of the EEF.

104. CDC Minutes, June 29, 1920; Coventry EEA, Executive Committee Minutes, January 17, 1921; Carr, "Engineering Workers and the Rise of Labour," pp. 178–179.

105. CDC Minutes, March 2, 1922.

106. Calculated from ibid., reports of Complaints Subcommittee, July 3–September 12. The exact total of cases *reported* is 1,890, but in several instances the Subcommittee reports do not include numbers. The committee further complained that branches were not providing information on defaulters and referred some cases to the District Committee as a

whole. Thus the 1,890 figure is an understatement. Carr, "Engineering Workers and the Rise of Labour," p. 246, puts local AEU members at 10,450 in May 1922.

107. CDC Minutes, September 12, 1922.

108. Carr, "Engineering Workers and the Rise of Labour," p. 246.

109. CDC Minutes, April 21, 1922; Carr, "Engineering Workers and the Rise of Labour," pp. 207–209.

110. CDC Minutes throughout the 1920s report sanctions against members for ignoring union rules. For action taken against shop stewards, see, e.g., CDC Minutes, May 28, June 29, September 7, 16, 1920, April 19, 28, 1921; Coventry EEA, Executive Committee Minutes, January 17, 1921.

111. CDC Minutes, May 26, 1925.

112. Ibid., October 3, 1922.

113. Ibid., August 13, 1927.

114. Carr, "Engineering Workers and the Rise of Labour," pp. 251–253.

115. CDC Minutes, April 28, 1921; Coventry EEA, Executive Committee Minutes, March 3, April 24, 1924; Carr, "Engineering Workers and the Rise of Labour," p. 258.

116. CDC Minutes, November 23, 1920.

117. On the 1930s and early 1940s, see Carr, "Engineering Workers and the Rise of Labour," pp. 467, 483–486, 500–507; James Hinton, "Coventry Communism: A Study of Factory Politics in the Second World War," *History Workshop Journal* 10 (Autumn 1980): 90–118.

Chapter 7

1. For the United States, no general study of rank-and-file movements in the wartime metal trades exists. There are many insights scattered in David Montgomery's *Workers' Control in America*, and there is an excellent case study by Cecelia Bucki ("Dilution and Craft Traditions"). The following overview is pieced together largely from Montgomery, *Workers' Control in America*, and the *MMJ*.

2. *MMJ*, August 1915, p. 753.

3. Montgomery, *Workers' Control in America*, p. 95.

4. *MMJ*, September 1917, p. 756, October 1917, p. 853, September 1918, p. 822; Bing, *War-Time Strikes*, pp. 171–172.

5. Bing, *War-Time Strikes*, p. 157.

6. In April 1918, James O'Connell (president of the AFL's Metal Trades Department) urged the Shipbuilding Labor Adjustment Board to alter its procedure. "All requests for hearings or conferences from local representatives in any locality should be referred to this Department be-

fore any date is set for such a hearing, so that this Department may take the matter up with the internationals affected and make the necessary arrangements for the proper representation. . . . All hearings or conferences in connection with wages, hours, or conditions of employment in the shipbuilding industry should be given as far as possible a national scope so that local prejudices, the local situation, and local representation, may be avoided as far as possible." Everett Macy, Shipbuilding Labor Adjustment Board chairman, agreed, adding in his reply, "We believe that no hearings should be granted except the material to be presented has first received the approval of the international presidents." Letters quoted in American Federation of Labor, Metal Trades Department, *Proceedings of the Tenth Annual Convention* (1918), pp. 10–12.

7. American Federation of Labor, Metal Trades Department, *Proceedings of the Eleventh Annual Convention* (1919), p. 7. See also report of IAM President Johnston for 1918, *MMJ*, June 1919, p. 512; letter from O'Connell to MTD affiliates, February 3, 1919, *MMJ*, March 1919, p. 233; Montgomery, *Workers' Control in America*, p. 125.

8. *Labor Leader*, January 31, 1918.

9. Montgomery, *Workers' Control in America*, p. 95.

10. *MMJ*, January 1920, p. 49; *Labor Leader*, January 8, 1920.

11. *MMJ*, August 1919, p. 744. See also organizers' reports, *MMJ*, 1918–1919, passim, and *MMJ*, May 1919, p. 446, January 1920, pp. 15–16, 28; American Federation of Labor, Metal Trades Department, *Proceedings of the Eleventh Annual Convention* (1919), p. 108; Perlman, *The Machinists*, pp. 55–56; Meyer, *The Five Dollar Day*, p. 171.

12. Montgomery, *Workers' Control in America*, pp. 126–127.

13. See, for example, the agreements won by machinists at the U.S. Cartridge Company and the Newton Manufacturing Company in Lowell, Massachusetts (*MMJ*, April 1916, pp. 347–348, September 1916, p. 876, August 1917, p. 669, September 1917, pp. 737–738, February 1919, pp. 104–105); and demands made throughout the New York area by IAM District Lodge 15 (*Labor Leader*, January 31, 1918). See also Montgomery, *Workers' Control in America*, pp. 103, 124.

14. This problem of shop committee recognition is explored by David Montgomery, "New Tendencies in Union Struggles and Strategies in Europe and the United States, 1916–1922," in *Work, Community, and Power: The Experience of Labor in Europe and America, 1900–1925*, ed. James E. Cronin and Carmen Sirianni (Philadelphia: Temple University Press, 1983), pp. 103–109.

15. United States Bureau of Labor Statistics, *Monthly Review*, April 1916, p. 19; Manufacturers' Association of Bridgeport, Minutes, March 4, 1915.

16. Information on the 1915 strikes is taken from the *Bridgeport Post*

and *Bridgeport Herald* throughout July, August, and September and from *MMJ*, September 1915, pp. 836, 839, 848, October 1915, p. 941.

17. On the latter point see Hewes, *Women as Munitions Makers*, pp. 40–44.

18. "A.W. Reports," July 3, 1916.

19. *Bridgeport Herald*, September 19, 1915.

20. *Iron Age*, December 9, 1915; *MMJ*, January 1916, p. 63; "A.W. Reports," June 8, 1916.

21. *Bridgeport Herald*, April 16, 1916; "A.W. Reports," April 20, July 31, 1916; statement by B. J. Strzelecki, National War Labor Board, Hearings, July 2, 1918, N.A., RG2, Box 3, Docket No. 132, re: Liberty Ordnance.

22. "A.W. Reports," April 5, 1916.

23. "A.W. Reports," passim; statement by John Hart, Remington tool room steward, National War Labor Board, Hearings, July 2, 1918, N.A., RG2, Box 3, Docket No. 132.

24. *Labor Leader*, April 18, 1918.

25. "A.W. Reports," September 19, 22, 1916; Manufacturers' Association of Bridgeport, Minutes, November 2, 1916; *Bridgeport Herald*, July 15, September 23, 1917; advertisement in *Bridgeport Herald*, June 24, 1917; Perlman, *The Machinists*, p. 54; Bucki, "Dilution and Craft Traditions," p. 112.

26. *Bridgeport Herald*, August 8, 1915; "A.W. Reports," May 5, 1916; *Bridgeport Post*, July 12, 1917.

27. *Bridgeport Herald*, August 8, 22, September 19, 1915; "A.W. Reports," June 8, 1916; *Bridgeport Post*, July 12, 1917; *Labor Leader*, August 15, 1918.

28. "A.W. Reports," July 13, 1916; United States Department of Labor, Records of the Conciliation Service, Series 33, File 567, National Archives, Record Group 280.

29. "The Bowen clique" is a phrase used by the employers' labor spy, "A.W."

30. "A.W. Reports," September 5, 1916.

31. Ibid., June 4, 1916.

32. Ibid., August 9, 1916. A similar case is reported November 10, 1916.

33. Ibid., April 11, 1916.

34. Ibid., April 7, 26, May 12, 1916.

35. Among these allies of Lavit was Edwin O'Connell (one of the militants discharged by Remington-UMC), who won the election for president of Lodge 30. *Bridgeport Herald*, March 25, 1917; letter from George Bowen to Department of Labor Conciliator Robert McWade, April 30, 1917, Department of Labor, Records of the Conciliation Ser-

vice, Series 33, File 347, N.A., RG280; Montgomery, *Workers' Control in America*, p. 128; Bucki, "Dilution and Craft Traditions," p. 114.

36. *Bridgeport Post*, July 14, 1917; National War Labor Board, Hearings, July 1, 1918, N.A., RG2, Box 3, Docket No. 132. A copy of District Lodge 55's proposed working rules is in Department of Labor, Records of the Conciliation Service, Series 33, File 817, N.A., RG280. See also the discussions in Montgomery, *Workers' Control in America*, pp. 103–104, 128, 132; and Bucki, "Dilution and Craft Traditions," pp. 113–114.

37. See Lavit's remarks on this point in the minutes of the Local Board of Mediation and Conciliation, November 21, 1918, meeting, National War Labor Board, Case Files, N.A., RG2, Box 21, Docket No. 132.

38. *Bridgeport Post*, July 12, 1917; *Bridgeport Herald*, July 15, 1917; Department of Labor, Records of the Conciliation Service, Series 33, File 567.

39. National War Labor Board, Hearings, July 17, 1918, N.A., RG2, Box 3, Docket No. 132.

40. *Bridgeport Herald*, March 25, 1917; Department of Labor, Records of the Conciliation Service, Series 33, File 357; statements by Edwin O'Connell and James Quigley, National War Labor Board, Hearings, July 2, 1918, N.A., RG2, Box 3, Docket No. 132; *MMJ*, May 1917, p. 430.

41. *Bridgeport Post*, July 12, 1917; *Bridgeport Herald*, July 15, 1917; Department of Labor, Records of the Conciliation Service, Series 33, File 567.

42. *Labor Leader*, April 18, May 9, 1918; *Bridgeport Post*, May 9, 1918; Bing, *War-Time Strikes*, pp. 171–172.

43. Statements by IAM Executive Board member Fred Hewitt and by B. J. Strzelecki, National War Labor Board, Hearings, July 1, 2, 1918, N.A., RG2, Box 3, Docket No. 132. Department of Labor, Records of the Conciliation Service, Series 33, Files 519, 819, 1026, N.A., RG280; *MMJ*, August 1917, p. 679, January 1918, p. 63; *Labor Leader*, February 21, 1918; *Bridgeport Herald*, July 7, 1918; Bing, *War-Time Strikes*, pp. 75–76.

44. *Labor Leader*, April 4, 1918; *Bridgeport Herald*, July 7, 1918; statement by Lavit, National War Labor Board, Hearings, July 2, 1918, N.A., RG2, Box 3, Docket No. 132; Bing, *War-Time Strikes*, p. 234, n.1.

45. *Labor Leader*, April 4, 1918.

46. Ibid., April 18, May 9, 16, 1918; statement by Fred Hewitt, National War Labor Board, Hearings, July 1, 1918, N.A., RG2, Box 3, Docket No. 132; Hearings before the Mediation Branch of the Industrial Service Section of the Ordnance Department, May 23, 1918. Reprinted by the Manufacturers' Association of Bridgeport. Copy in National War Labor Board, Case Files, N.A., RG2, Box 19, Docket No. 132; telegram

from Lavit to Kerwin (assistant to the Secretary of Labor), May 2, 1918, National War Labor Board, Case Files, N.A., RG2, Box 20, Docket No. 132; telegram from IAM Executive Board member Savage to Lavit, May 6, 1918, Box 20; May 4, 1918, memo, no author given, Box 21; *Bridgeport Herald,* May 5, 1918; *Bridgeport Post,* May 9, 11, 12, 1918; Manufacturers' Association of Bridgeport, Minutes, May 14, 1918.

47. Testimony by Fred Hewitt, National War Labor Board, Hearings, July 1, 1918, N.A., RG2, Box 3, Docket No. 132.

48. Statement by Fred Hewitt, ibid.; *Labor Leader,* July 18, 1918.

49. National War Labor Board, Case Files, N.A., RG2, Box 19, Docket No. 132. This characterization steers a middle course between David Montgomery and Cecelia Bucki. For Montgomery (*Workers' Control in America,* pp. 129–130), events during the first half of 1918 are of a piece with the program of 1917; for Bucki ("Dilution and Craft Traditions," pp. 114, 117–118), they mark a decisive retreat to craft exclusiveness. The ambiguity of craft versus class policies is, in fact, clear even in the August program, with its proposals for quite conventional apprenticeship regulations. Demands in strikes from March through June do abandon semiskilled production workers (versus Montgomery's interpretation), but not specialists or women (versus Bucki's interpretation); and those to the NWLB once again included production operatives and unskilled helpers.

50. National War Labor Board, Hearings, July 2, 1918, N.A., RG2, Box 3, Docket No. 132.

51. Testimony by Fred Hewitt, ibid., July 1, 1918.

52. Testimony by J. J. Keppler, ibid., July 2, 1918.

53. Testimony by Lavit, ibid.

54. Testimony by Lavit, ibid., July 5, 1918; and by Keppler, ibid., July 3, 1918.

55. E.g., Hewitt's response to William Wallace, ibid., July 1, 1918. See also the editorial reaction to NWLB decisions regarding classification in Bridgeport and elsewhere in *MMJ,* August 1918, p. 764.

56. Hearings before the Mediation Branch of the Industrial Service Section of the Ordnance Department, May 23, 1918.

57. The text of the NWLB's award is reprinted in *MMJ,* October 1918, pp. 915–918. For the disagreements within the NWLB, see the copies of proposed awards in National War Labor Board, Case Files, N.A., RG2, Box 19, Docket No. 132; minutes of executive session of the NWLB, August 16, 1918: Submission to Umpire, National War Labor Board, Case Files, N.A., RG2, Box 21, Docket No. 132.

58. On the strike, see *Bridgeport Post,* August 30–September 18, 1918; *Bridgeport Herald,* September 1, 8, 15, 1918; *Labor Leader,* September 5, 1918.

59. *Bridgeport Herald*, September 1, 1918.

60. Telegram from Isaac Russell (NWLB Field Representative) to Jett Lauck (NWLB Secretary), August 29, 1918, National War Labor Board, Case Files, N.A., RG2, Box 20, Docket No. 132.

61. *Bridgeport Herald*, September 8, 1918; *Bridgeport Post*, September 14, 1918.

62. Department of Labor, Records of the Conciliation Service, Series 33, File 1819, telegram from Agent Lane of the Department of Justice, Bureau of Investigation. See also *Bridgeport Post*, September 6, 1918.

63. *Bridgeport Post*, September 5, 10, 11, 12, 14, 1918.

64. *Bridgeport Post*, September 10–12, 1918; International News Service bulletin, September 14, 1918, quoted in *Bridgeport Herald*, September 15, 1918.

65. *Labor Leader*, September 19, 1918.

66. See, e.g., National Metal Trades Association, *Report of the Committee on Works Councils in the Metal Trades* (Chicago: NMTA, 1919); National Industrial Conference Board, *Works Councils in the United States* (Boston: NICB, 1919); National Industrial Conference Board, *Experience with Works Councils in the United States* (New York: The Century Co., 1922); and Carroll E. French, *The Shop Committee in the United States* (Baltimore: Johns Hopkins University Press, 1923).

67. *Bridgeport Herald*, March 23, 1919; George Hawley, "Bridgeport Employers Report Shop Committees Successful," *New York Evening Post*, April 22, 1920 (Hawley was the general manager of the Manufacturers' Association of Bridgeport). This was a feature of many government-sponsored representation schemes. See Bing, *War-Time Strikes*, p. 162. For Lavit's responses to the NWLB shop committee scheme, see telegram from Isaac Russell to Jett Lauck, September 4, 1918, National War Labor Board, Case Files, N.A., RG2, Box 20, Docket No. 132; *Bridgeport Post*, September 4, 1918; minutes of meeting of Local Board of Mediation and Conciliation, March 31, 1919, National War Labor Board, Case Files, N.A., RG2, Box 21, Docket No. 132.

68. Organization and By-Laws of Collective Bargaining Committees Instituted by the NWLB for Bridgeport, Connecticut. Copy in National War Labor Board, Case Files, N.A., RG2, Box 21, Docket No. 132.

69. Willard Aborn and William Shafer, "Representative Shop Committees: America's Industrial Roundtable," *Industrial Management*, July 1919, p. 29. Some examples of the issues raised by employee representatives, including the poor condition of floors or the need for an improved hot water supply, may be found in reports to the Bridgeport examiner from NWLB investigators of employee representation schemes instituted before NWLB elections. National War Labor Board, Case Files, N.A., RG2, Box 21, Docket No. 132.

70. *Bridgeport Herald*, September 29, 1918; *Labor Leader*, October 3, 1918.

71. Telegram from Lavit, Clydesdale, and Scollins to Jett Lauck, May 5, 1919; letter from Willard Aborn to W. D. Angelo (assistant chief administrator of the NWLB), May 12, 1919; telegram from Lauck to Lavit, May 6, 1919, all in National War Labor Board, Case Files, N.A., RG2, Box 21, Docket No. 132.

72. Bing, *War-Time Strikes*, p. 81.

73. Letter to the NWLB from Lavit, reprinted in *Labor Leader*, September 6, 1918.

74. *Bridgeport Herald*, March 23, 1919.

75. Hawley, "Bridgeport Employers."

76. Letter to the NWLB, reprinted in *Labor Leader*, September 26, 1918.

77. National Industrial Conference Board, *Experience*, pp. 17–18.

78. Manufacturers' Association of Bridgeport, Minutes, April 16, 1918.

79. National Industrial Conference Board, *Works Councils*, p. 10; Hawley, "Bridgeport Employers." See also Bureau of Industrial Research, *American Shop Committee Plans* (New York: Bureau of Industrial Research, 1919).

80. National Metal Trades Association, *Report*, p. 3; National Industrial Conference Board, *Works Councils*, p. 14; National Industrial Conference Board, *Experience*, p. 13; Don Lescohier and Elizabeth Brandeis, *History of Labor in the United States, 1896–1932: Working Conditions and Labor Legislation* (New York: Macmillan, 1935), pp. 349–350. Out of 225 employee representation plans surveyed by the NICB in 1919, 155 were in the metal trades (excluding iron and steel mills) and shipbuilding. National Industrial Conference Board, *Works Councils*, p. 14.

81. Manufacturers' Association of Bridgeport, Minutes, April 2, 1918.

82. *Bridgeport Herald*, December 19, 1915, November 19, 1916, January 7, 1917, February 24, 1918; Manufacturers' Association of Bridgeport, Minutes, March 3, 24, 1916, April 2, 16, 1918. Here, too, Bridgeport employers followed a national enthusiasm for company-sponsored welfare programs.

83. Exchange between Mr. Merritt and Mr. Edge (Locomobile factory manager), National War Labor Board, Hearings, July 17, 1918, N.A., RG2, Box 3, Docket No. 132.

84. The details of (and justifications for) these schemes are extensively documented in ibid., July 17–18, 1918. See also *Bridgeport Post*, May 13, 1916; *Iron Age*, May 25, 1916, p. 1274, July 25, 1918, pp. 204–206.

85. Manufacturers' Association of Bridgeport, Bulletin, March 17,

1915, March 21, 1916, March 22, 1919; Manufacturers' Association of Bridgeport, Minutes, December 15, 1915, October 3, 1916; pamphlet entitled "Plan in Relation to Turnover, Production, and Plant Management, Etc.," Bridgeport Public Library, Accession 1977.25, Box 1; *Iron Age*, June 5, 1916.

86. *New York Times*, January 16, 1916, sec. 4; *Iron Age*, February 3, 1916; Manufacturers' Association of Bridgeport, Bulletin, March 3, 1916, June 7, 1918; Manufacturers' Association of Bridgeport, Minutes, April 2, 16, 1918; *Bridgeport Herald*, January 20, 1918. The prounion sympathies of some foremen made employers especially eager to relieve them of authority over hiring and firing. See "A.W. Reports," June 15, October 28, 1916.

87. A good review is Nelson, *Managers and Workers*, ch. 8. See also the collection of articles in *Annals of the American Academy of Political and Social Science*, May 1916; *Handling Men*; Dwight T. Farnham, *America vs. Europe in Industry: A Comparison of Industrial Policies and Methods of Management* (New York: Ronald Press, 1921), pp. 319–331; National Metal Trades Association, Committee on Industrial Relations, *Industrial Relations in the Metal Trades* (Chicago: NMTA, 1929).

88. Manufacturers' Association of Bridgeport, Bulletin, September 19, 1921; *Iron Age*, May 3, 1923, p. 1300.

89. *Labor Leader*, March 14, 1918.

90. Examples include the Bullard Machine Tool Company (*American Machinist*, May 27, 1920, pp. 1137–1138) and the Bridgeport Brass Company (*Iron Age*, July 15, 1920, pp. 131–133).

91. Resolution approved at mass meeting, September 4, quoted in *Labor Leader*, September 5, 1918.

92. The worst of postwar unemployment would not hit until 1920. In March 1920, a sample of thirty-one firms surveyed by the manufacturers' association had an average weekly employment of 31,785. Because there were at least twice as many companies in the city (albeit of smaller average size), these employment figures do not appear dramatically lower than the wartime norm. By the end of November 1920, the same sample of firms employed only 21,475. Manufacturers' Association of Bridgeport, Bulletin, December 1, 1920.

93. *Bridgeport Herald*, December 29, 1918, January 5, 1919; *Labor Leader*, passim; Bucki, "Dilution and Craft Traditions," p. 119.

94. *Labor Leader*, July 24, 1919.

95. Information on the 1919 strikes is drawn from the *Bridgeport Post*, *Bridgeport Herald*, and *Labor Leader*.

96. *Labor Leader*, August 28, 1919; Bucki, "Dilution and Craft Traditions," pp. 119–120.

97. *Bridgeport Post*, July 25, 1919.

98. *Bridgeport Post*, August 6, 1919. See also *Bridgeport Herald*, August 3, 1919; Department of Labor, Records of the Conciliation Service, Series 170, File 649, N.A., RG280.

99. *Bridgeport Post*, July 24, 1919.

100. Hawley, "Bridgeport Employers"; *Bridgeport Post*, August 1, 2, 8, 13, 14, 1919; *Labor Leader*, August 7, 1919; *Iron Age*, July 15, 1920, p. 131; Department of Labor, Records of the Conciliation Service, Series 170, File 672, N.A., RG280.

101. *Bridgeport Herald*, September 8, 1918; *American Machinist*, May 27, 1920, p. 1137.

102. *Bridgeport Herald*, November 23, 1919.

103. Lavit's expulsion and subsequent conflicts over Lodge 30's charter are covered by the *Labor Leader* in almost every issue from August 7, 1919, until the paper's demise late in 1920. See also *Bridgeport Post*, August 10, 20, 1919; *Bridgeport Herald*, August 10, September 7, 28, 1919. The national view is in *MMJ*, September 1919, p. 853, October 1919, p. 953, April 1920, pp. 315–317.

104. *Bridgeport Post*, August 30, September 3–5, 1919.

105. *Labor Leader*, August 14, 1919, February 5, 1920; Perlman, *The Machinists*, p. 64.

106. *Bridgeport Post*, August 10, 1919.

107. *Labor Leader*, December 23, 1920.

108. Ibid., March 4, 18, 1920.

109. The AMWA at its peak had about eleven thousand members, mostly in New York City; most of those members were immigrant, semiskilled workers. Ibid., May 20, June 24, 1920. See also May 6, 1920, for the union's structure.

Chapter 8

1. See p. 254, n. 87.

2. The following distinction loosely resembles that made by Andrew Friedman (*Industry and Labour*) between "responsible autonomy" and "direct control," although his emphasis is on strategies for maximizing production and minimizing labor troubles. The focus here is on the more specific goal of keeping factory politics within sectional and economistic bounds, an achievement compatible with output restriction, strikes, and so forth.

3. Chapter Three evaluates the divergence in British and U.S. labor relations.

4. For prewar railroad shops, see Chapter Four. For postwar conflicts and strategies, see Ronald Radosh, "Labor and the American Economy:

The 1922 Railroad Shop Crafts Strike and the 'B & O Plan,'" in *Building the Organizational Society,* ed. Jerry Israel, pp. 73–87 (New York: Free Press, 1972).

5. The post-1901 NMTA definition of control problems reinforced the propensity of employers in the metal trades (as in other industries) to attribute strikes to outside agitators.

6. Aminzade, *Class, Politics, and Early Industrial Capitalism*, pp. xii–xiii.

7. Ibid., ch. 3–4.

8. In one overview of class formation in Toulouse (ibid., pp. 69–70), Aminzade does hint at this interpretation; his general model and historical analysis generally do not.

9. Foster, *Class Struggle and the Industrial Revolution*, ch. 3–4.

10. Katznelson, "Working-Class Formation and the State."

11. Naturally this division is also a simplification, the usefulness of which can be demonstrated only in practice.

12. The political conditions for sustaining rank-and-file movements for workers' control are emphasized by Antonio Gramsci, among others.

Bibliography

Aborn, Willard, and William Shafer. "Representative Shop Committees: America's Industrial Roundtable." *Industrial Management* 58 (July 1919): 29–32.

Aldridge, Alan. *Power, Authority and Restrictive Practices.* Oxford: Basil Blackwell, 1976.

Alford, L. P. "Introduction of Shop Management in Typewriter Plants." *American Machinist*, October 5, 1916, pp. 585–587.

———. "Ten Years' Progress in Management." *Mechanical Engineering* 44 (November 1922): 699–703.

Allen, G. C. *The Industrial Development of Birmingham and the Black Country, 1860–1927.* London: Frank Cass, 1966.

Amalgamated Society of Engineers. *Jubilee Souvenir.* London: Cooperative Printing Society, 1901.

———. *Notes on the Engineering Trade Lock-Out of 1897–8.* London: Charles Mitchell, n.d.

———, American and Canadian Council. *Monthly Report.*

"American and British Workmen." *Engineering* 76 (August 14, 1903): 205–207; (August 21, 1903): 242–244.

American Federation of Labor, Metal Trades Department. Constitution and By-Laws of the Metal Trades Department of the American Federation of Labor, 1909. Copy in AFL-CIO Library, Washington, D.C.

———. *Proceedings of the Annual Conventions.*

Aminzade, Ronald. *Class, Politics, and Early Industrial Capitalism: A Study of Mid-Nineteenth-Century Toulouse, France.* Albany: State University of New York Press, 1981.

Anderson, Gregory. "Some Aspects of the Labour Market in Britain c. 1870–1914." In *A History of British Industrial Relations, 1875–1914,* edited by Chris Wrigley, pp. 1–19. Brighton, Sussex: Harvester Press, 1982.

Annual Reports of the Registrar-General, 1916 [Cd 8206] and 1920 [Cmd 608].

Aronowitz, Stanley. *False Promises: The Shaping of American Working Class Consciousness*. New York: McGraw-Hill, 1973.

Arthur, James. "American and British Workmen and Machinery." *American Machinist*, November 24, 1892, p. 4.

Ashworth, John H. *The Helper and American Trade Unions*. Baltimore: Johns Hopkins University Press, 1915.

Aves, Ernest. "The Dispute in the Engineering Trades." *Economic Journal* 8 (March 1898): 115–124.

———. "Labour Notes: The Dispute in the Engineering Trade, &c." *Economic Journal* 7 (December 1897): 623–630.

"A.W. Reports." Typescript of reports from a labor spy, planted in the Bridgeport International Association of Machinists, to the Manufacturers' Association of Bridgeport. Bridgeport Public Library.

Bain, George Sayers, and Robert Price. *Profiles of Union Growth: A Comparative Statistical Portrait of Eight Countries*. Oxford: Basil Blackwell, 1980.

Barker, Arthur. *The Management of Small Engineering Workshops*. Manchester: Technical Publishing, 1903.

Barnes, George Nicol. Letter to *The Engineer*, May 19, 1899.

———. "Uses and Abuses of Organisation Among Employers and Employees: The Old Trade Unionism vs. Wisely Organised Labour." *Engineering Magazine* 20 (January 1900): 560–567.

Bell, Daniel, ed. *The Radical Right*. Garden City: Doubleday Anchor Books, 1964.

Bendix, Reinhard. *Work and Authority in Industry: Ideologies of Management in the Course of Industrialization*. Berkeley and Los Angeles: University of California Press, 1974.

Berger, Suzanne D., ed. *Organizing Interests in Western Europe: Pluralism, Corporatism, and the Transformation of Politics*. Cambridge: Cambridge University Press, 1981.

Berres, Albert J. "Metal Trades Department." *American Federationist* 23 (October 1916): 944–954.

Beynon, Huw. *Working for Ford*. East Ardsley, Wakefield: EP Publishing, 1975.

Biggs, Ken. "Coventry and the Shop Stewards' Movement, 1917." *Marxism Today* 13, no. 1 (1969): 14–23.

Bing, Alexander. *War-Time Strikes and Their Adjustment*. New York: E. P. Dutton, 1921.

Birmingham Small Arms Company. "History of the Birmingham Small

Arms Co., Ltd. 1861–1900." Unpublished manuscript, Modern Records Centre, University of Warwick, n.d.

Bloomfield, Meyer. "The Aim and Work of Employment Managers' Associations." *Annals of the American Academy of Political and Social Science* 85 (May 1916): 76–87.

————. *Management and Men: A Record of New Steps in Industrial Relations*. New York: Century, 1919.

Bogart, Ernest L. "The Machinists' Strike, 1900." *Yale Review* 9 (November 1900): 302–313.

Bonnell, Victoria. *Roots of Rebellion: Workers' Politics and Organizations in St. Petersburg and Moscow, 1900–1914*. Berkeley and Los Angeles: University of California Press, 1983.

Bonnett, Clarence E. *Employers' Associations in the United States: A Study of Typical Associations*. New York: Macmillan, 1922.

————. *History of Employers' Associations in the United States*. New York: Vintage Press, 1956.

Booth, Charles. *Life and Labour of the People in London*. Second series: Industry, vol. 1. New York: AMS Press, 1970 [1902–1904].

Bourdon, M. W. "Production Methods in the British Automobile Plants." *Automotive Industries*, June 24, 1920, pp. 1461–1462.

Brandes, Stuart. *American Welfare Capitalism, 1880–1940*. Chicago: University of Chicago Press, 1976.

Braverman, Harry. *Labor and Monopoly Capital: The Degradation of Work in the Twentieth Century*. New York: Monthly Review Press, 1974.

Brecher, Jeremy. *Strike!* Boston: South End Press, 1972.

————. "*Who* Advocates Spontaneity?" *Radical America* 7, no. 6 (1979): 91–112.

Briggs, Asa. "Social Background." In *The System of Industrial Relations in Great Britain: Its History, Law, and Institutions*, edited by Allan Flanders and H. A. Clegg, pp. 1–41. Oxford: Basil Blackwell, 1954.

Brody, David. "Radical Labor History and Rank and File Militancy." *Labor History* 16, no. 1 (1975): 117–126.

Browne, Sir Benjamin. "Uses and Abuses of Organization Among Employers and Employees: What Employers May Prevent and Effect by United Action." *Engineering Magazine* 20 (January 1900): 553–559.

Bucki, Cecelia F. "Dilution and Craft Traditions: Bridgeport, Connecticut, Munitions Workers, 1915–1919." *Social Science History* 4, no. 1 (1980): 105–124.

Buckler, William H. "The Minimum Wage in the Machinists' Union." In *Studies in American Trade Unionism*, edited by Jacob Hollander and George Barnett, pp. 109–151. New York: Henry Holt, 1907.

Bullard Company. *Yankee Toolmaker.* Draft copy in possession of Jack Stupakevich, Manager for Labor Relations and Security, Bullard Company, 1980.

Bunnell, Sterling H. "Jigs and Fixtures as Substitutes for Skill." *Iron Age* 93 (March 5, 1914): 610–611.

Burawoy, Michael. "The Anthropology of Industrial Work." *Annual Review of Anthropology* 8 (1979): 231–266.

———. *Manufacturing Consent: Changes in the Labor Process Under Monopoly Capitalism*. Chicago: University of Chicago Press, 1979.

———. *The Politics of Production: Factory Regimes Under Capitalism and Socialism*. London: Verso, 1985.

———. "Toward a Marxist Theory of the Labor Process: Braverman and Beyond." *Politics and Society* 8, no. 3–4 (1978): 247–312.

Bureau of Industrial Research. *American Shop Committee Plans*. New York: Bureau of Industrial Research, 1919.

Burgess, Keith. *The Challenge of Labour: Shaping British Society, 1850–1930*. London: Croom Helm, 1980.

———. *The Origins of British Industrial Relations: The Nineteenth Century Experience*. London: Croom Helm, 1975.

Burns, W. "New Shop Methods from the Machinist's Point of View." *Engineering Magazine* 31 (April 1906): 93–96.

Buttrick, John. "The Inside Contract System." *Journal of Economic History* 12, no. 3 (1952): 205–221.

Calvert, Monte. *The Mechanical Engineer in America, 1830–1910: Professional Cultures in Conflict*. Baltimore: Johns Hopkins University Press, 1967.

Cambridge Journal of Economics. Special issue, "The Labour Process, Market Structure, and Marxist Theory," 3, no. 3 (1979).

Carr, F. W. "Engineering Workers and the Rise of Labour in Coventry, 1914–1939." Ph.D. thesis, University of Warwick, 1978.

Chamberlain, L. "Replacing Piece by Premium Plan of Paying for Work." *American Machinist*, March 31, 1910, p. 581.

Chandler, Alfred. *The Visible Hand: The Managerial Revolution in American Business*. Cambridge, Mass.: Harvard University Press, 1977.

Clark, Victor S. *History of Manufactures in the United States*. New York: Peter Smith, 1949.

Clarke, R. O. "The Dispute in the British Engineering Industry, 1897–98: An Evaluation." *Economica*, new series, 24 (May 1957): 128–137.

Clawson, Dan. *Bureaucracy and the Labor Process: The Transformation of U.S. Industry, 1860–1920*. New York: Monthly Review Press, 1980.

Clegg, Hugh Armstrong. *The System of Industrial Relations in Great Britain*, 3rd ed. Oxford: Basil Blackwell, 1976.

———. *Trade Unionism Under Collective Bargaining: A Theory Based on Comparisons of Six Countries*. Oxford: Basil Blackwell, 1976.

Clegg, H. A., Alan Fox, and A. F. Thompson. *A History of British Trade Unions Since 1889,* vol. 1: 1889–1910. London: Oxford University Press, 1964.

Cole, G. D. H. *The Payment of Wages.* London: Labour Research Department, 1918

———. *Trade Unionism and Munitions.* Oxford: Clarendon Press, 1923.

———. *Workshop Organization.* Oxford: Clarendon Press, 1923.

Colvin, Fred H. *60 Years with Men and Machines: An Autobiography.* New York: McGraw-Hill, 1947.

Commission on Industrial Relations. *Final Report and Testimony.* 11 vols. Washington, D.C.: Government Printing Office, 1916.

Conlon, P. J. "Past, Present and Future of Our Association." *Machinists' Monthly Journal,* February 1909.

Connecticut Bureau of Labor Statistics. *Annual Reports.*

Coventry and District Engineering Employers' Association. "History of the Association." Typed manuscript, dated February 21, 1966, in "Historical Documents" box, offices of the Coventry and District Engineering Employers' Association.

———. Miscellaneous records in "Historical Documents" boxes.

Coventry District Committee, Amalgamated Society of Engineers. Minutes. Offices of the Amalgamated Union of Engineering Workers, Coventry District Committee.

Craig, John. "The Premium System and Its Relation to Discipline in the Factory." *The Open Shop* 4 (March 1905): 137–139.

Cronin, James. "Labor Insurgency and Class Formation: Comparative Perspectives on the Crisis of 1917–1920 in Europe." *Social Science History* 4, no. 1 (1980): 125–152.

———. "Strikes 1870–1914." In *A History of British Industrial Relations, 1875–1914,* edited by Chris Wrigley, pp. 74–98. Brighton, Sussex: Harvester Press, 1982.

Croucher, Richard. "The Amalgamated Society of Engineers and Local Autonomy, 1898–1914." M.A. thesis, University of Warwick, 1971.

Cuff, Robert D. "The Politics of Labor Administration During World War I." *Labor History* 21, no. 4 (1980): 546–569.

Danenberg, Elsie Nicholas. *The Story of Bridgeport.* Bridgeport: The Bridgeport Centennial, 1936.

Darlington, P. J. "Methods of Remunerating Labor." *Engineering Magazine* 17 (June 1899): 444–454; (September 1899): 925–936.

Dawson, Andrew. "The Paradox of Dynamic Technological Change and the Labor Aristocracy in the United States, 1880–1914." *Labor History* 20, no. 3 (1979): 325–351.

Dore, Ronald. *British Factory–Japanese Factory: The Origins of Na-*

tional Diversity in Industrial Relations. Berkeley and Los Angeles: University of California Press, 1973.

Drake, Barbara. *Women in the Engineering Trades.* London: Labour Research Department, 1918.

Drew, Walter. "Unionizing Industry as a War Measure." *Iron Age,* January 10, 1918, pp. 142–143.

"Economical Workshop Production." *Mechanical World,* twenty-part series, October 29, 1909, to October 7, 1910.

Edwards, Richard. *Contested Terrain: The Transformation of the Workplace in the Twentieth Century.* New York: Basic Books, 1979.

Elger, Tony, and Bill Schwarz. "Monopoly Capitalism and the Impact of Taylorism: Notes on Lenin, Gramsci, Braverman, and Sohn-Rethel." In *Capital and Labour: Studies in the Capitalist Labour Process,* edited by Theo Nichols, pp. 358–369. London: Athlone Press, 1980.

Elliott, John. *Conflict or Cooperation? The Growth of Industrial Democracy.* London: Kogan Page, 1984.

Engineering Employers' Federation. Correspondence. Offices of the EEF, London.

———. General letters. Offices of the EEF, London.

"English and American Methods in the Engineering and Iron Trades." *Engineer,* January 21, 1898, p. 66.

"Famous British Works: Messrs. Alfred Herbert, Ltd., Coventry." *Engineering Production,* August 18, 1921, pp. 146–149.

Farnham, Dwight T. *America vs. Europe in Industry: A Comparison of Industrial Policies and Methods of Management.* New York: Ronald Press, 1921.

Fireman, Bruce, and William A. Gamson. "Utilitarian Logic in the Resource Mobilization Perspective." In *The Dynamics of Social Movements: Resource Mobilization, Social Control, and Tactics,* edited by Mayer N. Zald and John D. McCarthy, pp. 8–44. Cambridge, Mass.: Winthrop Publishers, 1979.

Fitch, Charles. "Report on the Manufacture of Interchangeable Mechanism." U.S. Bureau of the Census, *Tenth Census* (1881).

Floud, Roderick. *The Machine Tool Industry, 1850–1914.* Cambridge: Cambridge University Press, 1976.

Foner, Philip S. *History of the Labor Movement in the United States,* vol. 2: *From the Founding of the A. F. of L. to the Emergence of American Imperialism.* New York: International Publishers, 1955.

———. *History of the Labor Movement in the United States,* vol. 3: *The Policies and Practices of the American Federation of Labor, 1900–1909.* New York: International Publishers, 1964.

Forbes, W. D. "Foremen vs. New Appliances." *Machinery* 5 (January 1899): 143.

. "Machine Shop Discipline." *American Machinist*, April 18, 1895, pp. 303–304.

Ford, C. "The Political Behavior of the Working-Class in Coventry, 1870–1900." M.A. thesis, Department of Social History, University of Warwick, 1973.

Forman, A. S. "Estimator, Rate Fixer and Inspector." *American Machinist*, March 16, 1911, pp. 503–504.

Foster, John. *Class Struggle and the Industrial Revolution: Early Industrial Capitalism in Three English Towns.* London: Weidenfeld and Nicolson, 1974.

Fox, Alan. "Industrial Relations in Nineteenth-Century Birmingham." *Oxford Economic Papers*, new series, 7, no. 1 (1955): 57–70.

Freeman, Richard B., and James L. Medoff. *What Do Unions Do?* New York: Basic Books, 1984.

French, Carroll E. *The Shop Committee in the United States.* Baltimore: Johns Hopkins University Press, 1923.

Friedman, Andrew L. *Industry and Labour: Class Struggle at Work and Monopoly Capitalism.* London: Macmillan, 1977.

Friedmann, Georges. *Industrial Society: The Emergence of the Human Problems of Automation.* Glencoe, Ill.: Free Press, 1955.

Garside, W. R., and H. R. Gospel. "Employers and Managers: Their Organizational Structure and Industrial Strategies." In *A History of British Industrial Relations, 1875–1914*, edited by Chris Wrigley, pp. 99–115. Brighton, Sussex: Harvester Press, 1982.

Gartman, David. *Auto Slavery: The Labor Process in the American Automobile Industry, 1897–1950.* New Brunswick, N.J.: Rutgers University Press, 1986.

Giddens, Anthony. *The Class Structure of the Advanced Societies.* New York: Harper and Row, 1973.

Gleason, Arthur. "The Shop Stewards and Their Significance." *The Survey,* January 4, 1919.

Golden, Clinton S. "The Militants of the Metal Trades—The Machinists." In *The Amalgamated Illustrated Almanac—1924*, pp. 142–144. New York: Amalgamated Clothing Workers of America, Education Department, 1924.

Goldthorpe, John H., ed. *Order and Conflict in Contemporary Capitalism: Studies in the Political Economy of Western European Nations.* Oxford: Clarendon Press, 1984.

Goldthorpe, John, David Lockwood, Frank Bechhofer, and Jennifer Platt. *The Affluent Worker: Industrial Attitudes and Behavior.* New York: Cambridge University Press, 1968.

Goodrich, Carter L. *The Frontier of Control: A Study of British Workshop Politics.* New York: Harcourt, Brace and Howe, 1920.

Gordon, David, Richard Edwards, and Michael Reich. *Segmented Work, Divided Workers: The Transformation of Labor in America.* Cambridge: Cambridge University Press, 1982.

Gore, Van. "Rank-and-File Dissent." In *A History of British Industrial Relations, 1875–1914,* edited by Chris Wrigley, pp. 47–73. Brighton, Sussex: Harvester Press, 1982.

Gospel, Howard F., and Craig R. Littler, eds. *Managerial Strategies and Industrial Relations: An Historical and Comparative Study.* London: Heinemann, 1983.

Gouldner, Alvin. *Wildcat Strike.* Yellow Springs, Ohio: Antioch Press, 1954.

Great Britain, Board of Trade. *Report of the Departmental Committee Appointed by the Board of Trade to Consider the Position of the Engineering Trades After the War.* London: HMSO, 1918.

Great Britain, Business Statistics Office. *Historical Record of the Census of Production, 1907–1970.* London: Government Statistics Service, n.d.

Great Britain, Census of Production, 1907. *Parliamentary Papers.* Cmd. 6320, 1912–1913 cix.

Great Britain, Commission of Enquiry into Industrial Unrest. *Report of the Commissioners for the West Midlands Area.* London: HMSO, 1917.

Great Britain, Committee on Industry and Trade. *Survey of Industrial Relations.* London: HMSO, 1926.

Great Britain, Ministry of Labour. Industrial Report No. 2: *Works Committees.* London: HMSO, 1918.

————. *Report of an Inquiry as to Works Committees.* Reprinted by the Industrial Relations Division, United States Shipping Board Emergency Fleet Corporation, 1919.

Great Britain, Ministry of Munitions. *History of the Ministry of Munitions.* London: HMSO, 1922.

————, Justice McCardie's Committee of Enquiry. *Interim Report on Labour Embargoes.* London: HMSO, 1918.

Great Britain, Parliament. *Report by a Court of Inquiry Concerning the Engineering Trades Dispute, 1922.* London: HMSO, 1922. Cmd. 1653.

Great Britain, Royal Commission on Labour. *Minutes of Evidence.* London: HMSO, 1893.

Gurr, Ted Robert. *Why Men Rebel.* Princeton, N.J.: Princeton University Press, 1970.

Habakkuk, H. J. *American and British Technology in the Nineteenth Century: The Search for Labor Saving Inventions.* Cambridge: Cambridge University Press, 1967.

Haber, Samuel. *Efficiency and Uplift: Scientific Management in the Progressive Era, 1890–1920.* Chicago: University of Chicago Press, 1964.

Haber, Samuel L. "A History of the International Association of Machinists." B.A. thesis, University of Wisconsin, 1924.

Habermas, Jürgen. *Legitimation Crisis.* Boston: Beacon Press, 1973.

Hanagan, Michael P. *The Logic of Solidarity: Artisan and Industrial Workers in Three French Towns, 1871–1914.* Urbana: University of Illinois Press, 1980.

Hanagan, Michael, and Charles Stephenson. "The Skilled Worker and Working-Class Protest." *Social Science History* 4, no. 1 (1980): 5–13.

Handling Men. Chicago: A. W. Shaw, 1917.

Hawley, George. "Bridgeport Employers Report Shop Committees Successful." *New York Evening Post,* April 22, 1920, p. 11.

Herding, Richard. *Job Control and Union Structure: A Study of Plant-Level Industrial Conflict in the United States with a Comparative Perspective on West Germany.* Rotterdam: Rotterdam University Press, 1972.

Heron, Craig. "Labourism and the Canadian Working Class." *Labour/Le Travail* 13 (Spring 1984): 45–75.

Hewes, Amy. "Bridgeport on the Rebound." *The Survey,* October 14, 1916, pp. 49–50.

———. *Women as Munitions Makers: A Study of Conditions in Bridgeport, Connecticut.* New York: Russell Sage Foundation, 1917.

Hiller, E. T. *The Strike: A Study in Collective Action.* Chicago: University of Chicago Press, 1928.

Hinton, James. "The Clyde Workers' Committee and the Dilution Struggle." In *Essays in Labour History, 1886–1923,* edited by Asa Briggs and John Saville, pp. 152–184. London: Macmillan, 1971.

———. "Coventry Communism: A Study of Factory Politics in the Second World War." *History Workshop Journal* 10 (Autumn 1980): 90–118.

———. *The First Shop Stewards' Movement.* London: George Allen and Unwin, 1973.

———. "The Rise of a Mass Labour Movement." In *A History of British Industrial Relations, 1875–1914,* edited by Chris Wrigley, pp. 20–46. Brighton, Sussex: Harvester Press, 1982.

———. *Unions and Strikes.* London: Sheed and Ward, 1968.

Hirst, F. W. "The Policy of the Engineers," *Economic Journal* 8 (March 1898). 124–127.

Hobsbawm, E. J. *Labouring Men: Studies in the History of Labour.* London: Wiedenfeld and Nicolson, 1964.

Hobson, S. G. "The Industrial Unit and the New Shop Steward." *New Age,* September 26, 1918, pp. 346–347.

————. "War Conditions and the New Shop Stewards." *New Age,* September 19, 1918, pp. 331–333.

Hodginson, George. *Sent to Coventry.* N.p.: Robert Maxwell, 1970.

Holton, Bob. *British Syndicalism, 1900–1914: Myths and Realities.* London: Pluto Press, 1976.

Hudson, Frank. "The Machinists' Side of Taylorism." *American Machinist,* April 27, 1911, p. 773.

Hunt, E. H. *British Labour History, 1815–1914.* Atlantic Highlands, N.J.: Humanities Press, 1981.

Hurwitz, Samuel J. *State Intervention in Great Britain: A Study of Economic Control and Social Response, 1914–1919.* New York: Columbia University Press, 1949.

Hyman, Richard. *Strikes.* Glasgow: Fontana/Collins, 1977.

————. "Trade Unions, Control and Resistance." In *The Politics of Work and Occupations,* edited by Geoff Esland and Graeme Salaman, pp. 303–334. Toronto: University of Toronto Press, 1980.

————. *The Workers' Union.* Oxford: Clarendon Press, 1971.

International Union of Machinists and Blacksmiths, New Jersey Union No. 5, New Brunswick. Miscellaneous records, Rutgers University Library, Accession 427.

Janes, George Milton. *The Control of Strikes in American Trade Unions.* Baltimore: Johns Hopkins University Press, 1916.

Jefferys, James. *The Story of the Engineers, 1800–1945.* London: Lawrence and Wishart, 1945.

Jones, Gareth Stedman. "Class Struggle and the Industrial Revolution." *New Left Review* 90 (March–April 1975): 35–68.

Katznelson, Ira. "Working-Class Formation and the State: Nineteenth-Century England in American Perspective." In *Bringing the State Back In,* edited by Peter B. Evans, Dietrich Rueschemeyer, and Theda Skocpol, pp. 257–284. New York: Cambridge University Press, 1985.

Kerr, Clark, et al. *Industrialism and Industrial Man.* Cambridge, Mass.: Harvard University Press, 1960.

Kimball, Dexter. "Basic Principles of Industrial Organization." National Metal Trades Association, *Proceedings of the Annual Convention,* 1914.

Kingsford, P. W. *Engineers Inventors and Workers.* London: Edward Arnold, 1964.

Kuhn, I. W. "Business Unionism in a Laboristic Society." In *The Business of America,* edited by I. Berg, pp. 284–309. New York: Harcourt, Brace and World, 1968.

Labor Leader. Weekly paper of International Association of Machinists Lodge 30, Bridgeport, Connecticut.

Labour Research Department. *Labour and Capital in the Engineering Trades.* London: Labour Publishing Co., 1922.

Laslett, John. *Labor and the Left: A Study of Socialist and Radical Influences in the American Labor Movement, 1881–1924.* New York: Basic Books, 1970.

Lawrence, J. D. "Prussianism in the Workshop." *Amalgamated Engineers' Monthly Journal,* September 1919, p. 53.

Lescohier, Don, and Elizabeth Brandeis. *History of Labor in the United States, 1896–1932: Working Conditions and Labor Legislation.* New York: Macmillan, 1935.

Levine, A. L. "Industrial Change and Its Effects upon Labour, 1900–1914." Ph.D. thesis, University of London, 1954.

————. *Industrial Retardation in Britain, 1880–1914.* London: Weidenfeld and Nicolson, 1967.

Lewis, J. Slater. "Works Management for the Maximum of Production." *Engineering Magazine* 18 (October 1899): 59–68; (November 1899): 201–208; (December 1899): 361–368.

"Life in a Workshop." Workers' Union *Record,* April 1915.

Lipset, Seymour Martin, and Earl Raab. *The Politics of Unreason.* New York: Harper and Row, 1970.

Litterer, Joseph A. "Systematic Management: Design for Organizational Recoupling in American Manufacturing Firms." *Business History Review* 37, no. 4 (1963): 369–391.

Littler, Craig. "Deskilling and Changing Structures of Control." In *The Degradation of Work? Skill, Deskilling, and the Labour Process,* edited by Stephen Wood, pp. 122–145. London: Hutchinson, 1982.

————. "Understanding Taylorism." *British Journal of Sociology* 25, no. 2 (1978): 185–202.

McCarthy, John D., and Mayer N. Zald. "Resource Mobilization and Social Movement: A Partial Theory." *American Journal of Sociology* 82, no. 6 (1977): 1212–1239.

McClelland, Keith, and Alastair Reid. "Wood, Iron and Steel: Technology, Labour and Trade Union Organization in the Shipbuilding Industry, 1890–1914." In *Divisions of Labour: Skilled Workers and Technological Change in Nineteenth Century England,* edited by Royden Harrison and Jonathan Zeitlin, pp. 151–184. Urbana: University of Illinois Press, 1985.

Maier, Charles. "Between Taylorism and Technocracy: European Ideologies and the Vision of Industrial Productivity in the 1920s." *Journal of Contemporary History* 5, no. 2 (1975): 27–61.

————. *Recasting Bourgeois Europe: Stabilization in France, Germany, and Italy in the Decade After World War I.* Princeton, N.J.: Princeton University Press, 1975.

Mann, Michael. *Consciousness and Action Among the Western Working Class.* London: Macmillan, 1973.

Manufacturers' Association of Bridgeport. Bulletin. Bridgeport Public Library, Accession 1977.25.

———. Minutes of Executive Board and Committee Meetings. Bridgeport Public Library, Accession 1981.06.

Manufacturers' Research Association. Records. Harvard Business School, Baker Library, MSS 883.

Marglin, Steven. "What Do Bosses Do? The Origins and Functions of Hierarchy in Capitalist Production." *Review of Radical Political Economy* 6, no. 2 (1974): 60–112.

Maxim, Hiram. "The Effects of Trade Unionism upon Skilled Mechanics." *Engineering Magazine* 14 (November 1897): 189–195.

"Men and Output." *The Times Engineering Supplement*, September 29, 1916, pp. 145–146.

Merkle, Judith A. *Management and Ideology: The Legacy of the International Scientific Management Movement.* Berkeley and Los Angeles: University of California Press, 1980.

Meyer, Stephen, III. *The Five Dollar Day: Labor Management and Social Control in the Ford Motor Company, 1908–1921.* Albany: State University of New York Press, 1981.

Miller, Fred J. "The Machinist." *Scribner's Magazine* 14 (September 1893): 314–334.

———. "Scientific Management: Its Installation and Operation." *Efficiency Society Journal* 5 (March 1916): 118–136.

Montgomery, David. "New Tendencies in Union Struggles and Strategies in Europe and the United States, 1916–1922." In *Work, Community, and Power: The Experience of Labor in Europe and America, 1900–1925,* edited by James E. Cronin and Carmen Sirianni, pp. 88–116. Philadelphia: Temple University Press, 1983.

———. *Workers' Control in America: Studies in the History of Work, Technology, and Labor Struggles.* Cambridge: Cambridge University Press, 1979.

Moore, Barrington, Jr. *Injustice: The Social Bases of Obedience and Revolt.* White Plains, N.Y.: M. E. Sharpe, 1978.

More, Charles. "Skill and the Survival of Apprenticeship." In *The Degradation of Work? Skill, Deskilling, and the Labour Process,* edited by Stephen Wood, pp. 109–121. London: Hutchinson, 1982.

Mosley, Alfred. "British Views of American Workshops." *Cassier's Magazine* 23, no. 3 (1903): 475–479.

Moss, Bernard. *The Origins of the French Labor Movement: The Social-*

ism of the Skilled Workers, 1830–1914. Berkeley and Los Angeles: University of California Press, 1976.

Murphy, J. T. *The Workers' Committee: An Outline of Its Principles and Structure*. London: Pluto Press, 1972 [1917].

Nadworny, Milton. *Scientific Management and the Unions, 1900–1932*. Cambridge, Mass.: Harvard University Press, 1955.

National Industrial Conference Board. *Experience with Works Councils in the United States*. New York: The Century Co., 1922.

———. Research Report No. 8: *Wartime Employment of Women in the Metal Trades*. Boston: NICB, 1918.

———. *Wartime Employment of Women in the Metal Trades*. Boston: NICB, 1918.

———. *Works Councils in the United States*. Boston: NICB, 1919.

National Metal Trades Association. *Report of the Committee on Works Councils in the Metal Trades*. Chicago: NMTA, 1919.

———. *Synopsis of Proceedings of the Annual Conventions*.

———, Committee on Industrial Relations. *Industrial Relations in the Metal Trades*. Chicago: NMTA, 1929.

National War Labor Board. Records. Docket No. 132, International Association of Machinists District #55 vs. Bridgeport, Connecticut, employers. National Archives, Record Group 2.

Nelson, Daniel. *Frederick Taylor and the Rise of Scientific Management*. Madison: University of Wisconsin Press, 1980.

———. *Managers and Workers: Origins of the New Factory System in the United States, 1880–1920*. Madison: University of Wisconsin Press, 1975.

Niven, M. M. *Personnel Management, 1913–1963: The Growth of Personnel Management and the Development of the Institute*. London: Institute of Personnel Management, 1967.

Noble, David. *America by Design: Science, Technology, and the Rise of Corporate Capitalism*. New York: Knopf, 1977.

———. "Social Choice in Machine Design: The Case of Automatically Controlled Machine Tools, and a Challenge for Labor." *Politics and Society* 8, nos. 3–4 (1978): 313–347.

Norris, H. M. "Actual Experience with the Premium Plan." *Engineering Magazine* 18 (January 1900): 572–584; (February 1900): 689–696.

Oberschall, Anthony. *Social Conflict and Social Movements*. Englewood Cliffs, N.J.: Prentice-Hall, 1973.

O'Connell, James. "Piece-Work Not Necessary for Best Results in the Machine Shop." *Engineering Magazine* 19 (June 1900): 373–380.

Offe, Claus, and Helmut Wiesenthal. "Two Logics of Collective Action: Theoretical Notes on Social Class and Organizational Form." In *Politi-*

cal Power and Social Theory: A Research Annual, vol. 1, pp. 67–115. Greenwich, Conn.: JAI Press, 1980.

O'Neill, P. J. "British and American Industrial Methods Compared and Contrasted." *Machine Tool Review,* June–July 1917, pp. 20–30.

Orcutt, H. F. L. "Machine Shop Management in Europe and America." *Engineering Magazine,* eight-part series, vols. 16–17.

Palmer, Bryan. "Class, Conception, and Conflict: The Thrust for Efficiency, Managerial Views of Labor, and the Working Class Rebellion, 1903–1922." *Review of Radical Political Economy* 7, no. 2 (1975): 31–49.

———. *A Culture in Conflict: Skilled Workers and Industrial Capitalism in Hamilton, Ontario, 1860–1914.* Montreal: Queen's University Press, 1979.

Panitch, Leo. "The Development of Corporatism in Liberal Democracies." *Comparative Political Studies* 10, no. 1 (1977): 61–90.

Penn, Roger. *Skilled Workers in the Class Structure.* Cambridge: Cambridge University Press, 1985.

Perlman, Mark. *The Machinists: A New Study in American Trade Unionism.* Cambridge, Mass.: Harvard University Press, 1961.

Perlman, Selig. *A Theory of the Labor Movement.* New York: Augustus M. Kelley, 1949.

———, and Philip Taft. *History of Labor in the United States, 1896–1932.* New York: Macmillan, 1935.

Peterson, Joyce Shaw. "Auto Workers and Their Work, 1900–1933." *Labor History* 22, no. 2 (1981): 213–236.

Phelps Brown, E. H. *The Growth of British Industrial Relations: A Study from the Standpoint of 1906–14.* New York: St. Martin's Press, 1959.

———. *The Origins of Trade Union Power.* Oxford: Clarendon Press, 1983.

Piore, Michael, and Charles Sabel. *The Second Industrial Divide: Possibilities for Prosperity.* New York: Basic Books, 1984.

Pope, Liston. *Millhands and Preachers: A Study of Gastonia.* New Haven, Conn.: Yale University Press, 1942.

Potter, Zenas. "War-Boom Towns I: Bridgeport." *The Survey,* December 4, 1915, pp. 237–241.

"The Present State of the Art of Industrial Management." American Society of Mechanical Engineers, *Transactions* 34 (1912): 1131–1229.

Prest, John. *The Industrial Revolution in Coventry.* London: Oxford University Press, 1960.

Pribicevic, Branko. *The Shop Stewards' Movement and Workers' Control, 1910–1922.* Oxford: Basil Blackwell, 1959.

Price, Richard. "The Labour Process and Labour History." *Social History* 8 (1983): 57–75.

————. *Masters, Unions and Men: Work Control in Building and the Rise of Labour, 1830–1914*. Cambridge: Cambridge University Press, 1980.

Radosh, Ronald. "Labor and the American Economy: The 1922 Railroad Shop Crafts Strike and the 'B & O Plan.'" In *Building the Organizational Society*, edited by Jerry Israel, pp. 73–87. New York: Free Press, 1972.

Ramirez, Bruno. *When Workers Fight: The Politics of Industrial Relations in the Progressive Era, 1898–1916*. Westport, Conn.: Greenwood Press, 1978.

Richmond, J. R. *Some Aspects of Labour and Its Claims in the Engineering Industry*. Glasgow: N.p., 1916.

Roberts, Wayne. "Toronto Metal Workers and the Second Industrial Revolution." *Labour/Le Travail* 6 (Autumn 1980): 49–72.

Roe, Joseph Wickham. *English and American Tool Builders*. New Haven, Conn.: Yale University Press, 1916.

Rogers, Fred, et al. "Developments in Machine Shop Practice During the Last Decade." American Society of Mechanical Engineers, *Transactions* 34 (1912): 847–865.

Roland, Henry. "The Revolution in Machine-Shop Practice." *Engineering Magazine* 18 (October 1899–March 1900); six-part series.

————. "Six Examples of Successful Shop Management." *Engineering Magazine* 12 (October 1896–March 1897), 13 (April 1897); six-part series.

Rolt, L. T. C. *A Short History of Machine Tools*. Cambridge, Mass.: MIT Press, 1965.

Sabel, Charles F. *Work and Politics: The Division of Labor in Industry*. Cambridge: Cambridge University Press, 1982.

Samuel, Raphael. "The Workshop of the World: Steam Power and Hand Technology in Mid-Victorian Britain." *History Workshop* 3 (Spring 1977): 6–72.

Saul, S. B. "The Engineering Industry." In *The Development of British Industry and Foreign Competition, 1875–1914*, edited by Derek H. Aldcroft, pp. 186–237. London: George Allen and Unwin, 1968.

————. "The Machine Tool Industry in Britain to 1914." *Business History* 10, no. 1 (1968): 22–43.

————. "The Market and the Development of the Mechanical Engineering Industries in Britain, 1860–1914." *Economic History Review*, second series, 20, no. 1 (1967): 111–130.

————. "The Motor Industry in Britain to 1914." *Business History* 5, no. 1 (1962): 22–44.

Schloss, David F. *Methods of Industrial Remuneration*, 3rd ed. London: Williams and Norgate, 1898.

Schwartz, Michael. *Radical Protest and Social Structure: The Southern Farmers' Alliance and Cotton Tenancy, 1880–1890.* New York: Academic Press, 1976.

Sewell, William H., Jr. *Work and Revolution in France: The Language of Labor from the Old Regime to 1848.* Cambridge: Cambridge University Press, 1980.

Shadwell, Arthur. *The Engineering Industry and the Crisis of 1922: A Chapter in Industrial History.* London: John Murray, 1922.

————. *Industrial Efficiency: A Comparative Study of Industrial Life in England, Germany and America.* New York: Longmans, Green, 1906.

Shorter, Edward, and Charles Tilly. *Strikes in France, 1830–1968.* Cambridge: Cambridge University Press, 1974.

Sirianni, Carmen. "Workers' Control in the Era of World War I." *Theory and Society* 9, no. 1 (1980): 29–88.

Slichter, Sumner H., et al. *The Impact of Collective Bargaining on Management.* Washington, D.C.: Brookings Institution, 1960.

Smith, Steve. "Craft Consciousness, Class Consciousness: Petrograd, 1917." *History Workshop* 11 (Spring 1981): 33–56.

Soffer, Benson. "A Theory of Trade Union Development: The Role of the 'Autonomous' Workman." *Labor History* 1, no. 2 (1960): 141–163.

Stearns, Peter. *Lives of Labor: Work in a Maturing Industrial Society.* New York: Holmes and Meier, 1975.

Stelling, Robert. "The Foreman in Relation to Workshop Organization." *Engineering and Industrial Management*, September 4, 1919, pp. 294–295.

Stone, Katherine. "The Origins of Job Structures in the Steel Industry." In *Labor Market Segmentation*, edited by Richard Edwards, Michael Reich, and David Gordon, pp. 27–84. Lexington, Mass.: D. C. Heath, 1975.

Tariff Commission. *Report of the Tariff Commission*, vol. 4: *The Engineering Industries.* London: P. S. King and Son, 1909.

Tilly, Charles. "Collective Violence in European Perspective." In *Violence in America: Historical and Comparative Perspectives*, edited by Hugh Graham and Ted Gurr, pp. 4–45. New York: Praeger, 1969.

————. *From Mobilization to Revolution.* New York: Random House, 1978.

Todd, Nigel. "Trade Unions and the Engineering Industry Dispute at Barrow-in-Furness, 1897–1898." *International Review of Social History* 20, no. 1 (1975): 33–47.

Towlson, J. T. "A British View of Shop Efficiency." *American Machinist*, August 24, 1911, pp. 361–362.

Trades Union Congress. *Premium Bonus System Report: Report of an Inquiry*. Manchester: TUC, 1910.

Turner, H. A. *Trade Union Growth Structure and Policy. A Comparative Study of the Cotton Unions*. London: George Allen and Unwin, 1962.

United States Bureau of Labor, 11th Special Report. *Regulation and Restriction of Output*. Washington, D.C.: Government Printing Office, 1904.

United States Bureau of Labor Statistics. *Monthly Review*.

United States Congress, House Committee on Labor. *Hearings Before a Special Committee of the House of Representatives to Investigate the Taylor and Other Systems of Shop Management*. Washington, D.C.: Government Printing Office, 1912.

————. *Hearings on a Bill to Regulate the Method of Directing Work of Government Employees*. Washington, D.C.: Government Printing Office, 1916.

United States Congress, Senate Commission on Industrial Relations. *Final Report and Testimony*. 11 vols. Washington, D.C.: Government Printing Office, 1916.

United States Congress, Senate Committee on Education and Labor. *Report of the Committee of the Senate upon the Relations Between Capital and Labor*. Washington, D.C.: Government Printing Office, 1885.

United States Department of Commerce, Bureau of the Census. *Thirteenth Census of the United States*, vol. 8: Manufactures, 1909. Washington, D.C.: Government Printing Office, 1913.

United States Department of Labor. Records of the Conciliation Service. National Archives, Record Group 280.

United States Industrial Commission. *Reports*. 19 vols. Washington, D.C.: Government Printing Office, 1901–1902.

United States War Department. *A Report of the Activities of the War Department in the Field of Industrial Relations During the War*. Washington, D.C.: Government Printing Office, 1919.

Upp, John. "The Woman Worker." American Society of Mechanical Engineers, *Transactions* 39 (September 1917): 1129–1140.

Urwick, L., and E. F. L. Brech. *The Making of Scientific Management*, vol. 2: *Management in British Industry*. London: Management Publications Trust, 1949.

Wagoner, Harless. *The U.S. Machine Tool Industry from 1900 to 1950*. Cambridge, Mass.: MIT Press, 1968.

Waldo, George C. *History of Bridgeport and Vicinity*. New York: S. J. Clarke, 1917.

War Labor Policies Board. Records. National Archives, Record Group 1.

Warner, W. Lloyd, and J. O. Low. *The Social System of the Modern Factory. The Strike: A Social Analysis*. New Haven, Conn.: Yale University Press, 1947.

Watson, Egbert P. "The Changes in One Lifetime in the Machine Shop." *Engineering Magazine* 30 (March 1906): 883–890.

Watson, W. F. *Machines and Men: An Autobiography of an Itinerant Mechanic*. London: George Allen and Unwin, 1935.

———. *The Worker and Wage Incentives*. London: Hogarth Press, 1934.

Weaver, G. G. "The Foreman—Past and Future." *American Machinist*, October 26, 1922, p. 652.

Webb, Sidney. *The Works Manager Today*. London: Longmans, Green, 1918.

Weekes, B. C. M. "The Amalgamated Society of Engineers, 1880–1914. A Study of Trade Union Government, Politics, and Industrial Policy." Ph.D. thesis, University of Warwick, 1970.

White, Joseph. *The Limits of Trade Union Militancy: The Lancashire Textile Workers, 1910–1914*. Westport, Conn.: Greenwood Press, 1978.

Whiteford, James F. "Development of Management in the United Kingdom." *Mechanical Engineering* 44 (November 1922): 703–704.

Wigham, Eric. *The Power to Manage: A History of the Engineering Employers' Federation*. London: Macmillan, 1973.

Williams, Alfred. *Life in a Railway Factory*. Newton Abbot, Devon: David and Charles Reprints, 1969 [1915].

"The Works and Methods of Alfred Herbert, Ltd., Coventry, England—II." *American Machinist*, April 19, 1906, pp. 506–508.

"The Works and Some of the Product of Alfred Herbert, Ltd., of Coventry, England." *American Machinist*, October 17 and 24, 1901, pp. 1155–1159, 1179–1184.

"Works and Workers." *Times Engineering Supplement*, February 22, 1918, p. 46.

"The Works of the Daimler Co., Ltd." *Automobile Engineer* 11 (August 1921): 285–290.

"The Works of Messrs. Alfred Herbert, Limited, Coventry." *Engineering* 90 (July 22, 1910): 113–120.

Wright, Thomas. *Some Habits and Customs of the Working Classes*. New York: Augustus Kelley, 1967 [1867].

Yates, Morris. *Wages and Labour Conditions in British Engineering*. London: Macdonald and Evans, 1937.

Zald, Mayer N. "Issues in the Theory of Social Movements." In *Current Perspectives in Social Theory: A Research Annual*, edited by Scott G. McNall and Gary N. Howe, vol. 1, pp. 61–72. Greenwich, Conn.: JAI Press, 1980.

Zald, Mayer N., and John D. McCarthy, eds. *The Dynamics of Social Movements: Resource Mobilization, Social Control, and Tactics.* Cambridge, Mass.: Winthrop Publishers, 1979.

Zeitlin, Jonathan Hart. "Craft Control and the Division of Labour: Engineers and Compositors in Britain, 1890–1930." *Cambridge Journal of Economics* 3, no. 3 (1979): 263–274.

———. "Rationalization and Resistance: Skilled Workers and the Transformation of the Division of Labor in the British Engineering Industry, 1830–1930." B.A. thesis, Harvard University, 1977.

Newspapers and Trade Journals

Amalgamated Engineers' Monthly Journal
American Machinist
Automotive Industries
Bridgeport Herald
Bridgeport Post
Coventry Herald and Free Press
Engineering
Engineering Magazine
The Engineer
The Foreman
Industrial Management
Iron Age
Iron Trade Review
Labor Leader
Machinists' Monthly Journal
Midland Daily Telegraph
The Open Shop
Workers' Union *Record*

Index

Compositor:	Graphic Composition, Inc.
Printer:	Braun-Brumfield, Inc.
Binder:	Braun-Brumfield, Inc.
Text:	11/13 Caledonia
Display:	Caledonia